RAISED BY A
SERIAL KILLER

RAISED BY A SERIAL KILLER

DISCOVERING THE TRUTH ABOUT MY FATHER

APRIL BALASCIO

HARPER
element

Raised by a Serial Killer is a work of nonfiction.
Some names and identifying details have been changed.

HarperElement
An imprint of HarperCollins*Publishers*
1 London Bridge Street
London SE1 9GF

www.harpercollins.co.uk

HarperCollins*Publishers*
Macken House, 39/40 Mayor Street Upper
Dublin 1, D01 C9W8, Ireland

First published by Gallery Books USA,
an Imprint of Simon & Schuster, 2024
This edition published in the UK by HarperElement, 2024

10 9 8 7 6 5 4 3 2 1

Interior design by Kathryn A. Kenney-Peterson

April Balascio asserts the moral right to be
identified as the author of this work

A catalogue record of this book is
available from the British Library

HB ISBN 978-0-00-846666-4
TPB ISBN 978-0-00-846667-1

Printed and bound in the UK using 100% renewable
electricity at CPI Group (UK) Ltd

This book is produced from independently certified FSC™ paper
to ensure responsible forest management.

For more information visit: www.harpercollins.co.uk/green

For Dave and Judy Hack.
Their love and forgiveness fill my heart with gratitude.

Author's Note/Disclaimer

This book is a memoir, based on my recollections, recounted to the best of my ability. I am deeply grateful to the people from my past who willingly shared their own recollections. In addition, I consulted letters, newspaper articles, video and audio recordings, books, and websites. The dialogue within that is not directly quoted from research material is faithful to my memories. Except for a few names and details that have been changed, the names, places, and events described within these pages are real.

Contents

RAISED BY A
SERIAL KILLER

PREFACE

This is a story about a daughter and her father. It's a story about love and betrayal, about lost innocence and violence. It was never a story I wanted to tell, but I feel that now it demands to be told.

I was eleven when I came to realize that my father was a bad man, and that he was sometimes a bad father—a really, really bad father. Until then, he was just my dad and I loved him even while I feared his terrifying temper. But it's not that simple, is it? It never is.

When I think of the ideal father, I imagine someone who challenges his daughter to be her best self, who applauds her when she achieves her goals, even while inspiring her to reach beyond them, and who imparts vital life skills so she becomes independent and resourceful. It can be said that my father met those criteria. I can handle a chop saw and hang sheetrock better than most men. And I was on my own by the age of eighteen, fully able to support myself because I was not afraid of hard work. My father taught me that.

My ideal version of a father loves, protects, and cares for his child when she is sick or hurt. Even here, my father checks the boxes. I remember him packing my sprained ankles with ice when I'd jumped off a merry-go-round. It was he who brought me popsicles when I had strep throat.

In my parental ideal, I envision a father who creates a home where his children feel safe, where they thrive within the sense of security he provides.

Here is where my fantasy crumbles. I never felt safe under his roof—ever. He inflicted injuries in his rage, and I wore his marks: bruises, sprains, and once, when I was sixteen, a hickey on my neck. And yet, my father would defend his children against anyone he believed meant them harm. And if "love" means he would kill to protect me, then yes, my father loved me.

• • •

My childhood was not always unhappy. Alongside the memories of bewilderment and fear, I have good memories, too. In many ways my father enabled that happiness as truly as he inflicted the pain. Because he was impulsive, playful, and fearless, we had adventures that other children could not have had. We moved so often it was hard to say where home was, but even on the road—sometimes traveling crammed into a U-Haul truck with my dad driving, my mom in the passenger seat, our dog Happy at her feet, my baby sister on her lap, one brother and I squeezed in between them, with two other brothers standing in the space behind the seat—we always knew we were, without a doubt, a family.

We were poor, often hungry, moving from one dilapidated and filthy rental house to another, sometimes living in tents and campers and, once, in a barn. Between 1969, when I was born, and 1987, my family lived in Ohio, Florida, Georgia, Arizona, Colorado, Pennsylvania, and Wisconsin, and we passed through just about every state.

By 2009, I was a parent myself, living in an immaculate four-bedroom house that my husband and I had painstakingly renovated, with a four-car garage on five acres. Each of my three well-fed, well-dressed teenagers had their own bedroom. But I didn't feel like I had arrived at some pinnacle of success. My husband worked the swing shift, and my nights were long. Questions about my past nagged me. My childhood was like a jigsaw puzzle I couldn't put together because there were too many missing pieces. I couldn't even remember all the names of the towns we lived in, but at night, unable to sleep, I'd lie in bed and try to remember each school I attended as a child—a new one almost every year—as a mental exercise, but also as something more. I was looking for clues. Why had we left all those towns in such a hurry? I had vague memories of rumors of missing people, of bodies found. Did those dark murky echoes have anything to do with my childhood? When I remembered a town name, I'd sit up, grab my laptop, and obsessively scan my computer's search results for cold cases there. Each time, I was discouraged. Nothing struck me as significant or familiar. I was convinced I would never put my splintered memories back together. But one night, out of the blue, the name

Watertown, Wisconsin, came to me. We weren't there long, just the summer of 1980. I was eleven, but I remember with a strange clarity the old rambling farmhouse we stayed in there. It had an incongruous, giant stained glass window through which shards of colored light danced on the dining room table and floor.

I googled "cold case 1980 Watertown Wisconsin."

A case called "The Sweetheart Murders" came up on my screen. With my pulse pounding in my ears, I read a news story about two young people who disappeared on the night of August 9, 1980, after attending a wedding reception just outside Watertown, in rural Jefferson County, Wisconsin.

According to the article, nineteen-year-olds Kelly Drew and Timothy Hack were high-school sweethearts. He was a farm boy who loved tractor pulls. She was a town girl who had just received a cosmetology degree. And they were last seen alive at 11 p.m., leaving the wedding reception at a venue called the Concord House. Six days later, strips of Kelly's shredded clothing were found alongside the country road leading away from the Concord House, with dried semen on her pants and underwear. Their bodies were not discovered for two and a half months. Kelly's corpse was found by squirrel hunters at the edge of a field, eight miles away from the Concord House. The police found Tim's body not far from hers. Tim had been stabbed. Kelly had been bound and strangled and possibly raped. Despite one of the largest manhunts in the history of Wisconsin, the police were unable to find the killer.

I felt a shudder of recognition. The Concord House. We had camped next to it when we first moved to Wisconsin, and my dad had worked there. We moved into the beautiful old farmhouse that summer. I remember hearing that two teens in town went missing. Though we'd only arrived in Watertown a few months earlier, we left the state soon after the news broke.

In 2009, Jefferson County, Wisconsin, reopened the Sweetheart Murders case because there was biological evidence on file and they were asking the public for any leads. Flashes of déjà vu bombarded me. I could almost hear my memories clicking into place. But I was also afraid that what happened next would be like a row of dominoes. Once I tipped the first one, I wouldn't be able to stop the outcome, even if I wanted to.

The cold case website gave a number to call with any information on the murders. I tossed my laptop aside and leapt out of bed. I paced my bedroom from window to window, to my mirror on the wall, back to the windows, back to the mirror, stopping to stare at my reflection. My hair stood on end from running my trembling hands through it again and again. It was late in the evening. I thought I might just call the number and leave a message. Surely, I wouldn't have to talk to anyone.

Instead, I called my sister. She was only four when we left Wisconsin, so I didn't expect her to corroborate my memories. I just wanted her blessing. But she was wary. "Think of what it will do to our families," she warned. She was thinking of hers and mine, but also of our three brothers', and Mom and Dad, of course. But I was thinking of Kelly Drew's family. Of Tim Hack's family. And there were others, I was sure of it, if only I could put all the missing pieces together.

My sister's words of caution unintentionally had the opposite effect. I was thinking about all the parents whose children never came home. My oldest son was nearly the age Tim had been on the night he'd died. My daughter was only a few years younger than Kelly had been. Like most kids their age, mine often went out at night with friends, and on those nights I felt a kind of dread beyond what was anywhere near reasonable. With my own children safely asleep in their rooms down the hall, how could I dare stay silent? How could I make any other decision? I told my sister I would think about what she'd said and hung up, but I had already made up my mind.

I dialed the hotline number, while mentally composing the message I'd leave, something vague like: "*Hi, my name is April. I might have information on the Sweetheart Murders.*" Then a voice answered, "Hello, this is Detective Garcia." And the first domino fell.

When I was a little girl, my world revolved around my dad. I loved him even as I feared his wrath. I studied him and learned his quirks and tells and I worked hard to earn his love. The events of my childhood eroded that adoration, but, even still, he never ceased to be the center of my universe, even as I tried to get out from under his control. And so when I tell you that it was me who pointed the finger at my father, who spoke the words that I knew—in the end—could bring him down, it is with profound sorrow, grief, and no sense of peace. What peace can be found in forcing the answer to the unbearable question: Was my own father more than a bad man? He had hurt people; I had witnessed that. But was I right to think that he may have gone further? Did all my memories of our leaving towns and schools and friends without saying goodbye qualify as evidence? Was there any truth to my growing suspicions that he may have been a killer? Was the man who cradled me in his arms when I was a young child a monster?

What is it that I seek in telling my story? Is it absolution, redemption, forgiveness? I don't yet know the answer. But if others find even a little bit of closure in their own lives, then my journey will have been worthwhile.

PART ONE

1

How He Met My Mother

I sometimes try to imagine the moment Mom and Dad first laid eyes on each other. They met on a city bus in Akron, Ohio. He was thirty-five and she was twenty-one. What Kay Lynn Hedderly first saw in Edward Wayne Edwards is easy to imagine. She might have been drawn to this rakish bad boy on parole from prison. He was handsome and gregarious, full of exuberance. Dad had a boyish grin, playful blue eyes, and sandy-blond hair, and with his warm deep drawl, his strong build, and good looks, he must have seemed like John Wayne to Mom. Though he preferred to describe himself as a cross between John Dillinger and Don Juan. Like Dillinger, he'd robbed a bank and escaped prison twice. Like Dillinger, he courted fame—and never wore masks during robberies because he wanted to be recognized. And the Don Juan comparison speaks for itself. But whoever he reminded Mom of, he rode into town and swept her off her feet.

What Dad saw in Mom is harder to guess. She was the kind of person people overlook. She lived with her parents and was a good Christian girl who wore plain dresses, no makeup, and seemed not to want to stand out. She was tall and slim and kept her dark brown, nearly black, hair short. She would have been the shy girl at the school dance who was hoping not to be noticed, and Dad would have been the kid tearing it up in the middle of the dance floor.

When they met, Mom was already engaged to a promising young man who her parents approved of. Mom was from an average American family of five, with an older brother and a younger sister and two responsible upstanding parents. Mom's parents lived their entire lives in the Akron area, went to the Lutheran church, and were active community members. Her father,

Howard Russel Hedderly, worked for forty-two years at the Firestone Tire & Rubber Company. Her mother, Mary Elizabeth, worked in a department store. Her parents encouraged Mom to go to college and become a teacher.

Dad was an Akron native, too, but their hometown was about all they had in common. He was born to an unwed mother and spent much of his childhood in an orphanage and reformatory. He proposed just two months after meeting Mom, and she accepted. Even when he told her about his past, including his time on the FBI's Ten Most Wanted List, an achievement he was proud of, she didn't change her mind. He admitted to being fresh from a federal penitentiary having served five years of a twelve-year sentence for armed bank robbery. And his entire life before this prison sentence had been one of crime, scams, arson, and women. But now, he claimed, he had been inspired by a kindly prison guard to change his ways. He spoke of his reform with the fervor of a man born again. He was so full of confidence and bravado that he had become a motivational speaker, giving talks at police academies about his experiences, providing insights into the criminal mind. One police officer told him that he would have made a damn good detective.

After telling Mom about his past, he claimed to have said, "If you want to end the engagement, I'll understand. But if you'll marry me, I will bend every bone in my body to make you the happiest woman alive." According to him, she loved him even more than ever for his confession. They married six months later.

Mom got her teaching degree, but she didn't teach for long, because she and Dad got married and had me all in the span of a year. Dad's job description on their marriage license is "Truck Driver." He was a proud member of the Teamsters union, thanks to Jimmy Hoffa, whom he had actually met and become friendly with in prison.

Why did Mom choose someone so different from the sort of man she was familiar with? I can only think that she was conned by him like so many others. Or maybe the sheer force of his charisma overpowered her ability to think clearly. He considered himself to be very persuasive with women. He had been married to at least three other women before her (one of them three times).

Mom simply fell under his spell. They hid the fact that he was on parole from her parents, but even without knowing his backstory, Mom's parents were not impressed. They must have been mortified to have this smooth-talking con man as a son-in-law. They saw clearly that he was luring their daughter from the stable life they'd imagined for her and into the gutter, or at least into a life beneath her station. And Dad never forgave their disapproval. But Mom must have been helpless to resist his charm. Or maybe it was because she got pregnant with me before she'd had a chance to change her mind.

2

Bend Every Bone

1970

I was a year old when we moved into a little gray house on Avon Street in the North Hill section of Akron. Mom had just given birth to my brother David. She was never much interested in housekeeping, so the house on Avon Street was a mess. There were piles of dishes on the kitchen counters, dirt on the floor that stuck to my bare feet like breadcrumbs, and tangles of extension cords like snakes crisscrossing the floor.

Mom got pregnant again with her third child before I turned two. By two-and-a-half I was used to doing things by myself. Because I had a younger brother who seemed fairly helpless, I felt extremely capable. If I could figure something out, I could do it. Shouting "I do it!" might have been my first sentence. One day, I stomped into the living room wearing nothing but my white undies and saw that my very pregnant mother was on the sofa, trying to wrestle my brother David into a clean diaper. I had to step over all the extension cords to find a clear spot to sit on the floor. I wanted to plug in my night-light. The night-light, in the shape of a blue buffalo, was my favorite toy. I talked to it, long into the night, and I carried it around with me during the day.

I studied one of those long, winding cords. There was a lamp plugged in there, however, which had to come out so I could plug in my buffalo. Determined, I grabbed onto the lamp's cord and pulled. But my hands couldn't get a good enough grip to pull it out. I didn't want to ask for help because I never liked to ask for help, and, besides, Mom was clearly busy. So I used my mouth. I bit down hard on that electric cord and before I could yank it out, I was jerked off my feet. The pain was sharp, like a whip crack to my mouth. I smelled a terrible odor, and the shriek of my own scream rang in my ears, merging with Mom's screams. After this, I only recall flashes of images and impressions. Someone lifting me onto the dining room table. A neighbor's face hovered over mine. I don't know how I got to the hospital. Mom didn't drive, so it might have been the neighbor. I just remember the pain like an explosion in my head.

I woke up in a hospital room. My head still ached and my mouth felt bound like a mummy. I just wanted my dad to make everything okay. *Where is he?* And then I heard him. The smooth rumble of his voice as he spoke to the nurses. I heard his low chuckle as he joked with them. He was always joking with women.

"Hey honey," he said when he saw I was awake. He gave me his big warm grin.

I drifted in and out, Dad's face fading and coming into focus. I had just had my first surgery to reconstruct the side of my mouth where the cord had melted my lips and cheek.

Dad came to my bed and put his hand on my forehead and stroked it. I felt tears leak out of my eyes and down both temples. I whimpered through the bandaging.

He handed me my baby doll from home, and I clutched her to my chest. Dad lifted me up off the bed and then sat in the rocking chair beside it, holding me on his lap, soothing me while we rocked back and forth. I was safe now.

When Dad brought me home a week later, he carried me to the sofa. Mom stared at my bandaged face, while she bounced David on her hip. She looked frightened. David took one look at me and began to bawl. He didn't recognize his sister. I didn't want Dad to leave my side. And I dozed off with his reassuring weight on the sofa cushion beside me.

Every morning Dad had to change the itchy, sticky bandage that covered the right side of my face. It felt like he was ripping my whole bottom lip off. But I trusted him. Mom brought me broth and ginger ale and fed me through a big eye dropper. Dad showed Mom how to change the bandages. She trembled when she unwound the bandages the first few times. This was not her strong suit. But it was Mom who shaped my mouth with her fingers so I could drink through a straw.

Dad had been trained in first aid at prison, and we kept him in practice. We got hurt a lot.

I was an accident-prone child. Or maybe just independent and adventurous. I had several injuries in a row when I first learned to walk. I had waddled over to the hot, open oven door and grabbed it, burning my hands badly. I have a picture of myself as a toddler with a black eye; I had gotten ahold of one of Dad's hammers and hit myself with it. It got so Dad didn't want to take me to the emergency room because he thought he might get accused of child abuse.

I still have the scar from biting the electric cord. I've learned that many people assumed Dad had something to do with it. That one was self-inflicted, but I bore other scars caused by him, most of them not visible.

When Mom's third baby was born, he didn't look like David and me. David and I had dark, almost black hair, and dark brown eyes, like Mom. The new baby, John-John, had blond hair and blue eyes like Dad. And he was always in Mom's arms. Strangers stopped her on the street to say what a beautiful child he was. They didn't say anything about me. But they would sometimes stare at the scar on the side of my mouth.

With two little brothers to occupy Mom, I gravitated toward Dad, who became the center of my world. There were two versions of Dad. The one to be wary of and the one who was caring, tender, and loving. That one could cajole you out of a bad mood, cheer you up if you were sad, or tickle a tummy ache away. On a typical evening, when I heard his big tan sedan pull up in the driveway, I ran outside to greet him, David toddling after me.

In a second, I could tell what kind of mood Dad was in. If he was happy, he looked at me and smiled wide. I ran to him and he picked me up and threw me in the air. I shrieked with delight. "Again!" I said. And he did it again and again. Then we played my favorite game where he held me by my ankle and wrist and began to spin slowly around in a circle, spinning me faster and faster, high and low like a roller-coaster ride. "Faster?" he asked. "Faster!" I yelled. He twirled me until I felt dizzy and then he'd set me down in our little grassy front yard. I knew he would never let me fall.

As soon as he lowered me to the ground, I checked his pockets. Yep, just as I suspected. I found a piece of hard candy that he'd put there just for me. I was Dad's favorite. Of this I was certain. David was too young for hard candy. Dad said he might choke on it.

If Dad was mad about something when he arrived home, he wouldn't look at me at all when he got out of the sedan, and the car door would slam. When that happened, I ran back into the house and hid behind the sofa.

There was one day when Dad came home early and surprised me while I was playing in the living room by myself. I sat on the beige carpet examining a bottle of Mom's red nail polish, which had been within easy reach on the small round end table by the sofa. Mom didn't like to wear makeup, but she did have this one tantalizing bottle of fingernail polish. I couldn't resist. I gripped the bottle in both hands and twisted the top off, reveling in the sharp, alluring scent that made my nose wrinkle. That's when Dad walked in and the bottle slipped from my hand. A thick, sticky splash of red appeared on the beige carpet. *Uh-oh.* I looked up at Dad, hoping he hadn't seen it. But he had. And he was furious.

"April, get over here!" he yelled.

I stood and bolted toward the stairs. He followed me, shouting. I reached the stairs before him and scrambled up them on all fours. I got to my room before he could overtake me and dove under the bed. I hoped he couldn't hear my pounding heart and jagged gasps of breath. But there he was, his enraged face peering sideways at me under the bed as he reached with an outstretched arm, his terrifying fingers extended. I cowered just out of reach. I thought I had outsmarted him, but with every passing second I could feel his rage mounting. I could see it in his reddening face and in his clenching fist. Finally, he picked up the bed by the frame and threw it. I covered my head with my arms, willing myself to be invisible. He grabbed me by the hair and yanked me up. He smacked me hard across my back and butt with his hand again and again. I heard Mom running up the stairs. She kept saying, "Wayne, stop it!" "Wayne, stop it!" until he finally did.

Mom rarely intervened when Dad lost his temper with me. There would be many times in my childhood when I would silently will her to speak up. But she had her own reasons for keeping quiet. I can count on one hand the rare times she told him to stop. She must have been as frightened for me as I was.

It was not the first beating I had received, it's just the first one that I remember clearly. Even then, I understood that Dad's fury was not only about me staining the carpet. It was also about me running away from him, me having the audacity to disobey him. For a brief moment I thought I could escape from him. But he righted that balance using brute force. On my small body. I had seen him use this force on Mom, too.

Just the night before, at dinner, Dad had taken his usual seat at the head of the scarred wooden dining room table. I knelt on a chair watching his every move. Mom strapped David into his highchair and then served Dad, piling white rice on his plate and forking a chicken breast on top. She added a spoonful of peas next. But Dad glared down at his plate. I held my breath. He picked up his knife and fork. Sometimes at dinner, he was chatty, telling Mom a story about what had happened during the day, but tonight he wasn't talking. He just looked intently down at the chicken breast sitting on the bed of rice. He sliced into it with his knife and then set his utensils down with a slow precision. Mom had taken her seat and was watching him, too.

His head swung toward her. "Dammit, Kay," he said in a sharp voice. "This chicken is undercooked!"

Then he lifted his plate and hurled it across the room, rice and peas flying everywhere. He lunged across the table, knocking over water glasses, and grabbed Mom by the arm. David, in his highchair, gave a nervous hiccup. Dad dragged Mom away from the table and he shoved her against the dining room wall. I put my hands over my eyes. I wished I had two more hands to cover my ears. I knew what was coming. I heard her say, "Wayne, please," in a pleading voice. Then I heard the horrible sound of his fist punching her. When I let myself look, she had dropped to the floor and curled into a ball, clutching her stomach. Dad stormed out of the house, kicking over a chair on his way out. David and I waited, staring at Mom until she pulled herself up. She didn't look at us. She just started cleaning up the bits of rice and peas from the floor and wall where Dad's plate had smashed. I felt sorry that she had to clean up the mess.

The night of the nail polish beating, Dad looked tired and sad, as he often did after he'd lost his temper. He lay on the stained beige carpet of the living room floor and patted his chest.

"Come here, honey," he said, inviting me to lay my head on his chest.

Still tender and bruised, I crawled up onto his chest. I listened to his big heart go *thump thump thump*. We lay like that, ear to heart, for a while. Dad could be so sad sometimes. And he didn't ever like for me to be mad at him. After he was angry, I knew he wanted to be forgiven. He didn't say he was sorry or ask to be forgiven, but I could just tell he wanted me to tell him that I loved him. It made him feel less sad. I wanted to make him feel better.

I said, "I love you, Daddy."

"I love you too, honey. I love you very much."

For a man with a hair-trigger temper, he also possessed a surprising degree of patience. Shortly after the undercooked chicken and nail polish incidents, I sat on the lawn, watching him paint the window trim on the second floor of the house. It looked like fun. Mom called him inside because he'd received a phone call. He backed down the twenty-foot extension ladder and walked into the house. He left the can of paint hanging from a hook on the ladder rung. As soon as he'd gone, I began to climb the ladder. I hauled myself up one step at a time, keeping my eye on the dangling can of paint the whole time until I reached the rung where it hung. A paint brush lay across the opening of the can. I reached through the rungs and grabbed the brush handle and plunged it into the paint, all the way up to my elbow. I caught a whiff of its rubbery odor as I pulled my dripping white arm out of the can. I stretched as far as I could and moved the white brush back and forth across the gray clapboard siding, making a pleasing wet slapping sound. This was even more fun than it had looked! I heard Dad's voice from below.

"Hey April, honey," he said. "Whatcha doing?"

"Painting the house," I said.

He didn't yell or threaten. He just calmly talked me down the ladder and then went back to painting.

• • •

My third brother, Jeff, was born two weeks before my fifth birthday. I wouldn't have minded a baby sister. I would have loved that. But another brother? I was so mad at Mom, I decided to run away. I carefully packed my favorite belongings in a plastic laundry basket: my baby doll, my buffalo night-light, my princess tiara, my favorite clothes, and my Cinderella coloring book and jumbo box of crayons.

I marched out of the house to the sidewalk and began striding down the block, the laundry basket banging against my shins, my hands gripping the handles so firmly they hurt. This running-away business was hard work. I got a few houses down when Dad's tan sedan appeared next to me. He rolled down the window.

"Hey April, honey," he said. "Whatcha up to?"

I was blessed with a loud voice, and I projected it through the open car window. "I'm mad," I announced. "And I'm running away and never coming back."

"Well, I'll miss you," he said. "Where you goin'?"

I had to think about that. Where was I going? I hadn't quite gotten that far in the plan.

"Do you have money?"

"No."

"How're you going to eat?"

Hmmm, I hadn't considered that, either. I didn't want to admit it, though. I hated to be wrong. I weighed my options, and none of them seemed good. But now that Dad mentioned food, I realized that it was lunchtime and I was hungry. I began to trudge back up the sidewalk. Dad turned the car around and drove home. The laundry basket felt heavier with every step as I walked back, and I was glad to get home simply to be able to stop carrying the awkward load. Dad was waiting for me on the porch.

"Want me to carry that for you?" he asked. I could tell he was trying to look serious and not smile.

I sighed and handed the laundry basket over to him as if I were doing him the favor. I had too much pride to admit I was relieved. We walked inside together as if nothing had happened.

3

"Sister, I'm Gonna Be a Crook"

1933–1948

Dad always told me I was lucky to have so many siblings. As far as he knew, he didn't have any. When he was born in Akron on June 14, 1933, his biological father had wanted nothing to do with him. His mother, an unmarried woman named Lillian Myers, was sent to prison during Dad's first year of life. She had been caught stealing a hundred dollars from a house she had been hired to clean. She'd arrived at the job wearing an evening gown, having come straight from wherever she had been the evening before.

At nine months old, Dad—born Charles Edward Myers—was adopted by Lillian's sister Mary Ethel and her husband, Fred Edwards, They had no other children. They changed his name to Edward Wayne Edwards. As an adult, Dad went by his middle name, Wayne. Lillian died of complications of a failed suicide attempt when Dad was five, though he thought of her as an aunt if he thought of her at all. He didn't learn that he'd been adopted until he was an adult. When he discovered the truth of his birth mother, and the circumstances of her self-inflicted death, his own childhood seemed all the more tragic.

Dad was a difficult child, even when he was very young. Any parent would have struggled with him. He often lied and got in trouble at school and couldn't stand having anyone tell him what to do. Mary Ethel developed a degenerative disease and Fred traveled a lot for work and had a drinking problem. By the time Dad was seven, they could no longer care for a child who was so hard to manage. Mary Ethel's parents, Dad's grandmother and grandfather Myers, whom he called Grammy and Po-Po, stepped in to care for their daughter. But they could not also take in their unruly grandson. Dad was sent to an orphanage, the infamous Parmadale Children's Village outside Cleveland, where the nuns would crack a stick across his palms or backside if he forgot to say "Yes, Sister" and "No, Sister."

For a boy who couldn't stand being told what to do, Parmadale was a nightmare. For a bedwetter, which Dad was, it was more like a medieval torture chamber. His nemesis was a tall nun named Sister Agnes Marie. She forced him to stand in a cold shower with his wet sheets. He had to stand out in the playground holding his sheets, yelling, "I am a bedwetter! I am a bedwetter! Here are my wet sheets!" The worst punishment was when Sister Agnes Marie made him hold on to a tree and instructed the other boys to line up to take turns kicking him in the rear. After each kick, the boys moved to the back of the line to await their next turn. He remembers being kicked two hundred times that day. When he tried to escape, she told the bigger boys to hold him to the tree. His hatred for the nuns grew with each day. Over the course of his five years at the orphanage, he tried to run away fifteen times. When a nun asked what he wanted to be when he grew up, he liked to brag that he told her, "Sister, I'm gonna be a crook, and I'm gonna be a good one."

Dad was visited at the orphanage by Grammy and Po-Po, and one of their daughters, his aunt Lucille. They always brought him candy. But Sister Agnes Marie gave most of it away to the other boys. According to Dad, Sister Agnes Marie said, "Ed, you're a bedwetter. You don't deserve all these nice things." But he saw the candy as the only evidence that anyone cared about him. When one of the boys was sent a birthday cake and none of it was shared with Dad, he stole the remaining cake and devoured it. Sister Agnes Marie accused Dad of the cake theft and he denied it. She grabbed him and beat him with a stick on his head and back and legs. When he finally confessed, she stopped and turned to the other boys: "I'm going to my room for five minutes. If you think this lad should be punished for breaking the seventh commandment, that's your business."

When she left the room, the other boys jumped on him and beat and kicked him savagely. He had learned that confessing had been a grave error and he vowed never to be defenseless again.

When Dad finally left the orphanage at the age of twelve, it was into the custody of his grieving grandmother. Both Mary Ethel and Po-Po had died. Now his grandmother was on her own to raise her deeply troubled grandson. She did her best, but he stole money and cigarettes from her purse. He skipped school and got into fights. Stolen bicycles became a regular mode of transportation for him. He became known, in his words, "as one of the roughest young hoods in town." He was caught shoplifting and began starting fires and setting off fire alarms. He loved to watch fire trucks roaring onto the scene, sirens screaming, knowing that it had been his actions that had brought all that noise and manpower.

When he was nearly thirteen, he fell in love with a neighbor, a divorced young woman—a brunette (even then he had a preference for them)—with children. The neighbor had a boyfriend who would show up in a dry-cleaning company's truck. Dad became convinced that if he could scare his rival off, the woman would marry him. Even as a pubescent boy he believed himself irresistible to women. Even then he believed he could bend their will to please him, using violence. He set fire to the boyfriend's truck, using his grandmother as an alibi. To his immense frustration, the man returned in a new truck a few days later, so he plotted to blow the truck up. He was beyond any parental control.

His aunt Lucille and her husband, Al, considered taking Dad in, but they knew they couldn't trust him. After two years of custody, Grammy sent him off to reform school when he was fourteen, a place that served as a breeding ground for criminals. He took this banishment as proof that no one loved him. He was darn sure that if he had kids, they would never doubt they were loved.

And this he achieved. He had five children, and we did not doubt that we were loved.

4

To Tell the Truth

1972

The four years my family spent on Avon Street were unique in Dad's life because he was not on the run. It was during this period that he wrote his memoir, *Metamorphosis of a Criminal*, an account of his time in the orphanage and his subsequent life in crime until his self-proclaimed transformation in prison at the age of thirty-four. His book was published in 1972 by Hart Publishing Company. It became his calling card, and he gave out copies to neighbors and friends. He was invited to speak on prison reform. After all, he had sampled several different prisons throughout his life, and had escaped from two. That alone made him something of an expert.

He went on a book tour, spoke to schools, church groups, and Rotary clubs on the importance of good parenting—a topic the book covers in depth. He rehearsed for his talks in our living room. He would dictate to Mom, who was an excellent typist. He'd practice his talk until his delivery was smooth. I listened to him rehearse his lines over and over again. I loved to hear his deep, resonant voice. He sounded wise and important.

He brought his family with him to hear one of his talks. When we walked into the big auditorium, his radiating smile drew all eyes to him. He took his position on the stage, and we settled into seats at the back. I looked around at the assembled crowd and saw that when he spoke, people listened with rapt attention. His topics ranged from marital love to parenting to prison guard training, and he would ask questions like, *What is society?* Then he'd answer, *Society is composed of families, and what the heads of families make it. The well-being of society and the prosperity of the nation depend upon home influences.* Heads in the audience would nod.

He would talk about the problems with today's parents and children. He'd ask, *What is lacking in those homes?* Had I been asked, I could have parroted the response: *Love and discipline.* The audience would have big nods again for this one.

In his presentations, Dad had sounded so sure of himself, but there were times at home when even he seemed like he was lost. Usually, he was full of the authority conferred upon him as the "head of the family," but now and then the veneer would crack and the vulnerable child inside would show.

In the evenings, Dad was sometimes antsy. On those nights, he would take the family for car rides, and we would just drive around to nowhere in particular for hours. But one night he just took me. I sat in the front bench seat of the sedan and watched him in the light of the streetlamps. He seemed distracted and anxious. We drove around until he parked the car. Then he lay down on the front bench seat and tapped his chest. I crawled on top of him and put my ear to his shoulder and heard the *thump thump thump* of his sad heart. Dad said, as if I were the one who needed comforting, "Everything is going to be okay. I love you, honey. It's going to be okay. It's just going to be you and me." I couldn't tell if he was really talking to me. I was worried because Dad sounded distraught. But I was also a little thrilled because I had the impression that we were going to take off, just the two of us, and I would not have to share him with my brothers. I fell asleep and woke up the next morning in his arms, being carried into the house. We'd spent all night sleeping in the car.

During the book tour, Dad became a minor celebrity, and even appeared on the television show *To Tell the Truth* on October 17, 1972. On the night it aired, our little house on Avon Street was electric with excitement.

We settled into our positions in the living room. Dad usually watched TV in his recliner, but tonight we were all lined up on the sofa together. My brothers and I snuggled in between our parents. I looked at Mom and saw a spark of eagerness in her expression, and this delighted me.

Dad sat perched on the edge of the sofa cushion, leaning forward, almost vibrating with nervous energy. When the show's host announced the three contestants, we all stared in amazement. I thought I was going to burst with pride. *There's my dad! On TV!* He stood with two other men who wore dark suits. Dad wore orange slacks, a lemon-yellow button-down shirt, a cream jacket with thin zigzag lines of green and blue, and a wide, snazzy tie. I thought he looked so handsome. He was one of three men who introduced themselves as the reformed felon and author of the book *Metamorphosis of a Criminal*, Edward Wayne Edwards. He fooled them all.

5

The Farm on Taylor Road

1974

With the money from the book sales and engagements, Dad bought an empty lot in Doylestown, Ohio. It was just twenty minutes outside Akron, but it was in the country. He planned to build a big house; we needed more space now that he and Mom had four children. Doylestown was a rural farm community. The kind of place where your neighbors might have cows and people leave the keys in their cars and their houses unlocked. But the house would take a long time for Dad to build, so he rented a farmhouse on Taylor Road a mile from the empty lot for us to live in in the meantime.

When I stepped out of our wood-paneled station wagon and looked around the farm, it felt as if I had entered an enchanted world. In Akron, houses were squeezed in next to each other with little neat front yards. But on Taylor Road there were no other houses visible. Here, fields of tall grass stretched before me, cherry trees lined the driveway, and fragrant mint grew everywhere. The whole farm smelled like peppermint candy. Dad looked at me, smiling at my astonishment.

"Pretty sweet, right honey?" he asked.

I took in the two-story farmhouse with a sagging front porch. The garage was missing its bay door. None of that mattered. I had my eye on another building—an unpainted barn. Chickens pecked busily in the dirt around the big sliding barn doors. *Chickens!* David and John-John, four and three, bolted from the car and started chasing them around the yard. A rooster gave them the stink eye.

Inside the barn it was dark. Shafts of light streamed in from a window, bits of dust floated as if suspended by magic. As my eyes adjusted, a hayloft came into focus above me with a rope swing and a pile of hay below it. Rusty farm equipment sat covered in cobwebs. An orange cat stretched and blinked at me from a tractor seat. Best of all, two shaggy ponies stood munching hay in the cool shadows. *Ponies!*

I walked up to the ponies with caution, hardly believing my eyes. I was five years old and considered myself a big girl, at least bigger than my brothers, but next to the ponies I felt small. One of the ponies, the dark brown one, sidled away from me like the chickens had done, but the rust-colored pony lifted its head. I held out my hand and the pony sniffed, its long chin whiskers tickling my palm. Then it took a step toward me. I stood like a statue. It lifted its nose to sniff my hair. I breathed in the scent of sweet grass and earth as the velvet muzzle explored my face. I was in love.

Dad's silhouette appeared in the barn door.

"One of them is Max and the other is Cindy," he said.

"Which is this one?" I asked. Dad walked up slowly and laid his hands on the rust-colored pony's back. Then he leaned down and looked underneath its big round belly.

"This one's Cindy," he said. "She's a girl. The other must be Max."

Dad had once worked on a farm, so he knew all about animals. I thought there was nothing he didn't know, or couldn't fix, or couldn't figure out. He told me that the ponies and chickens and the barn cat had come with the farm. I could hardly wait to be a real farmer.

Max kept his distance, but Cindy continued to nudge me with her nose. Dad plucked a big round brush from a nail on the wall and showed me how to groom Cindy, brushing the mud off her back and legs with the stiff bristles.

"Can I ride them?" I asked with reverence.

"Sure!" Dad said, giving Cindy a last pat on the rump. "Just don't fall off."

Outside the barn, David and John-John were running around with their arms out like windmills. They came dashing into the barn and startled the ponies. They took in the old tractors and jumped up and down with glee. Immediately they hopped up on one, side by side, and pretended to drive it. I guess they were looking forward to being farmers too.

The next morning, I wolfed down my cereal and ran out to the barn to check on the ponies. They were grazing in the field and looked up when I approached them.

Max let me pet him. But when I reached up to his halter, he pulled his head away. He pinned his ears back and moved off. Cindy looked at me, and I thought she had a sweet expression. She let me take her halter and lead her to the barn. She ate hay while I brushed her coat and removed the tangles from her mane and tail.

Now was the moment I'd been waiting for. I led Cindy by the halter to a stone wall. She was compliant enough to let me situate her next to it and stand there as I climbed onto the wall and slid my leg over her back. As soon as I was aboard, I threw my arms around her neck to hold on. She dropped her head to eat grass and I went tumbling down onto the ground in front of her. She looked at me as if to say, *Well, what did you expect? Do cowboys lie down on their ponies' necks?*

On the next try, I slid my leg over her back and sat up straight and grabbed her shaggy mane in my hands. I kept my shoulders back as she took a few steps forward, and then she broke into a jog and jostled me right over the side. This time she didn't look at me. She just kept going and then stopped to graze a few yards away.

Every day I tried again, and each time I lasted longer on her back. I learned to use my weight and my balance, and she learned new ways to unseat me. She liked to run through the field with me on her back, dodging the elderberry trees, and I learned to lean with her as she turned. I had no bridle or saddle and no control. Cindy was in charge. She would move off at a walk, and then tear across the fields until she got tired. Then she'd drop her head to eat grass and there was no motivating her to play cowboy with me again until she was good and ready. If I fell off, she didn't stick around to let me get back on. Sometimes I would walk up to her after she dumped me in the field and just lie in the grass next to her. She would stay close, and I would listen to the sound of her chewing grass or munching on an apple she'd found on the ground. And we would enjoy our companionship. Sometimes I talked to her and told her stories. She was an excellent listener.

There were a few times when I set off riding Cindy and ended up walking back to the house without her. I never wanted Dad to know I'd fallen off.

But Dad seemed to know everything. He would appear in the yard with a look of great amusement and say, "Hey Cowgirl. You get dumped in the back forty?" like he was living in one of his beloved John Wayne movies.

"I'm fine," I assured him, and I was. But even if I'd been hurt, I would have said the same thing. I knew I was not supposed to complain. Complaining was annoying to Dad, and I was eager to keep in his good graces.

"Good girl," he said.

To hear Dad's praise meant everything to me. One of my missions in life was to make him happy. Things that made him happy included Camel cigarettes, hard candy, Wrigley Spearmint gum, liver and onions, well-behaved children, and a little terrier named Scottie.

Scottie was Dad's dog. This little brown-and-white, wiry, adorable little dog followed Dad everywhere. Unless there was a chipmunk to be run to ground. Then no one could distract him.

He barked happily while chasing the chickens and the barn cats with David and John-John, but as soon as Dad appeared outside, Scottie made a beeline for him and followed him around doing whatever chore he had to do.

One such chore was fixing the electric fence that surrounded the ponies' paddock. On our first day at the farm, it was obvious that the fence wasn't working, because the ponies were leaning into it to get the grass on the other side.

It wasn't until Max started getting out of the paddock that Dad decided to fix the fence. The fence had a gate near the barn, and the electric wires that were buried under the gate had become detached. David, John-John, and Scottie had been watching Dad work when I came into the barnyard just as Dad finished. He turned the fence on by flipping a switch on a box on the barn wall.

As he walked away, he said over his shoulder, "Don't touch the fence."

"Why can't we touch it?" David asked as soon as the words were out of Dad's mouth.

"Yeah, why not?" John-John echoed.

Dad turned around and looked hard at David and John-John as if he was trying to see into their heads.

"Go ahead and pee on the fence," he told them.

"What? Why?" David asked.

"Just do it," Dad said, almost daring them, but also ordering them to do it. And he expected to be obeyed.

They pulled down their shorts and peed. As soon as their stream of urine hit the fence they screamed and fell to the ground, rolling around in agony. I watched in mute horror. Scottie barked hysterically. My brothers convulsed in pain. I wondered if I should run to get Mom. But Dad just laughed. "That'll teach you!" he said to them. And he kept laughing. The hilarity for Dad was that the boys hadn't believed him and had suffered for it. But I didn't see what was funny. In fact, it made my stomach hurt.

When Dad taught us a lesson, it often involved pain. I tried to hide pain from him. But David and John-John weren't afraid to cry if they got hurt, especially if I was the one to hurt them. If we argued over a toy and I smacked one of them, they would tell on me, and I would get in trouble. Even at five years old I was aware that in some ways it was "them" against me, the big sister. When they told on me, Dad would beat me hard on the butt with his belt.

Dad instilled in me that my brothers were my responsibility. If they got hurt, it was my fault for being careless. If they misbehaved, it was my fault for letting them. If they got punished for misbehaving, I got punished too. This didn't seem fair, but I never argued. He said it was to teach me a lesson. What did the lesson teach, exactly? It mostly taught me to expect pain. Whenever Dad changed his clothes, which he did at any time in any room in the house, and I heard the clank of his belt buckle on the floor, I would flinch and my stomach would clench.

One day Dad called me and my brothers into the living room. Something bad had happened, I could tell. Mom sat on the sofa by the living room window with Jeff on her lap and her expression offered no clues.

Dad lined us up—me, David, and John-John—in a row and demanded, "Who was using the nail clippers last?"

David, John-John, and I looked at each other and said nothing. There was silence.

Dad continued to demand a confession. I looked at him with an intentionally blank face. It was an expression I had mastered. If you gave no sign that you were nervous, then you must have nothing to hide. If you showed any sign of guilt or gave any show of fear or tears in advance, you would be punished. Dad might grab you and smack you across your backside just for acting scared.

None of us spoke up because we had no idea where the clippers were. The house, as usual, was a mess. It was hard to find anything. Dad pulled his belt off and grabbed John-John and spun him around. John-John wailed as Dad lashed him with his belt. I could tell David wanted to run, but he and I both knew to stand still. Running would have made the beating worse. David cried when it was his turn. He and John-John grabbed their butts and ran around in circles, high-stepping, their faces scrunched. Then Dad grabbed me and whipped me hard across the butt. It stung so bad I cried out, and I too grabbed my butt and did the same awful dance as my brothers.

Dad put his belt back on.

"You have fifteen minutes to find the clippers," he said.

When we just stood gaping at him, he shouted, "GO!"

Mom had watched this entire scene in silence from the sofa. Jeff, who was about a year old, watched, wide-eyed as he sucked his thumb.

Fifteen minutes later we returned empty-handed and full of dread. I had looked under the kitchen table, in the kitchen junk drawer, in the bathroom medicine cabinet, behind the sink, and even in the toilet. I double-checked where my brothers had looked, too, because boys can never find anything. After a second round of beatings, I looked over at Mom and I noticed the clippers on the windowsill behind the sofa. And now I remembered that she had been using them to cut Jeff's nails. Dad left the room, saying he'd come back in another fifteen minutes, and we'd better find them or else receive another beating.

"Mom!" I whispered, and pointed to the nail clippers resting just beyond her shoulder where she'd left them on the sill.

She looked at me with panic in her eyes and whispered back, "Don't tell your father."

I grabbed the clippers from the sill. There was no question in my mind about what she was asking me to do. I had to take the blame. If I told on Mom, she'd get beat, and I didn't want her to get hurt. Dad always said if we told the truth we'd still get in trouble, but we'd get in even more trouble if we lied. This was going to be bad. Dad would think I'd lied and, worse, I'd let my brothers get beat for it. When Dad came back, I stepped forward, my fear mounting. I couldn't look him in the eye. My chin began to quiver, and I was desperately holding back tears. I handed him the clippers.

I was afraid to look at Mom, so I stared at my feet. From her seat on the sofa, she said nothing. She was not going to save me. It was up to me to save her.

"I left them on the windowsill," I said. "I forgot."

Dad's face contorted in rage, and he roared, "What did you say?!"

"I forgot!" I pleaded.

He grabbed me by my wrists and whipped out his belt and whaled on my bottom again and again and again. Winding up each time for more power. As if from a distance, I heard my cries. My mind went somewhere else in these moments. It was like I left myself. I was galloping on Cindy, clinging to her mane, the wind whipping my tears away. I was swinging on the rope in the hayloft or climbing an apple tree or hiding out in the tall grass. In the magical world of the farm, I could let my mind take me anywhere I wanted to go.

6

Paradise Lost

1975

Dad sometimes took us with him to the construction site, which was still just a pile of lumber. The lot was a field ringed by trees, and my brothers and I loved to play in what we called "the woods," a strip of giant trees along the back border. The place where the house was going to be was littered with construction materials, including nails.

The first time he brought us, he told me, "April, keep an eye on your brothers." But it was hard to keep an eye on both of them at the same time because they ran off in different directions. John-John approached a stack of boards, assessed it, and walked around it. David was more reckless and he threw himself headlong at the pile, stumbled over it, and then staggered to his feet. Immediately, he let out a yowl and began hopping up and down on one foot. Dad came over and glowered at me. He sat down on the pile and pulled David onto his lap and took off his sneaker, which had a nail sticking straight through the sole. Dad took off David's sock and forced the blood out of the puncture wound while David squirmed and groaned. We got back into the car and drove home. I worried the whole time about what Dad would do to me when we got home. But he didn't do anything to me. He just soaked David's foot in Epsom salts. But I felt terrible. It had been my fault because David had been my responsibility. I had gotten off easy that time.

Later in the summer, while the fruit grew plump on the trees, David and John-John and I played in the tall grass, making forts and lying on our backs looking at the sky while I told them stories about princesses and ponies. We climbed the pear and apple trees and helped Mom weed the garden that grew strawberries and rhubarb. Mom made tart pies with flaky crusts, following the recipe on the sticky pages of her old Betty Crocker cookbook. She let me help her roll out the buttery soft dough—not too much!—and when she laid it carefully in the pie pan, I pressed my thumb along the edges to make a pretty ruffle. I salivated as she filled the crust with sugary fruit all the way to the top.

Collecting the fruit was almost as fun as eating it.

"Let's make a pear cobbler tonight," Mom said one afternoon.

David, John-John, and I all scrambled into the pear tree in the yard. Jeff sat on the ground examining earthworms nearby. Mom had a basket and was collecting the pears from the ground that weren't too bruised or rotten. From my perch on a low branch, I could toss pears right into the basket. David climbed into a sturdy notch in the tree not much higher than I did. But John-John was an agile tree climber, and he climbed the highest. I looked up from my safe spot, firmly wedged between two thick branches, to see how high he had climbed. He was silhouetted against the bright sun, his knobby knees sticking out of the legs of his shorts. He had found his own perch high above me and stretched to pick the harder-to-reach pears. I got back to tossing the low-hanging fruit to Mom.

Then I heard a snap and a yelp, and John-John came crashing through the branches. He fell past me, screaming, and he hit the ground with a thud. He writhed on the ground, opening and closing his mouth like a fish. I was terrified that he was about to die. But then came his howl, and I knew he would live.

I don't know who took him to the hospital, because Mom still didn't drive and, besides, we only had one car and Dad was at the construction site. But that night, when Dad brought John-John home from the hospital, he had casts on both wrists. Within a few weeks, he was back to running around the farm like any other rambunctious three-year old, despite the casts. One of the games John-John loved was similar to the one Dad used to play with me. John-John would run to me with his arms held out in front of him. I would lock hands with him and swing him around. I was able to swing him so fast, his feet would come off the ground, and I'd sail him in a circle around me. It should have occurred to me to wait to play this game until John-John's casts had been removed, but it didn't. He offered up his arms and I took his casts in my hands and swung him around in a circle, both of us laughing with the sheer joy of it, until John-John went flying. I looked down at my hands, shocked that I still held his casts. I was scared that I'd hurt him. But John-John just got up and raced over to me, face full of worry, but not pain. He and I were able to slip the casts back on without Mom or Dad ever knowing any better.

But I knew I had done something that could bring Dad's wrath, and that night I couldn't hold my fear in any longer. I found Mom in the bathroom where she was bathing Jeff and confessed what I'd done.

"Do you think John-John's okay?" I asked her.

"He seems fine to me," she said.

"Do you think Dad's going to be mad at me?" I said.

"Does Dad know?" she asked.

"No," I admitted. "I haven't told him yet."

"Well that's okay. John-John is fine. No need to worry Dad about it."

Okay, I would not tell Dad. That was a relief, but I still worried that what I'd done would catch up to me somehow and that I'd get the belt. The anticipation of the punishment was almost as bad as the real thing.

The end of summer was sneaking up on us, and I would be starting kindergarten soon. I felt important to be old enough to have a place to go on my own. The night before my first day, I slept in my new blue gingham dress that Grandma Hedderly had made for me. That morning, Dad did my hair in tight pigtails. Mom couldn't get them tight enough, but Dad did them just right. Mom had explained that the bus would pick me up at the end of our driveway, and I strode out the door, only to see the rear of the bus heading away. I ran as fast as I could down the driveway, hoping the bus driver would see me. I thought if I missed the bus, I wouldn't be allowed to go to school, and I stood at the end of the driveway and wept in an agony of despair. My relief was great when the bus turned around and came back for me. The driver kindly didn't comment on my tear-stained face.

From the first day, I loved my teacher, Mrs. Brown, who had soft hands and never raised her voice. When she corrected us, it wasn't in a harsh tone, just a firm one. I wanted to please her, not out of a fear of punishment, but out of a desire for her to like me. I wanted her to think I was wonderful. When gold stars were placed next to students' names on the wall, I wanted the most stars by my name. When she gave out certificates for achievement, I wanted one. The first certificate she awarded me was for tying my shoes. Mom had taught me before kindergarten, so that one was easy. I'd even timed myself at home to see how fast I could do it. I brought the certificate home to show Mom and Dad.

"I'm proud of you, honey," Dad said, which made the day even better.

I hung it on the wall of my room.

Meanwhile, work on the new house continued. Dad had accumulated an entourage of half a dozen young men and teenagers, using the promise of beer and food and general good times in exchange for helping with the construction. Often, they would come to help on the farm, too. They came to harvest elderberries for Dad's elderberry wine project that he had going on in the basement in big glass jugs. To gather the berries, we sat on the rooftop of Dad's station wagon, the guys and me, while Dad drove through the bumpy farm field going from elderberry tree to elderberry tree. The same trees I had to dodge while riding Cindy.

Dad stopped the car at each tree so the pickers could jump off and collect the tiny berries with their purple-stained fingers, then climb back aboard the station wagon's roof until the next tree. The friendliest was a guy named Billy. He was around nineteen, which seemed like a grown-up to me. He would help me get down from the top of the car and then lift me back up. Dad stayed in the driver's seat with Scottie sitting next to him. Scottie loved to go for car rides and sit next to Dad, who was happy not to have to get out of the car. He liked to conserve energy whenever someone else could do the work.

These young men became sort of an extension of the family. Sometimes after school, I got a ride to the construction site in a car full of the young men. I remember sitting on Billy's lap and the guys asking me to sing the songs I'd learned in kindergarten. I sang and acted out "Little Bunny Foo Foo" and

"Where is Thumbkin?" which I sang as "Where is Pumpkin?" to applause and laughter. I was delighted to entertain them.

Billy and the others were often at big backyard neighborhood parties Dad threw on the weekends, serving up his famous barbecue chicken, which he'd marinate the day before in Open Pit BBQ sauce. He'd boil the whole batch on the stovetop, adding butter and beer, then he would crisp and brown the pieces on the grill. Everyone said Dad's was the best barbecue chicken they'd ever tasted.

The adults would sit around drinking beer and pop, and the kids and Scottie would tear around the farm, playing hide-and-seek and chasing chickens. And Dad was always in the center, standing at the grill in his Bermuda shorts, holding court with a loud story of some past youthful antic or close call, always with an unfiltered Camel in hand. He was happy and funny when he had an audience. He was in his element—a real Family Man. He must have felt like he had arrived.

Sometimes he liked to show off in front of the assembled friends and neighbors. The first time he held his twenty-foot ladder straight up in the air in front of the crowd, I wondered what he was doing.

"April," he called to me. "Come here."

I approached cautiously.

"Climb up to the top rung."

I wasn't sure I'd heard him right. The ladder wasn't leaning against anything. He was just holding it straight up.

"Go on," he encouraged me. I knew his tone was not forceful because he had an audience. I obeyed him anyway and climbed the ladder as he held it almost steady, bracing it against his own weight.

"David!" he called next. "Climb up to the middle."

I couldn't look down. My limbs felt tingly, and my heart was pounding. The ladder quivered as David climbed.

"John-John!" I heard Dad say. And again, I felt the ladder shake slightly as John-John took his position somewhere below David.

"Hold on tight!" Dad demanded, and then the ladder began to shake violently. I screamed and heard my brothers scream as I held on with all my might. I felt the edge of the metal ladder cutting into my palms. I pressed my feet into the rung as the ladder swayed, spun, shimmied, and shook.

Finally, the ladder got still again and Dad let us climb down one by one. With wobbly legs we ran off, putting distance between us and the showman. The strength it took each of us to hold on was more than we knew we possessed. The strength it must have taken to pull the feat off on Dad's end was more than we could contemplate.

Dad did not just perform this stunt once as an experiment. It became a regular trick at backyard parties. Mom shot a home movie of it that he liked to show guests. He was the main attraction in the center ring in the big top of his own circus. We were just props.

Having moved out into the country beyond the city limits of Akron had many advantages—the fresh air, the freedom, the open spaces—and it also had the advantage of being farther away from Dad's disapproving in-laws, who, while not being out-and-out forbidden from visiting, were discouraged from doing so. They did, however, send gifts and money for Christmas and birthdays each year. On rare occasions, we would visit them with just Mom. I knew even then that Dad didn't like us to go anywhere without him.

The only relatives to join us for the holidays were Dad's aunt Lucille, who had visited him at the orphanage when he was a boy, and her husband, Al. They didn't have kids of their own. They sent money in advance so that Christmas could be a lavish affair—with gifts and feasting. Their arrival at our house was always a joyful moment.

I loved Aunt Lucille. She was a heavy smoker, like Dad, and she wore cat eye glasses with jewels on them. She smelled like her clean house—which we sometimes visited in Cuyahoga Falls—a mix of cigarettes and Murphy Oil Soap. She wore bright red lipstick on her thin lips, and her hair was curled at the beauty parlor. She wore a hairnet all the time, and a kerchief over her head when she went outside. I admired how well put together she was. Uncle Al had had a stroke and walked with a limp. One of his arms was paralyzed and he spoke in a way that only Aunt Lucille could understand. But he always seemed happy to watch the festivities.

I loved to hear Aunt Lucille tell stories. One of my favorites was about how she met Uncle Al. She had been walking down the road in Akron with a group of friends, and Al drove by with his friends. Apparently, he liked her "shelf" butt. Love at first sight. She always laughed when she told me that story.

When Aunt Lucille sat on the sofa, I liked to curl up in her lap and inhale her scent. That scent meant safety to me. When she was there, Dad was lighter, less irritable, and when she broke out in her loud laugh over something he said, his whole face would light up. She'd say, "Oh, Wayne." No one knew him better. And she loved him anyway.

Aunt Lucille was so unlike Mom. It wasn't just the makeup and her robust laugh. She loved to dance and tell stories. She sat on the floor around Chutes and Ladders, playing with as much gusto as me and my brothers. She had wanted kids, and we were her surrogate grandchildren.

Every year, Dad went all out at Christmas. In the run-up to the season, he decorated the house with garlands strung from corner to corner. He and Mom hung wreaths and trimmed the windows in lights. This year we had a giant tree and it stood in the slightly sagging corner of the farmhouse living room. Dad hung colorful strings of lights on the branches. We all took turns hanging ornaments and shiny silver tinsel.

"I made this one in school," I told Aunt Lucille as I proudly hung an ornament on the tree.

"April, that's lovely!" she said as she reached high to spread silver threads on the upper branches.

After we had put everything on the tree, Dad stood back to assess our work and then redistributed the tinsel and ornaments so the tree looked symmetrical.

On Christmas Eve, we made popcorn on the stovetop in a giant canning pot. We watched *Frosty the Snowman* and *Rudolph the Red-Nosed Reindeer* on TV, the whole family piled on the floor with pillows and blankets, while

Aunt Lucille and Uncle Al looked on from the sofa. I liked to lean back into her knees.

Dad loved the Christmas specials on TV as much as his kids did, but when they were over, he sent us to bed and we reluctantly crawled up the stairs. We never had to wait until morning to open our presents, because Dad couldn't wait. He woke us in the middle of the night.

"Wake up, kids," he said, bouncing up and down like a big kid. "Come see what Santa brought you." We all fervently believed in Santa.

We ran downstairs, and there under the tree was a mound of brightly wrapped gifts. The decorative lights around the dark windows bathed the living room in color. David, John-John, and I each picked a spot around the tree far enough away from each other that our presents wouldn't get mixed up. Mom sat on the sofa with Jeff on her lap. She would help him open his. Dad picked up each gift, then he passed it to one of us. One by one he handed out all the gifts—this year there were five each—which we stacked beside us. We had to be patient and take turns opening one gift at a time. Aunt Lucille and Uncle Al watched each gift being opened; they weren't about to miss this. John-John squirmed as he watched David unwrap his first gift—a Tonka Toy dump truck. We all "oohed" and "aahed." Each gift had to be admired by all before the next person could unwrap a present.

When it was my turn, I chose the biggest box first. I couldn't imagine what it was. I tore the wrapping paper off and opened the box to find a giant Barbie head that you could apply makeup to and shorten or lengthen her silky blond hair. Aunt Lucille clapped. This was by far my favorite gift that year.

After all the gifts were open, Aunt Lucille got down on the floor with me to examine the little makeup kit that came with the Barbie head. Soon, David fell asleep on top of his new truck, and Dad said, "Back to bed."

When we woke on Christmas day, we were greeted by the intoxicating smell of roast turkey and gravy. Dad had cooked up a feast, including stuffing, mashed potatoes, beets, yams, French-cut string beans, corn on the cob, and rolls. For dessert there was cherry pie, pumpkin pie, Christmas cookies, and eggnog.

With the festivities and feasting of the holiday over, we were back to our usual rations of tuna casserole or mac and cheese. I missed Aunt Lucille and her neutralizing effect on Dad. The winter turned brutal with record snowfalls and power outages, but Dad knew how to survive a storm. When the power went out, we simply gathered in the garage around a burn barrel like hobos. He cooked up pots of boiled cold cuts on the grill. I thought it was an adventure, as if we were acting in my favorite TV show, *Little House on the Prairie*.

When winter finally passed, the longer days felt like heaven. Early that spring, I was in the front yard with Scottie, who was chasing chipmunks. He also had a bad habit of chasing cars. That morning, Dad left the house, eating an apple, and got in his station wagon. He drove off fast down the road, and Scottie took off after the car, ignoring my frantic calls to him. Scottie was faster than the car, and Dad didn't even see him before he hit him. The car screeched to a halt and Dad got out, still holding on to his apple. When he saw Scottie, he threw the apple hard against the road in disgust. It splattered like apple sauce. He knelt by Scottie's limp body and wept. This was the only time I ever saw my father cry. Dad buried Scottie in the backyard of the farmhouse. He would not let us watch this.

With Scottie gone, Dad's mood was dark. When he came home from the construction site, it wasn't the same without Scottie running up to greet him. I hadn't greeted him enthusiastically in a while. I was too busy with my farm chores—feeding the ponies and chickens, shoveling poop, making outside work for myself that wasn't strictly necessary—just so I could minimize my time indoors with Dad.

Then, in May, the month of heaven-scented cherry blossoms and bright yellow daffodils, I woke one night to strange popping sounds. Through my open bedroom door I saw the glare of lights flashing against the wall in the hallway. I ran into the hall to look out the window. From there I could see the barn ablaze. The ponies were in the barn! I screamed and screamed as I watched sparks fly out into the darkness. Fire trucks crowded the yard and the strobe of their lights hurt my eyes. Flames had consumed its roof. I was still screaming when finally, Mom came to me. She held me close and brought me back to my room.

"But the ponies!" I sobbed. "Will Dad save the ponies?"

Mom was quiet. She had no answer, but she told me to stay in bed, in my room, and not come out. As soon as she left, I snuck back to the window and watched in horror as the barn roof came crashing in. My legs felt like rubber, and I collapsed by the window in a hiccupping heap. In the morning I found myself back in my bed. I had no memory of leaving the window.

I leapt out of bed and ran outside in my nightgown. There, in the garish daylight, where the barn had stood, was a pile of charred timbers.

The firemen were gone. It was just Dad walking around the site where the barn used to be. Max and Cindy were in the field. I felt a wave of relief that almost knocked me off my feet. The chickens survived, though the rooster had scorched tail feathers. I never saw the barn cats again.

The fire happened on a Friday night. All weekend I tried to catch Cindy. But the ponies wouldn't let me get near them. When I approached, even Cindy would pin her ears back. Her head would shoot up and her eyes would roll and she'd bolt away. I didn't understand why she suddenly didn't like me anymore.

When I got home from school on Monday, the ponies were gone.

"Where are Max and Cindy?" I asked Dad as soon as he came home.

His answer was so confusing that I still don't understand it. He said, "I'm sorry, honey. They were so traumatized by the fire, they became crazy. A man came to take them away."

"Well," I said, not comprehending this story at all. "Can't we get them back?"

"No, April," he said, looking truly sorry. "They were too wild. They had to be put down."

"What?!" I knew what "put down" meant. We'd had to "put down" one of the barn cats who got an infected tail. I couldn't make sense of Dad's explanation.

Dad wouldn't say any more to me. He just walked away.

The barn itself was now just the sharp broken bones of the building, with none of the softness of the animals inside. We never spoke of the barn fire again. That summer there were no ponies to care for, no Cindy to ride. We spent nearly every day at the Kevin Drive site while Dad worked on the house, slowly transforming the piles of lumber into walls and floors and roof.

In early September, exactly four months after the barn fire, Dad bundled us all into the station wagon one night and said we were going to the movies. I wondered what movie we were going to see. It was strange to be going out at night in our pajamas. But Dad just drove around until we fell asleep. When I woke up in the car, we were parked on Taylor Road in front of the farmhouse. I thought I was still dreaming, because what my eyes perceived couldn't possibly be correct. Fire trucks blocked the driveway. The farmhouse was engulfed in flames. But the strobing lights from the fire engines pulsed through the car and flames leapt out of the living room windows, and I knew that I could not wake up from this nightmare.

A piercing cry split the air, and I didn't realize it had burst from me until Dad whipped around, his face red with fury, and backhanded me from the front seat.

"Shut up!" he screamed.

My brothers were now awake, confused and crying. I stifled my sobs, burying my face in my hands, choking on my swallowed screams. I imagined my giant Barbie head with her hair on fire. I could hardly catch my breath. My heart was pounding so hard it felt like it was going to break.

Dad got out of the car and walked toward the fire trucks. I looked to Mom, expecting her to be desperate too. She was silent. I couldn't tell what she was thinking. There she was in the front seat, looking infuriatingly indifferent, eyes downcast on Jeff, who was hiding his head in her lap. Why wasn't she crying? Why wasn't she shocked? Why did she look like this wasn't a catastrophe?

Watching that house burn, I wanted to be far, far away. Something hurt so bad inside me, like it had when I learned Max and Cindy were dead. The sorrow welled like a wave that overtook me. I was drowning in it. And there was no one to rescue me.

I mourned that house and that barn and those ponies and that paradise for years. The farm on Taylor Road had been my Eden, and I had been cast out.

7

Practical Joker

1976

After the fire, we stayed in another rental house in the area. It was from there that I caught the bus for first grade, and we had a Christmas there, but it didn't feel like home. By summer, we moved into the new house on Kevin Drive, even though it wasn't ready for us.

And by not ready for us, I don't mean it didn't have furniture yet. I mean it had no running water or plumbing or heating system. Our water source was an ice-cold spring that was piped into the basement. Our toilet was a five-gallon bucket framed in a plywood box. The floors were rough plywood. The walls were just studs with pipes and electric wires visible between them. Dad told us that eventually, upstairs would have a large master bedroom and bathroom, a second bathroom and three more bedrooms. It was an ambitious project. But Dad and his crew of young men were working on it, and they just moved around the makeshift living quarters that Dad set up for us on the first floor. On one end of the house was a sunken living room with a kitchen off to the side. The other end had a giant fireplace with an area that would become a dining room/family room, and that was where we set up our makeshift bedroom with two sets of bunk beds. The fireplace would be our only source of heat come winter. Mom and Dad set up a bed in what would become Dad's office just off the family room.

The kitchen was barely functional: a stainless steel sink with countertops of loose plywood sheets. Instead of cupboards, there were shelves made of two-by-fours. Our table was an old metal one with a Formica top. The metal chairs had cracked yellow vinyl seats that pinched my legs.

In the sunken living room, there were two secondhand couches that were covered in a scratchy material with orange and brown flowers. And there was a big recliner for Dad that no one else was allowed to sit in.

Had I been older and wiser I might have figured out the reason behind why my giant Barbie head was still among my possessions. When I had first pulled her out of a box in the rental house, I was so happy to see her I didn't think to wonder how she had been saved from the fire. Her retractable hair was by now a frizzy mass from me playing with her so much. David's Tonka truck had been saved, too. So had all our Christmas presents and favorite books. I would eventually understand the implications, but I didn't then.

Kevin Drive was a dead-end street, and our property was surrounded by farmland. The field around our house was so large that Dad could have built a mansion on it. But the house he was building seemed mansion-like to me. It had an attached garage. None of it had siding, but Dad was more focused on getting the inside done than the outside. He traded in the station wagon for an El Camino, which was only sort of useful as a truck and only sort of useful as a car. When we went anywhere as a family in it, we all squeezed into the front row seat. Dad acquired a few other odd vehicles too, including an old out-of-commission police car that sat in our yard and which we pretended to drive until the grass grew high around it and a family of mice moved in. An old school bus also appeared among the junk and construction debris in the yard, which was taking on a hillbilly character.

Indoors, our home may have been rough, but the outdoors was a giant playground. In the patch of trees at the edge of our yard, Dad helped David, John-John, and me build a treehouse in a sprawling oak, using scraps of plywood and boards. We swung like monkeys from the thick vines hanging from the treetops.

There was a pile of concrete blocks in the yard left over from the foundation that became a playhouse big enough for me and my three brothers to fit inside at once. Dad gave us a piece of plywood for the roof. I pretended it was a hospital and I was a doctor, fixing my brothers' broken bones. Or it was a Wild West fort and we acted out scenes from the John Wayne movies we watched with Dad.

Dad made us a tire swing with a stout rope tied to a limb of a tree. We took turns spinning each other until we were so dizzy we fell off.

Dad missed Scottie, and one day he brought home a beagle named Snoopy. Snoopy had all the bad habits of his breed. He would get a whiff of something interesting and be off like a shot. Dad built a doghouse and tied him to it with a short chain, and Snoopy actually pulled the doghouse off its foundation, taking off after a scent. Dad got so frustrated that one day he took Snoopy for a drive and returned without him. He must have simply dropped him off somewhere, though, because Snoopy returned on his own, using that powerful nose of his to find his way back. We kids were delighted to see him again and he seemed just as happy to see us. But Dad had had it with Snoopy and put him in the car again and drove off. This time Snoopy didn't come back.

Shortly after we moved to Kevin Drive, another new family moved in across the street, and they had a daughter, Diane, who was of babysitting age. Dad welcomed them to the neighborhood. He introduced himself like he had to all the neighbors, handing them his published memoir and explaining his background and new career as a motivational speaker. He said he kept an eye on the neighborhood because he had a lot of friends who were cops.

Then he asked the mom, Lynn, if their daughter would be available to babysit. Maybe it was the title of the book he handed to Lynn, *Metamorphosis of a Criminal*, or the state of our yard, or just careful parenting, but she required that she first come check out the house before allowing her daughter to babysit.

When she came over later that day, Dad ushered Lynn in as if he were the benevolent king of a castle. While Dad shared with her his excitement about the plans he had for the upstairs master bedroom and how far along he'd come with the wiring, she gazed around at the bunk beds in the family room with a look of dismay. I tried to see our home through her eyes. It was filthy. Construction dust covered the rough floors. Dirty dishes were stacked in piles on the plywood counter by the sink. Our mattresses were bare, with no sheets or pillows, covered with only a thin blanket. Piles of laundry filled one of the sofas. Extension cords snaked across the floor. There were no curtains or homey touches. Yet Dad was oblivious to her obvious alarm and gave her a full tour, including the basement. Dad was describing the ingenuity it had required to set up the water pipe in such a way.

"How do you bathe?" she interrupted.

"Oh, we do it down here!" he said proudly. "We bring buckets up for dishes and cooking, though." Then he added with a charming chuckle, "Just like the old days!"

Lynn seemed genuinely shocked by the primitive conditions. However, for whatever reason, she did allow her daughter to take the job. Maybe she felt sorry for the children who lived in a construction site and wanted to help us. Or maybe Dad's good intentions and winning smile convinced her it was safe.

When Diane first came over to babysit, Dad and Mom were getting ready to go out. Things were tense, because, as usual, Dad wanted Mom to put on makeup and she didn't want to. She said mascara hurt her eyes.

Diane was introduced to me and Jeff, who had turned two that spring when I turned seven.

"Where are the other two boys?" Diane asked.

"Oh, they're in the garage," Dad said.

He brought Diane to the mudroom, which connected the main house to the garage. We never used the garage for cars because it had no foundation and the ground was too muddy. But Dad used it for other things.

Diane peered into the garage expecting to see a six-year-old and four-year-old playing with blocks or something innocent like that. But instead, to her utter amazement, there on one wall were David and John-John, suspended from their belt loops by nails. They looked up forlornly, but said not a word.

"What are they doing there?!" Diane asked in a shaky voice.

"They're being punished," Dad explained.

"For what?" she asked, incredulous.

"For not listening," he said. He'd caught them playing when they were supposed to be cleaning up their crayons.

And then he brought Diane back into the house and continued the tour as if what she had witnessed was perfectly normal. Dad retrieved David and John-John before he and Mom went out. I could tell Diane was not keen on staying, but David and John-John didn't seem injured, and she may have felt it was too late. After all, Mom and Dad were backing out the door. Dad smiled and said, "Be good!" to us as they left.

Diane just shook her head in wonderment, and after the door closed, she said, "Well, what do you kids want to play?"

"Chutes and Ladders!" we all chimed in, and that's what we did.

Hanging David and John-John by their belt loops was a common punishment for minor infractions. Like telling them to pee on the electric fence at the Taylor Road farm, it was also a kind of practical joke that he played on them. Sometimes it was just a way to show off. As party entertainment, like the ladder trick, he would randomly hammer a nail into a stud and hang up his sons by their belt loops, gesturing to his guests, as if to say, "This is the kind of control I have over my family!" Practical jokes were big with Dad, and he thought up one for me and me alone. He would never have hung me by my belt loops. For one thing, I was too big, and for another thing, my pants and shorts never had belt loops.

His special torture for me on Taylor Road had been to force me to eat canned beets, which I loathed. The last time he did this at dinner, I threw up all over the table. Aunt Lucille had been there, and she'd said, "Wayne! Don't make her eat them!" I loved her all the more for it.

Here on Kevin drive, the prank was taken to a new level. It combined my dread over bathing in the icy water of the basement and my other aversion— buttermilk.

I hated washing my hair, which was thick and hard to detangle. If washing my hair had been a chore on Taylor Road, where we had hot water and a shower, now it was an event that I obsessed over days in advance. I'd think about stripping naked in the cold basement and dunking my head under the freezing water that gave me an instant headache and I'd start shivering. Even the idea of going down the wooden steps to the basement filled me with anxiety. This was the perfect set up for Dad.

Buttermilk made me throw up. I hated the smell and the taste and the texture. Dad loved it. He'd drink it right out of the carton.

The first time it happened on Kevin Drive was just after Mom had helped me wash my hair down in the basement and I had come upstairs and changed into clean clothes. I had just taken a seat on the scratchy sofa with my coloring books and box of crayons when I heard the refrigerator door open and close. Dad walked into the living room drinking from a quart carton of buttermilk.

"Come here, honey," he said.

I got up and went to him.

"April," he said, indicating the carton. "Either drink it or wear it."

"I don't want to drink it," I said. "It'll make me throw up." He already knew this.

"Dad, please," I begged.

"Drink it or wear it. Your choice."

If I threw up, I knew Dad would hit me. So I refused to drink it. This answer pleased Dad and he poured the rest of the nearly full quart over my head. The sour smelling buttermilk ran down my hair onto my face, down my collar, into my socks, onto the floor. I began to gag.

"Better get cleaned up!" Dad said, and off we went to the basement. I had to strip down and wash my hair again, freezing my brain as Dad held my head beneath the spigot of icy water.

This happened just often enough to keep me worrying whenever Dad opened the fridge door. I'd feel the panic rising inside me. There was nowhere for me to go. I had no bedroom. The rooms had no doors. I felt like a rabbit waiting for the beast to come get me.

Dad always laughed at my worry. I should be able to take a joke, he said.

I noticed that the bigger my reaction to his "practical jokes," the more he seemed to enjoy them. My brothers learned this too. We developed poker faces during these events, and that took some of the fun out of it for Dad.

He, himself, couldn't take a "joke." For him, a prank must always be at someone else's expense. Mom had learned this the hard way when we lived at the farm on Taylor Road. One of the jokes he liked to play on us there was to sneak up when we were showering and pour a pitcher of cold water on our heads. One day Mom decided, in an uncharacteristic flash of impishness, to pull the prank on Dad. He must have been in a good mood before the shower, because she never would have tried it otherwise.

"Come on," she said to me with a rare smile as she filled a pitcher with cold water at the kitchen sink.

I followed her down the hall and we stopped at the bathroom door and listened. I heard the muffled sound of Dad singing in the shower.

"Do it, Mom, do it!" I said.

She flashed me a nervous smile and, pitcher in hand, opened the door and disappeared into the steamy bathroom. I waited for her, bouncing on my toes. I couldn't believe she was doing this! I kept waiting for the sound of Dad squealing with surprise like we did when he did it to us. I expected to hear him burst out laughing. Instead, I heard a crash and a scream, and Mom came bolting out of the bathroom looking terrified.

She ran to her bedroom. I followed her. "What happened!?" I asked.

She told me that as soon as the cold water had hit him, Dad's fist flew through the glass shower door, shattering it. Mom closed her door. I ran to my room and did the same. I was worried that he would hurt her and that I would also get in trouble for cheering her on. A few minutes later, I heard Dad's voice talking calmly in the kitchen. I tiptoed out of my room and down the stairs and saw that he and Mom were at the kitchen sink. He had cut himself badly and was coaching Mom in how to stitch up his right hand.

Dad's response was more reflex than anger. He was someone you never wanted to surprise by touching him when he was asleep. Once, I tapped his shoulder when he was napping on the couch, and he snapped awake and snatched my neck in a grip like a boa constrictor before he even registered who I was. I never did that again. I came to think of him when he was sleeping as a wild animal that you should never disturb.

That winter, Dad threw great parties at the Kevin Drive house even though it was still a work in progress. At the New Year's party, we kids were allowed to stay up until midnight. The house was crowded with adults, including Dad's crew of guys and their girlfriends. I made my way through the partygoers, who seemed slightly off-balance.

A guy named Billy, the friendliest of Dad's crew, was sitting on the sofa with his girlfriend, Judith. "Come here, April," he said. He patted his lap, indicating I should get on. I did, and he bounced me on his knee. I sat for a while, listening to the adult conversation around me, more chaotic than usual and punctuated by barks of laughter. I saw Dad look over at me with a stern expression and I jumped off Billy's lap and joined David and John-John milling around the tipsy adults. I hoped I wasn't in trouble for anything.

Dad distributed hundreds of balloons, and we all blew them up. We hung them on the Christmas garlands and taped them along the walls and doorframes. Just before midnight, Dad passed a box of straight pins around, and the sense of anticipation was thick in the house. At the stroke of midnight, everyone started popping all the balloons. Colorful bits of rubber flew everywhere. David and John-John covered their ears. But I looked around at all the smiling faces. The moment the popping stopped, it was like the room took a collective breath, and we were all made new again. Maybe in the new year everyone would be happy. I made a wish—the same wish I'd made for my past two birthdays. I wished for a baby sister, just like Laura Ingalls had on *Little House on the Prairie*.

In fact, I thought we'd have an adventure like the Ingalls family when we moved to Kevin Drive. I envisioned us lugging buckets of water up from the basement like they brought water from the well, and I learned that that wasn't actually very fun. However, I thought helping to carry firewood into the house from a woodpile like a hardy pioneer girl would be. That winter was another one for the record books. One of our chores was indeed to bring firewood into the house, just like I'd hoped. But David, John-John, and I could each carry only one or two logs at a time from the woodpile to the house, sometimes with frozen fingers in stiff mittens in temperatures below freezing and in high winds. We trudged back and forth through deep snow in the yard, which was still a rutted construction site. Sometimes Dad would send us out at night to bring in more logs to stack on the floor by the fireplace. Outside, in the dark, while the cold wind howled, I thought monsters might grab me from behind as I stumbled back to the house with my heavy burden.

Our wood supply came from a lot a short drive away, where Dad would fell trees, cut and split the logs, and David, John-John, and I would throw the firewood into the back of Dad's El Camino. It *was* hard work, but if we hadn't been in the woodlot, we never would have met Happy.

One day, we were collecting firewood and looked up to see what I thought at first was a tall, scrawny wolf staring at us. Dad told us to back away, and he got between us and the wolf. He walked toward her, and she lay down. When he got close enough, she licked his hand.

On our way back home, we all squeezed into the front seat of the El Camino, including the dog, a sort of German shepherd–husky mix. When we got to the house, she jumped out, tail wagging. Dad gave her water and some leftovers in bowls he placed near Snoopy's old doghouse. That day she came home with us, she became part of the family—just one that didn't come into the house. She smiled so much, we named her Happy.

Dad's job, while we lived at Kevin Drive, was mostly working on the house and doing handyman and construction work for other people. But he was still getting occasional speaking engagements. We would listen to him rehearse his lines over and over again. One of the rhetorical questions he liked to ask was: "What are some of the definitions for love?" He answered: "Love is being called Wife and Mother . . . Love is having friends, but more important [dramatic pause], it's being one . . . Love is still waiting for him to come home from work as if it were your first date . . . Love is your husband running up the hospital stairs every night for a week to be the first visitor because the elevator is too slow . . ."

These days, Mom was hardly waiting for him as if it was their first date. She was always trying to avoid anything that could trigger a fit of rage, but it was a guessing game. We all tried to gauge his moods before committing to any interaction with him, when we could help it.

Now, when I heard his car pulling into the driveway, I didn't run outside to greet him. I consciously did the opposite. I would try to find something to do that would make me invisible, like picking up a book and getting engrossed in a story. My brothers would look up worriedly and take their blocks into a corner of the room to build a fort or in some other way be engaged quietly to avoid detection. Dad's moods coming home were increasingly dark.

But it was harder for Mom to avoid him. By spring that year, Mom was visibly pregnant with her fifth child. I was so excited. I prayed every night, the way Mom had taught us, that the baby would be a girl. One night after dinner, Dad got mad about not being able to find his cigarettes and lighter and he zeroed in on Mom. He punched her right in the stomach. In front of me. Mom grabbed her stomach and doubled over. Her eyes were squeezed shut and her brow was etched in pain. I'd never seen her in so much distress. She went straight to bed.

All night I worried about her and the baby. The next day, Mom caught me staring at her belly and gave me a sad little smile. She knew what I was thinking. What if Dad had hurt the baby. If it hadn't been for the baby, Dad punching Mom hard in the stomach wouldn't have seemed like an extraordinary event. I watched the bump nervously for days. But Mom's belly must have been strong, because the bump kept growing.

The house had come a long way since we'd moved in. Now we had indoor plumbing. We had hot water and a real bathroom with a shower and tub. No more bathing in the ice-cold water of the basement. No more pooping in a bucket. The floors and kitchen counters were still plywood, though, and those were hard to sweep clean. I knew this because David, John-John, and I had been instructed by Dad in how to do the housekeeping chores, tasks that Dad taught us to perform as soon as we were old enough to stand on a chair at the sink or hold a broom. We now washed the dishes, dried them, and put them away on shelves that we still used instead of cabinets. The house was, of course, a mess, but when basic cleaning had to be done, we kids were the ones to do it. And this was helpful to Mom, who was approaching her due date.

Finally, the day came when Dad packed Mom into the car with her little overnight bag to take her to the hospital. We waited for news with a baby-sitter. While Mom was at the hospital, I thought of Dad's public talks, and I wondered if Dad, like the loving husband in his lectures, would run up the stairs to see his wife or if Dad would be lazy and take the elevator. I decided Dad would never take the stairs to see his wife unless the elevator was out of service.

Dad came home the next day and told us with a big smile and a hug that we had a baby sister named Jeannine. *Hallelujah!* I jumped up and down and thanked God that he had answered my prayers.

The night before Mom came home, Dad gathered me and David and John-John to him and said he had a job for us. Jeff was only two, and still not quite up to doing hard work.

"Mom's coming home tomorrow and the house needs to be clean for the baby."

It was already late, but David was directed to get the broom and sweep the floor. John-John was told to pick up dirty laundry, and I got to work on the pile of dirty dishes. Dad got out a bucket and mop and scrub brushes.

"Make sure the floor and everything is scrubbed spotless," he said. He wasn't going to scrub the floor himself. He was telling us to do it, and we were already tired—it was almost bedtime and we hadn't had dinner. After finishing the dishes, I began on the plywood floor. The house had never seemed so huge to me. My brothers joined me with scrub brushes gripped in their smaller hands. My arms began to ache. My knees were scraped and sore.

The minutes on the clock ticked by relentlessly as we scrubbed. Dad wouldn't let us eat or sleep until we'd finished scouring the house. Of course, it's hard to clean plywood. David, John-John—and even Jeff—and I worked our knuckles bloody scrubbing those floors. We labored well into the night. I wanted to say, "It isn't fair!" but I knew better. David, however, couldn't help whispering exactly that when Dad left the room. "It isn't fair," he sobbed quietly. I knew I had to keep my brothers on task, so I said, "Just do your work," and kept scrubbing. My knees hurt so much I switched to the mop, but I was so exhausted that I nearly fell asleep on my feet. Dad came back into the room as I began to sway and he smacked me on the head to wake me up, and I went back to mopping. When we were finally allowed to go to bed, we fell into them, still wearing our wet, soapy clothes.

But the next morning, our exhaustion instantly was forgotten when we heard Dad's car outside. There was Mom, emerging from the car holding a pink bundle in her arms.

I loved having a little sister. I treated her like a living doll, giving her bottles of formula and dressing her in cute outfits that Mom's parents had mailed us. I carried Jeannine around and burped her and helped Mom give her baths. Once when she was old enough for me to bathe by myself, I brought her into the bathroom and ran warm water in the tub. But first, I needed to change her poopy diaper, so I removed it and I swished the cloth diaper in the toilet bowl like I'd seen Mom do a million times. I flushed. But the force of the flush sucked the diaper right out of my hand, and it disappeared down the toilet. I was sure that I'd clogged the toilet and it would overflow. If that happened, I knew I'd get a beating. I flushed and flushed and flushed to force that diaper as far away as possible, and to my great relief, the toilet kept flushing fine.

I gave Jeannine a bath as if nothing had happened, but this diaper down the toilet bothered me. I came into Mom's room and handed Jeannine over, now squeaky clean and in a new diaper. I hadn't planned on telling Mom about my worries, but I had to warn her in case the toilet gave her trouble. I sat on her bed, and as she put pajamas on Jeannine, I fessed up. Mom looked at me. I had hugged a pillow to my chest in my nervousness. She smiled and said, "Don't worry April. I think it's going to be fine." I hoped she was right. I wasn't convinced I was out of the woods.

If Dad was in a foul mood, he would fly off the handle for something like this. But when he was in a good mood, he might think it was funny. Funny that I'd had the diaper snatched from my hand by the toilet monster and funny that I'd been afraid I'd get in trouble. That night, Mom told Dad. She must have gauged that Dad was in a good mood. She was right. He thought it was hilarious. She laughed too. She didn't laugh often, so this was a treat for me to see. Even rarer was hearing them laugh together. She never laughed so hard she was out of control, like Dad. He loved to laugh to the point where he almost couldn't breathe.

I liked to think I could always tell what kind of mood he was in, like I had special powers to see inside his head, but I would sometimes get it wrong. Like the time we were all sitting in the living room. Mom was on the sofa knitting baby booties. Dad was in his recliner with a stack of white typing paper in his lap. My brothers and I were at his feet coloring in our coloring books on the floor.

"Look," he said, "I can draw a perfect Santa." And he picked up one of the sheets and drew for a moment, and then held it up for his children to admire. It was a perfect pencil drawing of Santa. David and John-John were impressed. But I had looked at those sheets of papers and I had seen that they already had faint lines, like something photocopied from a coloring book. Dad was just tracing those lines and I said so.

"No. I just drew that," he insisted.

I challenged him again, and again he denied it. "But there are lines on the paper already," I said.

"No there aren't."

"Yes there are. You're a liar!"

I had heard kids call other kids liars all the time. "Liar, liar, pants on fire," was a common refrain at recess. But here, I had just called my own father a liar to his face. I don't think I realized what I had just done. I just knew I had said the wrong thing.

Like a cobra striking, he grabbed me by my hair and my arm. I felt my body yanked back and then lifted in the air. I went flying across the room and struck the wall hard with a sickening whack.

I came to on the sofa, with Dad sitting beside me, holding a cold compress to my head. I kept my eyes closed for as long as I could. I was afraid to open them. I didn't want him to know I was awake. My head ached. When I finally opened my eyes, he stared at me with a worried expression. He asked, "April, honey, you okay?"

It took me a few minutes to reconstruct what had happened. I shuddered as I remembered the impact with the wall. I had called Dad a liar, insulting his honor, breaking a code that I didn't realize existed. And for that, he had thrown me across the room. I wondered if he looked so worried because he thought he might have killed me. Good, I thought. He should worry. I wasn't only hurt and scared, I was mad.

What I had said was true: he was a liar. We all knew it. He could look you in the eye and tell you something you knew was not true, and he would do it with complete sincerity. His truth was the only truth that existed. My truth, that I had seen with my own eyes, was not the truth at all. If what I knew to be true was false, then I must be the one who was the liar.

8

Self-Defense

I was about to start second grade and David was going into first, and it would be our first year going to school together. David was buzzing with excitement to take the bus with me, but I could not share his enthusiasm. I had much bigger things to think about. I had just had another surgery to repair the scar on the right side of my mouth from the burn I had given myself on Avon Street, and the fresh scar was bright red and raw. It was my fervent but irrational hope that no one would notice.

There was one particular boy I dreaded seeing on the bus. He was a redheaded kid two years older than me, who I hadn't seen since the end of first grade. He had asked me on the playground if I would be his girlfriend and I had said, "No way!" He took my rejection badly and threw a milk carton at me.

Now, on the first day of second grade, I got on the bus, my face ablaze with the scar and embarrassment. As I walked down the aisle on my way to the back of the bus, I passed the redheaded boy. He took one look at me and said, "Ew, what happened to your mouth?" That was all it took.

After that, every morning he, and what seemed to me to be every kid on the bus, joined in a chorus of ridicule. Every day when I made my way down the aisle, they called me Scar Face and Grape Ape, that ugly purple cartoon character. I took to wearing a wool cap that I could pull down over my face and sat hunched over in the back corner of the bus. The bus driver never said a word. David didn't sit with me.

A few weeks into it, I mentioned to Dad that I didn't like the bus anymore because the kids were mean to me. I regretted the words as soon as they were out of my mouth. His own child being bullied struck a deep chord in Dad. I was about the same age he had been at the orphanage when he had been unable to defend himself against the nuns and the other boys. He had told us those stories. I should have known better.

The next afternoon, when the bus stopped at our corner, I stood to get off. But when the door opened, Dad got on. I started shaking.

"Hey!" Dad began shouting at the bus driver. "Are you sleeping on the job or something? My daughter is being bullied and I'm not getting off this bus until I know who's doing it."

The bus driver sputtered, "I didn't know."

"Well if you were half-awake you should!" Dad shouted.

The driver looked at me, like this was my fault, and said, "Who's doing it?"

Mortified, I said nothing. I did not want to point out who the culprits were. But Dad yelled, "Which ones!?" I had to answer him.

I wanted to scream, "The entire bus!" but I only pointed to a few kids. Not the redheaded boy. Dad glowered at each one of them. Those kids I pointed to got in trouble at school, and after that day, the bus driver made me sit directly behind him, even though that seat was normally reserved for the kindergartners. David said nothing when he passed by me in my baby seat, taking his seat near the other kids in his class.

After the bus incident, Dad was determined that none of his children would ever experience the humiliation of being bullied again. He thought it was time for us to learn to defend ourselves. Thus began the ten-year program in self-defense taught by Edward Wayne Edwards, career criminal. His pupils were his three oldest children: me, age 7; David, age 6; and John-John, age 4.

For the first fight session, Dad called us into the living room and lined us up. He showed us how to throw a punch by demonstrating on an imaginary opponent and indicated on himself where the target of the punch needed to be for maximum effect. Then he said we would practice our moves on each other. David and I were up first because we were the closest in size.

Dad said, "Throw the first punch, April." I tentatively punched David in the shoulder.

"No good," he said. "Don't hold back. The day will come when your brothers will beat your ass."

I punched David's other shoulder slightly harder.

"I said don't hold back!" Dad yelled, and he punched me hard in the thigh, like he was giving me a Charlie horse—something he did when we least expected it, saying "Meet Charlie!" as he drove a punch so hard the muscle bunched and spasmed.

My leg hurt so bad my eyes watered. Was Dad serious? I was bewildered, but I did the only thing I could do—obey. I swung at David wildly, pummeling him with both fists, not caring where my punches landed. He fell to the floor, and I sat on him with fists still flailing as my blows rained down on his face. David held his hands up to defend himself, but I was faster.

"Good, good," Dad was saying, as David sobbed through his hands.

Afterward I felt sick. I was filled with rage at my father for making me hurt my brother. Hadn't he always told me it was my job to protect them? How could I fight them and protect them at the same time? I was so confused.

He stoked competition between us in other ways, too. Ridiculous ways, that were for his own amusement.

One weekend Dad devised a race to see who could finish two beers first. Mom wasn't home. David, John-John, and I were the contestants. Jeff was too little and watched, sitting on Dad's lap, sucking his thumb. There would be no second place. Only a winner. I was not about to let either of my brothers win. We sat down at the kitchen table with two cans of Budweiser in front of each of us. My first sip was disappointing. Why did grown-ups like this sour drink? But I sucked two beers down as fast as I could, and my head felt funny. Mom came home to find me raging drunk. I was standing on a chair singing and dancing to "I'm a Little Teapot." Dad was in hysterics, thinking this was about the funniest thing he'd ever seen. He roared with laughter and pounded the table with his fists.

"What in the world?!" Mom was saying to Dad as I ran upstairs and into the master bedroom. I ran straight to an open window and crawled onto the sill. I looked down at the yard and the ground looked like it was rising and falling, like it was breathing. The lawn looked squishy, like the floor of a giant green bounce house at the fair.

"April Lynn!" Mom yelled frantically from the doorway. "Come down from there!" She reached me just as I was about to jump. She grabbed me around my waist and pulled me back into the room as I scratched and clawed at her arms. She was in my way! She was wrecking the fun Dad and I were having! She held me close, pinning my arms to my side, and pulled me into the bathroom, where I vomited in the toilet. She held my hair and stroked my back, saying, "Oh dear, oh dear." I looked up at her, as the bedroom spun. She handed me a cup of water and I noticed that she was bleeding where my fingernails had gouged her arms.

As absurd as the drinking contest was, it did not do lasting harm, thanks to my mother getting to the window in time. If my brothers minded losing that one, they didn't mention it. But the regular gladiator sessions that continued for the rest of our childhoods, forced upon us by Dad, did not nourish sibling love. David and John never forgave me for beating them up; I would pay for that later. However, the fighting skills would serve me well in the coming years as a new kid in school every year between fourth and eighth grades.

As for fighting outside the home, Dad had two strict rules: (1) We must never ever start a fight. If he ever heard that we had started a fight, he would punish us severely. Punishment for infractions that weren't in the heat of the moment took the form of beatings with his belt across our butts; and (2) If someone else started the fight, then we had to finish it. If he ever learned that we'd lost a fight in self-defense, he would beat us worse than our opponent had.

I heard him loud and clear. If I had to fight, I had to win.

But not all of Dad's orders were clear. Mixed messages were everywhere. We were told not to start fights, but we saw him picking fights with Mom over the smallest things, like why didn't she like to wear makeup? Why was her hair so boring? Or he'd complain that she wasn't fun enough.

One night, after we kids were all in our bunks, Dad began screaming at Mom. Our bunks had been moved to the room designated to eventually become Dad's office, and it had thin walls to separate it from the rest of the open downstairs. I heard things crash in the kitchen. First John-John, then David, and finally Jeff, bringing his pillow, came scampering up to my upper bunk and squeezed into bed with me.

Together, we listened to the sound of Dad punching Mom on the other side of the wall.

We heard her screaming, "Wayne, stop! Wayne, stop!"

We huddled together, trying to be as quiet as possible. Jeff sucked furiously on his thumb and hugged his pillow close. I could feel his body shivering. We were all afraid not just for Mom, but also that in his frenzy Dad would run into our room and snatch us out of our beds and beat us, too. Sometimes this happened. I was often afraid he would find out that I hadn't folded the laundry like he'd told me to, and in the middle of the night he would yank me out of bed and spank me.

Jeff snuggled in closer to me and I pulled a blanket over all four of us, imagining that we could disappear and that if Dad came into the room, all he would see were four empty beds.

Beneath the false security of the blanket, David, John-John, Jeff, and I listened to Mom cry and Dad scream, "God dammit, Kay!"

To drown out the sounds, I whispered a story to my brothers. It was about a family just like ours—with five kids and a dog. I'd made up many stories over the years about this alter family. All my stories had happy endings. In this one, the kids went on a camping trip with their dog and discovered a buried suitcase filled with toys and dog treats.

The stories were close enough to our own lives that we could all picture ourselves playing the parts. In real life we often went camping—Dad loved camping—and we brought Happy. We actually did lots of fun things that other families did—like going to the circus or the amusement park. But in our real family, there were also the times when the children hid in bed and listened to the father scream and the mother cry against a backdrop of crashing dishes and smacks and punches. I didn't know what it was like in other families, but I had a sense that it was not like this, but I would never say a word to anyone to let on that we were not like them.

I told my brothers stories about the normal family that looked just like ours and I held them close and prayed that by the time morning came, things would be okay again.

In the morning Dad was being extra nice to Mom, cooking her breakfast. He was usually careful not to hit Mom where bruises showed. A stranger observing this scene would not have known anything was amiss. Just a husband cooking his wife breakfast. But we knew what he was doing. Even if we hadn't heard the fight the night before, we would have known by his ingratiating behavior that there had been one.

Dad was lord of his castle. My brothers and I were his minions, fetching things for him at his command when he sat in his recliner every evening. "April, fetch me a beer." "David, get me my cigarettes." "John-John, change the channel to eight." The posse of young men he surrounded himself with made him feel wise and admired. But they were not in the inner circle. Only we—Dad's wife and children—were extensions of himself. He was allowed to hurt us, but nobody else was. I never doubted he would do whatever it took to protect us from anyone who might cause us harm. I just didn't think anyone else would.

9

Billy

Summer 1977

Billy, one of the young men who worked on the house, attended parties, and generally hung around, was someone who paid attention to me, but I never felt threatened by him. I trusted him. I'd known him since I was five years old. I was eight now. One day, Billy was on his way upstairs to sheetrock what was going to become my room, and he paused as he passed me in the living room. "Wanna help me?" he asked. I felt very grown-up to be able to help out with construction.

"Sure!" I said, and followed him upstairs.

"You can be my assistant," he said, "and hand me drywall nails."

I stood beside him, handing him a nail each time he needed one. And he would gently take it from me, tickling my palm as he did. I giggled because I felt like he wanted me to, as kind of a way to acknowledge that we were playing a game that wasn't strange. I was sure he could have worked faster putting all the nails in his pocket, but this had been his suggestion. I liked his attention and he was funny, but I got tired of standing around and I sat down on the plywood floor to practice writing my name in cursive with a chalky piece of drywall. I loved how the loopy *A* connected to the loopy *P*. I wore a red skort with loose baggy legs that let you sit cross-legged. Billy reached over and put his hand on my leg. He asked if I wanted a piggyback ride. He often gave me piggyback rides in the yard, and I thought they were fun. He would put me down the minute Dad walked into view. But Dad wasn't in the room, so I hopped up on Billy's back. He took a few galloping strides and stopped in the middle of the room. Then with one hand he reached up behind him and ran his fingers into the leg of my skort and touched me. "Does that feel good?" Billy whispered.

I froze. This had never happened before. I knew that whatever was happening shouldn't be happening, but I didn't know what to do about it.

Then I heard Dad's voice calling up the stairs. "April, come here."

Billy dropped me and I scrambled to my feet.

He whispered, "Don't tell your dad."

I couldn't look at him. He didn't need to tell me that. I wouldn't have risked telling Dad in a million years. I was confused and frightened and the last thing I wanted was for Dad to know.

I felt sick, like I'd eaten something bad. I ran downstairs, terrified I was in trouble. But Dad didn't look mad. I couldn't read his expression, but it didn't seem that he was about to punish me. He seemed eerily calm, and his expression was as serious as I'd ever seen him. Not angry, but intense, which scared me. He asked, "Did Billy touch you where he shouldn't?"

"No!" I said.

"You sure?" he asked, squinting at me.

"Yes, I'm sure." I didn't want it to happen again, but I also didn't want to get Billy in trouble. And I was most afraid of what Dad would do to me.

I worried that Dad knew I was lying. I knew his every expression and every tone of voice. I came to know what I called his Lying Voice. It would be something I would recognize throughout my life, even after he was gone. I would hear it on tape recordings, and I would think, "There, right there. That's not true. He's lying." I figured Dad might know me in the same way. When I said that Billy hadn't touched me, I wondered what it was that my father read when he studied my face so intently. I didn't think he believed me.

Dad hadn't liked Billy's friendliness with me for a while. When Dad called me from the bottom of the stairs, had he already silently observed what had happened in the room? Billy stopped coming around. Every now and then, I would think of him and feel queasy at the memory. But I was busy with school and siblings and playing, and I pushed the memory of what happened upstairs that day way deep down.

• • •

As a family, we watched the news every night in the living room. Dad watched the news the way some people watch sports, yelling at the TV as if he knew better than the reporters. I'd seen young men shouting at a ref's call while watching a football game on TV. Dad would do that to the newscaster. If there was a crime being reported, Dad would say things like "No, no, it didn't happen that way"; or scoff, "Don't be an idiot. He wouldn't have done it like that"; or speculate, "I bet they find the gun in . . ." Like he should have been part of the team of investigators, like he was more of an expert than the police at solving crimes. He also talked to Mom and to us kids about crimes that he'd read about in the paper or that people in town were talking about. He was particularly obsessed with violent crime—murders and stabbings, that kind of thing.

One day, Dad called me from the front yard. I was in the kitchen and heard him shout, "April. I want to show you something."

I ran to the door and saw him holding a big gun in his hand. "It's a shotgun," he said. "I'm going to show you how to use it."

"Get over here," he said when I hesitated.

I approached cautiously. I wasn't sure what he was up to. He handed me the gun and told me to hold it to my shoulder. It was heavier than it looked. I struggled to even hold it up to my shoulder.

"Aim for the burn barrel," he said. The barrel sat next to the driveway and was already full of holes.

"Here's the trigger," he said, showing me.

"Pull it," he said, and I did.

I was knocked flat on my back when the shotgun went off. It went flying out of my hands and Dad caught it midair, laughing. My shoulder felt like it was broken. He hadn't warned me about the kick.

"You're lucky you didn't break your nose," Dad said.

I was baffled. If I could have broken something, and I wasn't sure I hadn't, why hadn't he warned me about it? He hadn't "taught" me how to shoot the gun, he'd just told me to shoot. I was once again, literally this time, the butt of his joke. Humiliated, I fought back tears as I ran back into the house.

• • •

A few days later, Dad took us on a strange field trip. We drove to Silver Creek Metro Park, four miles from our house, and all got out of the car. We had been to this park before for picnics, and Dad would always bring chicken to grill up for us. We'd spend hours playing on the mowed grass, kicking a ball or playing tag, and walking through the well-trod trails in the woods.

That's what I expected us to do that day, but I would be disappointed, because Dad didn't bring any food for a picnic and Mom didn't have our basket of toys. Instead, we parked in the parking lot and then Dad instructed us to get out of the car and walk together, not on the mowed grass or on a clear trail, but through weeds as high as my chest. I had to use my hands to part the way for myself. My brothers stumbled in my wake. Dad was walking a zigzagged course through the tall grass and seemed to be looking for something. He spoke rapidly to Mom, in the same way he did while watching the evening news on TV—as if he were speculating about a crime, searching for clues. I didn't know what we were searching for.

We kids fell behind, and my brothers were jostling each other. This worried me because the weeds seemed like a place you could get lost in. I looked for landmarks so I could find our way back just in case. And then Dad stopped abruptly and held up his hand. He said something like "I was right . . ." and "It's here . . ." Then he told us to turn around and go back to the car.

We stumbled back through the weeds to the parking lot and piled into the car and drove back home. *Well*, I thought, *that was a waste*. We hadn't even had a chance to play.

I didn't know it then, but Dad had taken us to a crime scene.

A few days later, we were sitting in the living room in the evening, watching the news as we did every night. Dad watched from the comfort of his recliner. Jeff sat in Dad's lap, sucking his thumb, eyes on the screen while his free hand stroked Dad's cheek. This was Jeff's preferred way to watch TV. Mom always sat on the sofa with Jeannine. My brothers and I were usually splayed on the floor, coloring or playing with toys, only peripherally aware of what was on the news.

"Hey," Dad said to Mom as the man on TV droned on. "You know those kids who went missing in the park?"

I heard this as if from a distance, the words *kids who went missing*, entering my head like an afterthought. What kids, I wondered? I imagined the missing kids were my age. *In the park.* Those words terrified me. I thought of the overgrown weeds in the park that we had just tramped through. How easy it would be to get lost in there.

Dad went on, "Their bodies were found."

Bodies? I understood what this meant—that they were dead. But my mind refused to focus there. I kept thinking of how frightened the kids who went missing in the park must have been, and I wondered if something bad like that could happen to me.

10

Boogeyman

I began third grade when John-John started in first grade and the three of us took the bus each morning to Hazel Harvey Elementary. (The same school that Jeffrey Dahmer attended in first grade ten years earlier.) I excelled academically and athletically. When I got a gold star on an assignment or a 100% on a spelling test, I drank up the praise. I wanted to be the best. In gym class, I wanted to be the fastest. And I was. I was scrawny and small, but strong and quick.

I loved school so much that in the afternoons I played school in the unfinished upstairs master bedroom with my siblings. Dad never finished the upstairs enough for us to use the bedrooms as bedrooms. Sitting on the floor, I pretended boxes were desks and I handed out homework and graded it just like a real teacher. At night, I pretended it was classroom story time and I read to them on blankets on the floor. Jeff listened wide-eyed to stories, sucking his thumb, holding the old pillow that he dragged around everywhere, like Linus with his blanket in the Charlie Brown comics. My favorite Disney book club selection was *The Haunted House*, where Mikey, Pluto, and Donald run out of gas and encounter bank robbers in a deserted house. They help the police catch the bad guys. Which was something Dad often said he was doing.

And it did seem like he was doing that. It wasn't uncommon to come home from school in the afternoon to find a police car in our driveway, because Dad made friends with the police wherever we lived. At night he would go to a bar, not to get drunk but to listen to the local male gossip. He'd feed information that seemed pertinent to the local cop he had befriended. He was a snitch, in other words. This chummy relationship with the local police was a way of reinforcing his image in the community as a reformed criminal and a friend of law and order. It was also an insurance policy. Who better to owe you a favor than a cop?

One day, after I'd just come home from school, I answered the door to find two men in slacks and blazers standing very straight. These two weren't in police uniform and they looked much more serious than the men who were dad's cop "friends." They said they were from the FBI and asked if Dad was home.

I called Dad and he came to the door and greeted the men warmly. "Oh, hey there! Come on in!" he said. Then they went off to talk privately.

Before they left, one of the men gave us kids small gifts. The little treasure chest they gave me was the perfect size in which to store the "Happy Grams" rewards I got at school. The visit by these men stumped me. I couldn't imagine why they had come. But I loved the little treasure chest. It moved with me to every bedroom I lived in for the next ten years.

After they left, I heard Dad talking to Mom. She must have asked the questions that were burning in my mind. Who were they and why had they come? Dad said that they had come to ask him questions about Jimmy Hoffa. Dad had just sent a book proposal to a publisher, which pitched the new book he was working on about the famous criminals he had met while in prison, including Jimmy Hoffa, who the FBI was still searching for. Somehow, the FBI must have found out that Dad had information about Hoffa. Whether he really did or not, the visit thrilled him. He was flying high for days. He'd managed to place himself at the center of attention again with the feds, and this time not for being on their Most Wanted list.

I thought Dad really missed his calling. He enjoyed being around policemen so much that I thought he should become one. He loved to watch true crime documentaries, which we would all watch with him, no matter how gruesome the crimes being discussed—and they almost always involved a murderer. Dad really perked up when the show was about some guy called the Zodiac Killer. I didn't think it was odd—if shows about one murder were appealing to him, a show about multiple murders would naturally be even more interesting.

To avoid becoming a criminal like he had been, and like the bad guys on TV, Dad felt it was important for us to have a strong moral education, and for this we needed church. Dad was not a religious person—the nuns had seen to that—but he insisted we join a local church and attend Vacation Bible School. Almost any denomination of Christianity would do except for Catholicism and Jehovah's Witnesses. Dad hated the Catholic church because of the nuns, he said. (Yet my brother John's middle name is Paul, after the Pope.) That suited Mom just fine because she herself was a devout Christian. She took us to services every Sunday morning. Dad drove us there but did not attend with us. Mom still did not have a driver's license. I didn't question why Dad didn't go to services. It was just another example of him having a different set of rules for himself.

Dad also wanted us to become Boy and Girl Scouts. David, John-John, and I joined the local troops.

Up until then, my closest friends had been my brothers, but in Brownies I met a girl named Stephanie and we became best friends. She would come over and we would play house using my sister as our baby. Once Jeannine started walking, she was less cooperative. She became impossible to dress or even keep a diaper on. Stephanie and I loved to play with my Hula-Hoop and practice our tumbling moves. I was competitive even with myself, keeping records of how many times I could twirl the Hula-Hoop around my waist without it falling or using my hands, and how many cartwheels I could do in a row.

Our yard became the place to go in the neighborhood to play tag or have water fights, with Dad being the one to orchestrate the games. He behaved like a teenage camp counselor, always inventing new variations on tag or setting up obstacle courses. Even Diane, our babysitter, would sometimes come over just to play.

While Dad welcomed kids into the yard, he didn't want anyone inside the house when he wasn't there. Once, when Mom and Dad went out to run errands, he left Diane in charge, instructing her to keep us outside, and even going as far as locking the door so we couldn't go in.

"What if they get hungry?" Diane asked, clearly surprised.

"They can wait 'til we get home," Dad said.

And that was that. The house was off-limits.

But then Dad began to discourage kids from coming into the house even when he was there. This was okay with me because I always hated it when anyone else was in the house when Dad lost his temper. When he began to yell, a heavy silence descended. We would all snap into survival mode, becoming quiet as mice, trying to busy ourselves out of his line of sight. Dad would ask the outsider to leave before the belt came out. The last time Diane came over, she was playing in the yard with us as a friend and not as a babysitter.

"Hey kids!" Dad shouted from the porch. "I have a new game for you!" he said as he came into the yard.

"Woo-hoo!" we shouted, thrilled to have a newly invented game of his. Or maybe a game involving getting sprayed with the hose. It was a hot day.

Instead, he instructed us to walk out to the woods and look for something special.

"Don't run," he said. "Walk."

We all headed off at a deliberate pace to the trees at the edge of the yard. Dad was kind of famous in the neighborhood for putting on fun scavenger hunts with prizes.

"What are we looking for?" I asked.

"You'll know it when you see it," Dad said, walking along behind us.

As we entered the trees, the air was just a bit cooler, the bright sun blocked by the canopy of leaves. He said, "Keep your heads down and keep looking."

"Are we close?" Diane asked.

"Not yet," he said. "Now spread out and go slow."

We did as he instructed, putting a few arm lengths between us. Diane was to my left. We were silent, the leaves and twigs snapping beneath our feet.

From behind us, he said, "Keep going."

We obeyed, fully engaged in the game. I kept my eyes on the ground in front of me, sweeping right and left, passing my gaze over roots and concentrating on scrubby bushes. I was looking for a splash of color or a flash of sparkle, some trinket he had cleverly hidden. And then BANG! We all spun around at once and saw Dad standing there with a black handgun raised at shoulder height. He had just fired a loaded gun in our direction.

The sound of it rang in my ears and pulsed along with my racing heart. Diane stood stock-still, as if she were made of stone. I could see her struggling to get her legs to cooperate. Then she slowly started moving, as if through molasses, and walked away, holding herself stiffly. I became aware of another sound. Dad was laughing. He laughed and laughed. "It was just a joke!" he said to our astonished faces.

When Diane made it to the driveway, she ran like she was on fire, not looking back. She never came over again—either to babysit or play.

I didn't blame her. Dad's erratic behavior was beginning to worry even me. It was over a dumb pile of clothes that I received one of the worst beatings I can remember. Dad had never poured the concrete floor in the garage, so we had never used the mudroom as a mudroom. Instead, for the two-plus years we lived on Kevin Drive, when we walked in through the door, we just threw our coats and jackets and other stuff on one of the couches. It's not like we had dressers. This was where the clean laundry ended up as well. Nothing changed, except that one night Dad had decided that this was totally unacceptable. It didn't matter that the rest of the house was dirty and in a state of clutter and chaos.

"Everyone, get over here!" he demanded.

He picked up each article of clothing to see who it belonged to. If it was Mom's or his, he threw it aside. But if it was mine or my brothers', we had to step forward. Whoever it belonged to got beat with a straw broom. The mound of clothes was huge. This would take a while.

He held up my raincoat.

"April, stand still!" he shouted, and picked up the broom like a baseball bat and swung, hitting me so hard on the butt, my whole body jerked with the impact and I was knocked down. I didn't understand why he was doing this. I had dozens of pieces of clothing—socks, shirts, sweatshirts—on the couch. I was the biggest offender, but my brothers had enough pieces to feel pummeled by him as well. Each time Dad found another article of clothing of mine, the beating was worse than the one before. Mom watched from the other couch, holding Jeannine. Jeff hid his face in her lap. Finally, Dad hit me with enough force I was sprawled on the floor and couldn't get up, and Mom said, "Okay, Wayne. That's enough."

My backside felt like he had flayed the skin right off my butt and cut into the muscle. I slunk on my hands and knees to my bunk.

That night I had to sleep on my stomach. I couldn't even lie on my side. My neck hurt like I had whiplash. Dad tried to ingratiate himself afterward. He crawled into my bunk and lay next to me as I sobbed.

He must have thought he'd gone overboard even by his own standards.

"Honey?" he said, tugging on my sleeve. "I wish you hadn't had so much clothes on the sofa."

Not "I'm sorry I hurt you." But "I'm sorry you made me hurt you." I knew the difference.

I wouldn't look at him or say anything. I didn't tell him I loved him. Or that it would be okay. I kept my face buried in my pillow. Dad crawled down from my bed when it was clear that I wasn't going to comfort him and he left the room.

He had gone far enough overboard this time that I couldn't go to school the next day. My backside was so bruised, it was too painful to sit down. I was always disappointed to miss school. As I lay in bed all day, wondering what my classmates were doing, a thought occurred to me for the first time. When I was younger, Dad would sometimes take me to construction jobs with him on school days. He told me it was because he needed my help. At the time, I thought it was because he was lonely and wanted my company. Now I wondered if those "bring your daughter to work" days corresponded with conspicuous bruises or injuries.

When the house was far from finished, Dad painted a large mural of a flamboyant peacock on the wall downstairs, greeting anyone coming into the house. He must have purchased the template, because I saw him tack enormous sheets of tracing paper onto the wall. The sheets had images and numbers corresponding to colors, like the paint-by-numbers set I'd received for my birthday. I liked watching him paint. He'd put on an Elvis Presley record album and sing as he worked. Sometimes it would be Frank Sinatra or Bing Crosby. He smoked and sang while meticulously applying paint to the wall. I could sit on the floor and watch him for hours.

The glorious result was the first thing that greeted people when they came into the house. They would ooh and aah. Dad boasted that the mural was a design of his own creation. Of course, I knew that part wasn't true, but by now I knew to keep my mouth shut.

It surprised me when Dad said he'd sold the house. He said that we'd be moving soon, but not right away. Not until the school year was over.

Moving was something I had done a lot in my eight years. From Avon Street to Taylor Road to the other rental house to the house on Kevin Drive. I didn't want to move, but a part of me thought that maybe if we moved, Dad would be happier.

"Where are we moving?" I asked.

"It'll be a surprise!" Dad said. "But here's a hint. No more cutting and hauling firewood!" he said, looking at me and smiling. "Soon you'll be running on the beach and swimming in the ocean every day!"

Running on the beach! That did sound good.

The couple who had bought the house had a Winnebago, and they parked it in our yard for about a month before we moved out. They often stayed in the camper, and I would see them when I played outside or when I walked up the street to catch the bus. Dad didn't seem to like them. They had a habit of walking into the house uninvited, without knocking, and this infuriated him. One day I was in the living room doing homework on the couch and Dad walked in and saw, through the picture window, that the woman was walking toward the house.

"I'll show her what you get for walking into someone's house without knocking," he said. Then he stripped naked and stood in front of the door ready to greet her as she walked in. He stood, expectant.

She opened the door and her jaw dropped. She was stunned to see him standing fully nude before her, with his flamboyant peacock mural directly behind him. I was shocked too. I wanted to crawl under the couch. It was the first time I'd seen Dad do something to intentionally embarrass someone outside the family. He often walked around naked when it was just his family, but he'd never taken his clothes off in front of other people. I don't know who was more horrified, the woman or me. But Dad thought it was hilarious. She mumbled something that might have been an apology and ran out the door.

Dad was bent over with laughter. "She got what she deserved," he said between gasps.

The money from selling the house made it possible to start a new chapter in our life. To celebrate, Dad bought a brand-new green Ford Econoline van. We also bought the Winnebago from the couple. I think Dad sold the El Camino to one of the young men who had helped build the house. I know it wasn't Billy, because we hadn't seen him around since the previous summer. Once school was out, we left Kevin Drive and Doylestown and Ohio itself, setting out in the Winnebago towing the new van. When John-John had asked why we were leaving, Dad said that he turned over information to the police about some bad men and now they were after him. I believed we were on the run from the boogeyman. It did not occur to me for several more years that perhaps the boogeyman was my father.

11

The Federal Reformatory at Chillicothe, Ohio

1950–1952

The map of Dad's young adult life looks like a wagon wheel. With Akron as its hub, spokes reached out to cities in Florida, Georgia, North Carolina, Colorado, Oregon, Montana, Pennsylvania, Texas, Idaho, and Arizona, where he returned again and again. Each spoke of his journey began with a young woman to whom he promised a new life, or marriage, or an adventure—a woman he would quickly replace with another along the way. A woman and a scam. That was his MO. Once he wore out the young woman and the scam, he moved on, always returning to his home base of Akron to regroup.

After running away from the reformatory, he joined the marines two days before his seventeenth birthday. He thrived in basic training at Parris Island. He was strong and fit and good at it. After boot camp, he was sent to Camp Lejeune in Wilmington, North Carolina. But when his unit got shipped out to Korea, he wasn't yet eighteen, and that was the age requirement for combat. He could not accept this. He wanted to fight. He was ready. But rules were rules, and he could not get around them. He took the disappointment badly and quit. Going AWOL is a bad idea. But it isn't surprising that Dad took this route. In his young life, according to his own account, he was wildly impulsive.

Upon going AWOL in Wilmington, he headed off in a stolen car to Florida, where he was arrested for car theft and ended up being held in the Jacksonville County Jail. He received a five-year suspended sentence and didn't have to serve a minute more. Free, he was so relieved that he had a meal in a restaurant and shocked himself by actually paying for it rather than running out on the tab. Maybe this was the beginning of a new chapter, where he would live honestly, he thought. But his motivation didn't last long. He got a job in a garage. He was still only seventeen, but claimed he was twenty-two, with five years of military service under his belt. When his boss called him out for lying, he quit the job. He met Linda, "a petite brunette," and convinced her to run away with him to Texas.

In Houston, they rented a room in a house and he got a job in a super-market. But within two weeks he got severe food poisoning and was taken to a VA hospital by his well-meaning boss to whom he had bragged of his military service.

While at the VA, two events occurred that derailed his immediate plans. The first was that he attracted the attention of a psychiatrist who looked into his military record of dishonorable discharge and his history of compulsive lying and became convinced that my father needed to be admitted to a psych ward. He was not the first professional to feel alarmed. Dad's case file from his period of juvenile detention at the age of thirteen includes a report from the Bureau of Juvenile Research dated 1946. It states: "According to the police department, he was involved this summer in bicycle stealing and will not tell the truth even when the truth would be advantageous to him." Before he was sent to the detention center, he'd been a student at St. Joseph's school, but he was kicked out. "Parents of little girls had complained that he had been mo-lesting their daughters on the way home from school." This report describes him as "impulsive, indifferent and careless . . . changeable . . . erratic." Later, a report of a psychiatric examination in 1950, just before he joined the marines, concluded: "The personality picture is one of a highly disturbed individual who needs psychiatric help. This will probably be impossible since it would take a very long-term treatment to make any change. It is a case of a boy who has multiple difficulties, most of which it is too late to correct . . . Wayne is neurotic and possibly psychotic. His behavior is definitely psychopathic."

The second thing that happened while he was hospitalized was that Linda took up with another man. My father went ballistic when he found out. In his memoir, he recounted his assault on Linda, blow-by-blow. He wrote, "I hit her in the stomach with every ounce of strength I had. She doubled up and let out a pathetic groan." He shouted at her, "I'll mess your face up so bad, you'll never be looked at by a horse, let alone a man." And he proceeded to do that, beating her so savagely, he wrote that it was "miraculous" that he didn't break any of her bones. With eyes "practically swollen shut" she pleaded with him, but, he wrote, "I was unmoved."

Remember, this is the book he passed around to neighbors by way of a calling card. "For my own sake," he wrote, "I didn't want to kill her." Then he fled with the battered Linda to Akron, where she got help from a stranger to return to Florida, though not before he kept her one more night and raped her.

He returned to petty crimes in Akron, stealing hubcaps, batteries, and tires off parked cars and selling them to junk yards. That's when he met Nancy. She was "an overweight dishwater blonde who idolized me," he wrote. She wasn't his favorite type, but she was easily manipulated, and after being betrayed by Linda, he needed to be back in control. He and Nancy embarked on a car stealing spree that began in Arizona and ended in South Carolina when he fell asleep at the wheel, crashing a stolen car, and woke up in a hospital. With Nancy's help, he gave the hospital the slip, stole another car, which he traded in at a car dealership for yet another car, and headed back to the familiar grounds of Wilmington. There he met Anna, "dark-haired and quite feminine," and ditched Nancy. He and Anna headed out to Norristown, Pennsylvania, a town he'd gotten to know well when he'd run away from reform school. Here, he purchased a uniform and paraded around as a Marine Corps corporal. The police got wind of him because he'd been seen in uniform at a bar with a different woman every night. Suspicious that he was impersonating an officer, they brought him in. He ended up back in Ohio, sentenced to two years in the Chillicothe Federal Reformatory for multiple car thefts, his first time actually serving time as an adult. He was eighteen years old. When he emerged two years later, he had honed his craft as a criminal and his talent for the hustle.

12

Florida Hustle

As we piled into the Winnebago, Dad revealed the surprise that we were going on a road trip to Florida. He was sure we'd love it.

But first, we had to pick up a passenger in Akron. Dad's adoptive father, Fred Edwards, had remarried after Mary Ethel had died. His second wife was named Lucille (not to be confused with Aunt Lucille), and we hardly ever saw her. But she had a niece in Atlanta who she wanted to visit, and Dad agreed to drop her off there on our way to Florida.

Atlanta was one of the cities Dad had lived in before . . . a few times. I knew Dad didn't like Grandma Lucille—he often said things like, "She's nasty . . . She treats Grandpa bad . . . [and] She lies all the time." But Grandma Lucille gave Dad money to take her to Atlanta, and that was probably the only reason he agreed to have her along at all. We all piled into the Winnebago, towing the new Econoline van. Dad drove with one hand on his thermos of coffee that he filled every time we stopped for gas. Mom sat in the front passenger seat with Jeannine on her lap and Happy at her feet. The rest of us rode in the back of the camper and played cards with Grandma Lucille at the galley table as we sped down the highway. Her red nails flashed as she shuffled the deck. She taught us how to play gin rummy.

When my brothers got too rambunctious Grandma Lucille raised her voice and said, "Boys! Behave yourselves!"

Since it was usually my job to keep my brothers in line, I was glad she was the one to speak up. But Dad blew up and said, "No one disciplines my kids but me!" I thought he was going to backhand her from the front seat. She didn't even flinch.

"Don't be such a mean SOB," she snapped back.

He just stiffened, and I heard him call her a bitch under his breath, but loud enough for her to hear. She just said, "Hmph!" I was amazed at her bravery. Maybe, I worried, she didn't know him well enough to fear him. But she knew him in a way that his children did not. She'd been married to Grandpa Fred for a long time and saw right through her stepson's bluster and lies. She shook her head and muttered, "miserable two-bit, low-down crook." Never had I heard anyone speak to my father this way. I was appalled and awed. I admired her. I think Mom did too. Mom never said a bad thing about Grandma Lucille, but she never said a bad thing about anyone. She didn't have good things to say about her either, though, so as not to contradict Dad. Generally, she played it safe and wasn't inclined to talk about people, period.

If Grandma Lucille hadn't been with us, we probably would have taken our time driving from Ohio to Florida. But Dad was in a hurry to get rid of her, so he drove straight through the night to Atlanta. Once we got to the home of Lucille's niece, Sandy, Dad didn't seem like he was in a hurry anymore. I understood why: Sandy's house was big and beautiful, and her husband, Bob, was a policeman. As soon as we arrived, we parked in the driveway, taking up the entire space. Sandy brought us around back to the patio. Now I wasn't in a hurry to leave either. Behind the house was an in-ground pool with beautiful blue tiles along the edge. I thought I'd never seen anything so luxurious.

"Why don't you kids change into your bathing suits and jump in?" Sandy suggested. We didn't need to be asked twice. We were back in a flash in our suits and jumped in the pool. Sandy brought us cold lemonade on a tray like we were in a restaurant. Bob asked David and John-John what they wanted to be when they grew up. David said he wanted to be a policeman, just like him.

As I sipped my drink at the patio table, legs swinging, watching the ripples of light wiggle on the pool bottom, I thought, *I don't ever want to leave this house.* Of course, I knew saying that would hurt Dad's feelings.

As I lingered over my lemonade, I overheard the tail end of a heated exchange between Dad and Grandma Lucille about money, and I knew we would be leaving soon. Grandma Lucille seemed like she wanted to get Dad out of her hair—immediately.

Before we hit the road, Bob came outside with a gift for David. It was one of his old police uniform shirts. I could tell he was giving my brother the shirt because he felt sorry for us. David was thrilled, but now I wanted to leave too. It was one thing to want to stay and live in luxury, but another thing entirely to be pitied. This whiff of pity I detected made me feel jittery. The lemonade now felt sticky on my fingers, and it had given me a stomachache. Sandy and Bob didn't need to feel sorry for us. We were fine. We were a family.

Back in the Winnebago, we continued south, and Dad's mood lifted now that Grandma Lucille wasn't with us. Fast was Dad's default driving speed. I knew that he was going *too* fast when Mom gripped the dashboard. I didn't know where we were going, but I didn't care. We played car games to pass the time. One of our favorites was a game that Dad made up called Car Bingo. We would think of categories and Mom would write them down on two sheets of paper, one for each team. Categories might include: horse, cow, another Winnebago, swing set, swimming pool, school, fire truck, tow truck, along with some harder ones like pig and Ford Mustang convertible. Whoever was first to shout out that we spotted something in a category got the point for their team. Mom kept score. Dad and I both had eagle eyes, so we could never be on the same team. We all sat at the front of the Winnebago, with David, John-John, and me perched on an ice chest between the two front bucket seats. Jeannine was of course on Mom's lap. Jeff liked to stand behind Dad's seat, sometimes squeezing his upper body between the driver's seat and the door, so he could rest his head on Dad's shoulder or have his hand on Dad's cheek. His thumb was always in his mouth unless he spotted something in a bingo category.

Dad and I often spotted the same thing nearly simultaneously.

"Cow!" Dad and I both shouted at the same time.

"That's a point for me!" Dad said in triumph.

"No way!" I burst out. "I called it first!" I wouldn't back down in Car Bingo. This was the rare time when I wasn't afraid to stand my ground. Somehow the inside of that speeding Winnebago was a neutral zone that was purely reserved for fun.

"Oh, okay," he chuckled. "I'll give it to you this time."

I loved those games. It was the best feeling to be riding in that Winnebago, like we were in a pod, together, joined in a cocoon of coziness and safety. Dad was always his most relaxed when we were on the open road. These are my happiest memories of childhood. When I felt that the seven of us had a united purpose, giddy with excitement about our grand adventure.

We had just passed the WELCOME TO FLORIDA sign when Dad said, "Oh, crap." We were mid-Bingo and he was speeding, as usual. A police car appeared behind us and flashed its lights. Dad pulled over. "Be quiet," he instructed.

We watched as the officer got out of his car and walked up to the Winnebago.

"Everyone smile and wave when he comes to the window," Dad said.

The officer appeared and surveyed the scene. There we were, five waving, smiling children clustered close to their parents in the front row of the Winnebago. Even Happy wagged her tail in greeting.

"How can I help you, Officer?" Dad said politely, trying to swallow a giggle.

"Do you know how fast you were going?" the officer said, still looking us over.

Dad apologized and could no longer suppress his laugh. He earnestly explained the game we were playing as the reason he wasn't paying attention to his speed. Dad seemed genuinely warm and humble at this moment. I liked to see him in this mode. My heart would swell up with pride when Dad was this version of himself. This was the man that I loved—charming and funny and a little bit sheepish. The officer began to laugh with him. Soon we were all laughing, but he took Dad's license and walked back to his car. We all got quiet again, nervous.

When the officer returned, he leaned his elbows on the open window and said, "Well kids, stop having so much fun with your old man while he's driving."

Dad laughed again heartily.

Then the officer gave us a big grin and handed over not a speeding ticket, but a fistful of Tootsie Pops, which he gave to each of us five kids.

By the time we arrived at our third campground in Central Florida, we had a routine down. We scrambled out of the Winnebago to stretch our legs while Dad hooked up the camper and set up the screened bug tent over the picnic table so we could eat unbothered by mosquitos. Then he sauntered out to meet the fellow campers like he was running for campground mayor. I watched him size up the kids and then do what he knew the other dads couldn't resist. He bet them that his scrawny nine-year-old daughter could beat their kids in a race from here to there. Dad had takers. I knew the drill and I liked what was coming.

The course was set. It was a dash from our campsite to a line of trees in the distance along the road. I lined up with four boys about my age. They jostled and didn't seem worried.

At the sound of Dad's "Ready? Set? Go!" I took off like a shot, pumping my arms, sucking my breath in through my nose and blowing it out from my mouth. My legs burned and I dug in, pushing through the pain, propelling myself forward, toward the row of trees. I felt a sense of freedom running, like I was flying.

I won. After I crossed the imaginary finish line, I bent over, catching my breath, my hair matted to my sweaty face. I looked up at Dad. He was beaming. He collected his winnings and then upped the ante.

"Anyone want a rematch?" he said. "This time she'll race barefoot!"

Three of the boys lined up again. Running barefoot hurt, but it was worth it. Again, I dug into the hot asphalt with the soles of my feet and felt my legs burn. Again, I reached the trees first. Again, Dad collected.

"How about one last race!" he said to the assembled crowd of fellow campers. "Double or nothing." He added, "Now she'll run barefoot over the rocks!" And I did it again, barefoot over the rocks. And watched Dad pocket the winnings, grinning and joking around with the other dads. "Better luck next time," he told one of the boys, who had run all three races and seemed on the verge of tears.

I sat at the picnic table and Dad brought me a bucket of cool water to soak my sore feet in, then he gave me my reward—a pack of Bubblicious that I had to share with my brothers. I felt great. Proud. It was okay with me, sitting there blowing bubbles with my feet on fire, that I was in on the hustle, that Dad used me to make money. I felt like his partner, and I knew what my real prize was—Dad's approval.

Our next campground was at a beach, and this caused me some trouble. I still won, but that last barefoot race had been over a path of crushed shells that sliced the soles of my feet like tiny needles. Afterward, I soaked my feet in the ocean, feeling the sharp sting of the salt water on the little cuts. The pain felt like a necessary price or even a badge of honor, like a Purple Heart medal. I also felt relieved. By winning, once again I'd put Dad in a good mood.

At a campground near Ocala, one of the boys I raced and beat had an older brother and younger sister, Lisa, who was close to my age. Their mom, Abby, asked if I wanted to play with her daughter, and even invited me to sleep over in their kids' tent. I was delighted. That night before bed, Abby suggested the kids take showers in the campground bathroom.

Abby and Lisa and I walked into the ladies' shower area, and Abby brought a basket filled with bottles of shampoo and conditioner and bodywash and washcloths and combs. In my family, when we went to shower, we just brought a bar of ivory soap. That was it.

Abby stood outside the showers and dispensed pink shampoo into my hand and told me to scrub well. "Use your fingernails and get right to your scalp," she told me. It was the first time I had ever used shampoo that smelled like strawberry candy. And it was the first time I'd ever received actual instructions on how to wash my hair. I guessed that rubbing a bar of ivory soap over my hair must not have been the right way to do it, but this was news to me. Next came the conditioner, which was also strawberry-scented.

"Let it soak into your hair, sweetie," Abby said. Then she helped me comb out the tangles before I rinsed it out. Again, this was new. I'd never used conditioner before. I loved how silky it made my hair feel under the warm running water. It wasn't just the hair products that smelled pretty. Even the bodywash Abby squirted onto a washcloth smelled sweet.

"Be sure to scrub your neck, sweetie," Abby called into the shower.

We didn't use washcloths in my family. But more amazing to me was learning there was a different kind of soap for girls and boys. I realized this might be why other girls smelled good. Why was I just now learning this? Did my mom know? Should I tell her?

There was something else I noticed about Abby. She spoke to her daughter differently than she did her sons. She called Lisa sweetheart, and she played with her hair and laughed with her as if they were best friends. This was surprising, too. Being a girl gave me no special relationship of intimacy with my mom. I was just one of the five kids. But clearly, this mom and this daughter were on the same team—the girl team. My family didn't seem to have one.

That night, I slept in the kids' tent with Lisa and her two brothers. The younger one, who I had beaten in the race earlier that day, barely acknowledged my existence, but the older brother didn't like me and let me know it.

"What are you even doing here?" he hissed at me in the tent. I didn't answer. "You better watch your back, you ugly stupid cow," he said.

My feelings were hurt, but part of me felt like I deserved it. I was an imposter. I had no business sleeping in this tent, pretending for a night that I was part of this family. I wriggled my sleeping bag closer to Lisa, with my back to her. I had trouble falling asleep, with the menacing boy across the tent and with the smell of strawberry shampoo strong on my pillow.

The next morning, I crawled out of the tent and ran to our camper a few sites over.

After a quick bowl of cereal, David, John-John, and I rode our bikes around the circle of campsites, when I heard Lisa's dad call her older brother sharply into a tent. I was horrified to hear the sound of the boy being spanked. I crept closer to their tent and overheard the boy crying. He hadn't been hit that hard, I thought. But the boy wasn't crying from pain, he was crying from shame as he tried to explain to his father why he'd said what he had to me. So Lisa must have told on him. Interesting. He said that he was trying to make his little brother feel better for losing to me. I realized that he had been, in his own way, coming to his younger brother's defense. I had hurt his brother's pride by being faster, so he was hurting my feelings by being mean.

But his dad wasn't finished with him. I listened while the man began a long lecture on the importance of treating girls with respect and dignity. He told his son that women were precious and men needed to protect, not bully them. "Would you treat your own sister this way?" he asked. The boy cried and told his dad he was sorry.

I felt bad that the boy got spanked, but this lecture was fascinating. Back in Doylestown, I hadn't really spent any time with other families. Dad didn't like us to go to other people's homes. This experience in the campground, spending time with this family, was the first time I realized how differently other people lived. But it was more than sweet-smelling bath products. Hearing the father speak to his son with disappointment and concern, not fury, in his voice was a revelation. Hearing him talk about the importance of being kind to girls might have been the most shocking part. When Dad punished us, it was always out of anger that we disobeyed him. He just struck out, like a snake. He never said he wanted us to be kinder people. The beatings were not to teach subtle lessons. They were just the price of misbehaving and didn't mean any more to me than the pain they caused.

The next day, Abby and Lisa and their family were packing up to leave the campground, and I was sad to see them go. We were staying on. Abby and Lisa came to say goodbye before they left. Lisa, with her hair up in a pink scrunchy that matched her pink sandals. Me, with my long hair loose, feet bare. I saw something in Abby's eyes that made me uneasy. She looked like she felt sorry for me. Though she hadn't said a word, I defended myself in my own head. My family was who I was. It was where I belonged. Maybe my mom didn't treat me like a princess, and maybe my dad sometimes acted more like a teenage boy than a grown man, but I was fiercely loyal and I even felt insulted. We might not smell as good as them, but we *were* every bit as good as them.

A brand-new RV pulled into the campground and took the site next to ours. It was a young German couple who were touring the United States. Their little two-year-old blond-haired boy was the same age as Jeannine. We caught them kissing behind our camper. Our families hung out at the campground pool together. At night, the adults sat around the grill, drinking beers, Dad cooking chicken. After dinner my brothers and I gathered at the picnic table to play Go Fish. Dad and Mom and the German couple lounged in lawn chairs talking. At bedtime, Dad sent us off to the Winnebago. Long into the night, I listened to the rise and fall of the adult voices and laughter, the Germans quieter than their new talkative American friend. I wouldn't have minded camping forever. Dad was more carefree in campgrounds. The more primitive living—the fires in the evening, chatting with the community of fellow campers who didn't know us—felt safe. Dad was his most charismatic when he was meeting people for the first time.

How long did the German couple stick around? Long enough for Dad to seize a business opportunity. The couple's plan was to travel throughout the US in their RV, including a tour of the West, and end their trip in California. Dad made a pitch that they accepted: he would meet up with them at the end of their trip to take possession of the RV and would sell it on their behalf and send the money to them in Germany. Even as a nine-year-old listening to Dad make big promises to the couple, I wondered why they would trust him. They didn't even know him.

We were still living in the campground near Ocala when the school year started. By now we had moved into a furnished single-wide mobile home on the campgrounds, because the Winnebago was cramped with the seven of us. The campground had enough permanent residents that the school bus stopped to pick kids up there. Mom even signed up to be a substitute teacher. The first morning I woke up in the single-wide, I was covered in red bites that itched like crazy. I scratched my arms raw. This was my first encounter with bed bugs. But this wasn't Dad's first run-in with the little buggers, and he sprayed us down with insect repellent and pounded the mattress with a wet bar of soap before we got in bed at night. The little black bugs covered the bar of soap like poppy seeds on a bun.

Dad promised that we'd soon be living in a house. He had found a piece of property to buy with the remaining money from selling the house on Kevin Drive. With the help of the farmer and his tractor across the road, he cleared the shrubs and trees from the new lot and removed the stumps and roots. Without a bulldozer, though, Dad still had the problem of what to do about the mounds of dirt and debris. He tied a box spring to the back of the van and had me and my brothers lie on it for weight, and then he dragged the box spring around the lot to flatten the ground. We would sometimes fly off and have to run to scramble back on. It was like having our own amusement park ride.

We went with Dad when he picked out a brand-new double-wide mobile home, which had a plasticky smell that stung my nose. The new house was delivered in two sections and erected on our lot. Dad bought chairs and tables and beds on layaway. He promised me that later, he'd get me a new bedroom set with a white canopy bed and white dresser. Our family moved in, with Happy taking up residence in the crawl space beneath the trailer.

Florida was different from Ohio. Instead of apple and pear trees, there were orange and mango trees. Instead of chipmunks, there were lizards. We didn't live near the beach like Dad had promised—and I felt disappointed about that. It was hot. I sweat more than I could ever remember sweating. The double-wide came with AC window units, but we weren't allowed to use them. Dad said it made the electric bill too high.

We were still in the country, though. And that meant lots of room to run around, and it meant having neighbors with cows!

The family who owned the farm across the road had a daughter, Lucy, who babysat for us. She had blond hair and was in high school. Dad flirted with her and I thought that's just how men behaved with teenage girls. He was overly friendly with any young woman; the prettier the girl, the more friendly he was. I idolized Lucy. She introduced me to the movie *Grease*. I would go to her house to listen to the soundtrack. I imagined myself to be Sandy and sang "Summer Nights" at the top of my lungs as I walked to Lucy's house from mine. Lucy's was the first teenage girl's bedroom I had been granted entry to. With her posters of horses, collection of pop albums, the makeup and hair products arrayed on her vanity, I thought it was exactly the kind of room I would have someday when I was a teenager.

Living right across the street from a farm, Dad really embraced country life. He bought a Jersey milk cow from Lucy's family. Daisy moved to our property and was kept tied by a rope under a tree. It was my job to take care of her. I brought her water and grain and hay twice a day. Before and after school I sat close to her warm body and milked her. She smelled sweet, like clover. And I would carry the stainless steel bucket up to two-thirds full with steaming milk, to the house, where Mom would strain it with a cheesecloth. I didn't like the milk when it was warm, but cold it was good and creamy. Store-bought milk tasted like water by comparison. We had a hand-crank ice-cream maker, and Dad would make ice cream for us on special occasions.

Dad wanted to complete the Florida ranch lifestyle and surprised me one day after school by saying, "Hey April, want to come help me pick out a horse?"

"A horse?" I wanted to make sure I hadn't misheard.

"Yeah, like *Hi Ho, Silver!*"

I was in the van ready to go before he'd even finished the sentence.

The drive to the horse sale barn took us past flat green fields ringed by white fencing, until we turned off at a farm that looked like it had seen better days. The fencing wasn't painted, and it was patched with rope and mismatched boards. But I was not disappointed. There was a paddock filled with horses.

Dad and a man stood at the fence discussing each horse. I tried to listen in, but the man had such a strong accent, I only understood a word now and then. That was another thing about Florida. People talked funny.

Dad picked out a copper-colored horse with a striking white blaze down his nose. We were told he had a history of racing and then became a parade horse, but he retired from all that. Now big and fat, he was for sale to any interested party. That was us. His name was Keeper.

The next day, Keeper was delivered to Lucy's farm, where we would board him. When he stepped off the trailer, I thought he was the most beautiful horse I'd ever seen. He ran around the field for a few minutes, his coppery coat glinting in the sun, and then stopped and rolled in a muddy patch.

The first time I rode him I had to be lifted up high onto his back. I'd never ridden in a saddle before or held on to reins. Keeper amazed me by actually expecting me to tell him what to do. I was too afraid to get him into a gallop. His trot alone gathered plenty of speed. But he was so well trained that all I had to say was "*Whoa!*" and the horse would stop. He was careful with me and he loved when my brothers and I gave him a bath in the cool water from the hose.

When we drove our van along his fence line, Dad would beep the horn and Keeper would come tearing across the paddock and race us from his side of the fence. I imagined he was reliving his racing career. Dad probably got him because he liked to imagine himself as John Wayne, the way I pretended I was Olivia Newton-John. When Dad rode Keeper he made him gallop and he'd take him on trails through the woods. One day, running through the trees, Dad was knocked off by a branch and badly hurt his shoulder. After that he said we were selling Keeper. I cried that night and couldn't watch the next day as the beautiful coppery horse was loaded onto a trailer to leave us forever. I asked why he had to go? Dad said that we could no longer afford to keep a horse.

Money was always a topic of conversation—what we could afford and what was too expensive. Dad said food cost money and it was a sin to waste food, which I assumed meant it was also a sin to waste money. At mealtimes we had to eat what was put in front of us. We were not allowed to leave food on our plate. If it was food we didn't like (like liver and onions, one of his favorite dishes), we were not allowed to serve ourselves. Dad would serve us huge portions. And we had to eat it all while he watched to make sure we didn't spit it back out or hide it in our napkins. The only way I could get the liver down was drowning it in so much mustard that that's all I could taste. It was in the double-wide's kitchen that Dad taught me to cook. The first dish he showed me how to make was liver and onions, so I could make it for him. He instructed me on how to slice the onions, dredge the slimy liver in flour and cook it in butter. Then he took himself to his recliner in the living room and watched TV while I cooked, eyes streaming from the raw onions. I gagged at the smell of liver every time I made the dish.

Another rule in our family was that we were not allowed to eat between meals unless Dad gave us a snack. I was always hungry when I got home from school. My stomach would be growling all the way as I walked from the bus stop with my brothers. But I was afraid to ask for food. My brothers and I didn't go into the fridge if we were hungry. If we were caught helping ourselves to food, we would get beaten. The no-snacking rule did not apply to Dad. He had his own stash of candy and gum and soda, and he even had his own cereals that we weren't allowed to touch. When he wasn't home it was hard to resist sneaking some of his treats, but we were too scared that he would somehow know. I had seen him put a big multipack of Wrigley's Spearmint gum on top of the refrigerator. Days passed and my mind kept going back to this wealth of gum. Soon, wishful thinking took over, and I told myself that surely he would not know if I took one little stick from one of the many packs up there. And so, when no one was in the house, I pulled a chair up to the fridge and reached up and slid one piece of gum out of the open pack.

I chomped away on that stick of gum so nervously, I could hardly enjoy the sugary rush that temporarily quelled my hunger.

When Dad came home, from wherever he went during the day—I didn't know what kind of work he had—he went straight to the fridge. Earlier, I had spit out my piece of gum when the flavor was gone and had buried the chewed-up wad and the foil wrapper deep in the kitchen garbage where I knew no one would find the evidence. From the top of the fridge, Dad pulled a pack of gum down and looked at it. Immediately, he noticed that a piece was missing.

"April," he said. "Did you take a piece of my gum?"

"No!" I lied.

"You sure?" he asked. "Because you sure look guilty to me." I started to sweat. He picked up the phone and dialed.

"Hey Lucy, how you doing?" he said in a falsely nice voice, as if he hadn't been ready to whack me a second earlier. "Can you come over real quick? I need to ask you something." She showed up a few minutes later, looking confused when she saw me cowering in the kitchen.

He interrogated her. "Tell the truth. Did April take a piece of gum?"

"Uh," she said slowly and carefully, not sure what was going on. "I don't think so. I didn't see her take a piece of gum."

Dad dismissed her and he stood over me and asked "Are you lying to me?" His anger mounted as I shook my head in denial. He was about to boil over. I watched his fist and began to shake. My vision began to blur and my knees buckled. I thought I smelled mint, and I started to crumple. Suddenly, Dad burst into laughter. He was highly entertained by the fact that I was so afraid of him that I was about to faint. His desire to hit me drained from him when he started laughing, but I was left with a sense that the beating could come at any time when I least expected it. It was the last time I ever lied to him. It was better just to take the punishment and be done with it.

13

Jump Scare

All that campground racing over the summer paid off for me in school. I was the fastest runner in fourth grade, which gave me a certain social standing that compensated for my outsider status. I broke the school record for the 440-meter race. I also joined a gymnastics team and won sixth place on the balance beam at a district-wide competition. Dad was thrilled.

He decided that the glory of being a superb athlete was something all of his children should have. He got it in his head that he would train us for a local three-mile road race. As our coach, he would get in the van, with Mom and Jeannine, and drive along country roads slowly while my brothers and I would run behind it. He kept the van rear doors open to have us in his sights as we ran in the blistering Florida heat, sweating and getting cramps. If we fell too far behind the van, Dad would pull over to wait, and then as we approached, he'd pull away. It was like our carrot on a stick. We never knew when we'd be allowed to catch up to it and drive back home, sweat pouring from our bodies.

I had thought I liked to run, but I was a sprinter, not a distance runner. And I dreaded those runs. The day of the race soon came, and it was a hot one. People milled about the starting line, shaking out their legs and hopping up and down. I had only ever raced short distances and had no idea how to pace myself. Dad's training method wasn't designed with any strategy in mind. So when the start gun fired, I took off like I was running the 440-meter. About a quarter mile into the race, a thin crowd lined the road cheering. I thought I was nearing the end and picked up the pace, running as fast as I could, expecting the finish line to appear any minute. The minutes passed and my breath became ragged. I had to walk to catch my breath. Lots of people passed me, including other kids. I started getting nervous about what Dad would say if he saw me walking. I'd never lost a race before. I started running fast again until I had to walk. This was no good. Every time I walked, more people passed me. I started running again, but this time I set my eyes on a woman in front of me. She was older than Mom, but I tried not to think about that. She seemed like she knew what she was doing and I made sure I didn't pass her. She eventually pulled away. I couldn't keep up, but I kept her in my sights as she got smaller and smaller ahead. In this way, I got through the race at least without passing out.

At the awards ceremony at the end, Dad was eager and grinning to see what his kids had won. Jeff, only four-and-a-half, got a trophy for the youngest person to complete the race. Dad was proud of him. We all got little ribbons for completing the race, but mine didn't feel well-earned to me. I hadn't even wanted to do the race.

Next, Dad set his sights on another competition for me. This one had nothing to do with sports. It did require stamina, though. Scouting was an activity that had a lot of built-in opportunities to shine. There were badges to earn, and—in my case—Girl Scout cookies to sell.

Dad did his homework and learned that the Florida state record for cookies sold by an individual Girl Scout was nearly a thousand boxes. This was it. The new competition I would win, he decided. With his help, of course.

"Did I ever tell you I was the top Kirby vacuum salesman in my day?" He had told me that—lots of times, actually, from his days as a young man out West. The trick was to turn on the charm, he said. To sell cookies, Dad drove, with the whole family in the van, to campgrounds, trailer parks, and nicer densely populated areas and dropped me and David off to go door-to-door. David came with me because Dad said as a brother-sister team we would be more adorable. We'd go up and ring the doorbell to each house, and when the door opened, we'd smile and stand tall in our official scout outfits, with our matching brown eyes and brown hair, like twins. The man or woman at the door would invariably say, "What do we have here? Are you brother and sister?" David would proudly say on cue, the way Dad had coached him, "I'm helping my sister." It always worked.

Dad set daily sales goals. We didn't stop until we met our goals, even while John-John, Jeff, and Jeannine fell asleep in the car. There were times I wished I was napping with them. My feet hurt and I was hungry. Between neighborhoods, I'd hand over the orders and money to Mom, who kept close track of it. Sometimes we came home well after dark.

By the time I had to turn in all the orders, I had sold 1,368 boxes, setting a new Florida state record for Girl Scout cookies sold. Dad was elated.

This distinction earned me badges, and it was important to Dad that I earn more badges than anyone else at the badge ceremonies. He wanted me to be better than everyone else's kid. To be the best.

I knew he saw this as a reflection on him. I liked being the best, too, but this particular award for record cookie sales was really for him. And I was happy to provide him this satisfaction. Seeing him in the auditorium as I received my award for the most cookies ever sold, his grin was so wide it nearly split his face. I knew that when he was a kid, the nuns had made him feel worthless. Well, he was sure proving them wrong. He was the father of five excellent children—the "head" of the perfect all-American family.

Scouting itself was proof that we were wholesome. My brothers' Cub Scout troop's field day was one of Dad's finest moments. He was the master of ceremonies over dunking for apples, balloon-popping contests, sack races, and tug-of-wars. Like at his neighborhood barbecues, this was Dad at his best, most fun, most playful, happiest. In fact, I noticed that he had more fun than the other parents, and even more than some of the kids.

That Halloween, Dad had the Cub Scouts and their families over for a haunted trail in the woods adjacent to our lot. He set booby traps that dunked us with water and then dumped flour on our heads. Scary props popped out from behind trees. The other Cub Scout parents dressed in costumes and hid, jumping to scare us. We started out in groups of four children going through at once, but by the end, all the groups were clustered together, the kids clinging to each other as they walked along the trail, giddy at being scared in a way that thrilled us, because, despite the suspense, we knew we were safe.

There's a fine line between real terror and the excitement of anticipating fear when you know it's pretend. Dad liked to come very close to crossing that line with other people's kids, but I thought he only ever truly crossed it with his own.

Dad had not been wrong about winter in Florida. There was no snow or lugging firewood, and trees grew fruit and even bloomed in the winter. The other thing that was different were the people. In Doylestown, everyone was white and pretty much talked the same way. In Florida, people came in all colors and accents. Here we had friends for the first time that didn't look or sound like us. Two boys around David and John-John's ages—seven or eight years old—rode the school bus with us. I'll call them Curtis and Chris. They lived near a peanut farm in a small white cottage that sat back off the road. They walked to our house through an overgrown field nearly every day to play. We would go to the cow pasture next door to have cow paddy wars. They sometimes went to the drive-in theater with us. Dad snuck them in by hiding them under blankets in the van so he wouldn't have to pay extra.

Dad was always super friendly to the Cub Scouts who came over with their parents, but he was different with Curtis and Chris. I didn't know why for sure, but they were Black, and I often wondered if that was the reason. He made jokes in their presence that I later realized were racist. I didn't understand the jokes at the time, but I knew they were mean. Yet the boys were polite and never talked back or sassed him, even when he teased them about their hair or being afraid of Happy.

We had recently acquired an aboveground pool that someone was giving away. Curtis and Chris loved to play with us in the pool, but they hated getting their faces fully submerged. They kept a nervous eye out for Dad, because if he saw them, he would pick them up and throw them in the water. They would go all the way under and come up sputtering.

I was pretty sure that Dad wouldn't actually hurt them, but I knew he took particular joy in scaring them, which seemed different than the playful way he had of scaring us with his ghost stories that we loved just as much as he did, and his haunted trails that we begged him to make.

That year we saw *Jaws* at our favorite drive-in movie theater. Scary movies at the drive-in were extra fun, because Dad heightened the thrill by playing tricks on us during the movie. He would tell us to get out of the van and go get something at the snack shack. Then he'd hide outside the van and jump out at us when we returned. Even when we learned to expect it, the uncertainty of exactly when and where the jump scare would come was still deliciously exciting.

Curtis and Chris went with us to see *Jaws*. At one point in the movie, I was sent out for cups of orange soda and one small bag of popcorn for all of us to share. I could watch the screen the whole time, so I didn't miss anything. As I walked back to the van from the snack shack with my hands full, my eyes darted side to side waiting for Dad to jump out and scare me. But nothing jumped out at me. I guessed that Dad must have been too engrossed in the movie. When I got back to the van, I was safe, like I'd touched the base without being tagged. I settled on the bench seat between the boys and distributed the cups. I had a cup of orange pop in one hand and the bag of popcorn in my other. The boys reached over me to dig into the popcorn. I turned my attention back to the big screen. It was the part of the movie where they're all in the boat and the sheriff leans over the side chumming the water to attract the shark, and then *BAM!* My father screamed the second the enormous shark burst to the surface. My arms flew up involuntarily and orange pop and popcorn went everywhere, setting off a chain reaction. There was orange pop in John-John's eyes, up David's nose, on Jeff's pillow, in Curtis's hair, and our meager precious popcorn was everywhere. Dad convulsed in laughter. He'd outdone himself. My brothers and I and Curtis and Chris looked at each other and then we burst out laughing too.

By spring it was already hot again. "Hotter'in hay-dees," Dad liked to say. I didn't know what or where "hay-dees" was, but I agreed. Florida was hotter.

The pool was one of my favorite places to be, especially on those "hotter'in hay-dees" days. Ours was nowhere near as big as Sandy and Bob's in-ground pool. And it lacked the beautiful blue tile, but it served us well. We always had to check for snakes and alligators before we jumped in. The boys would beg me to make them a whirlpool, and I would run in one direction along the inside edge of the pool, around and around, creating an eddy so strong that it would pull us around like flotsam.

But when I could, I liked to be alone in the pool. I floated on my back, letting the air out of my lungs slowly, letting myself sink to the rubbery bottom, watching the bubbles leave my mouth and float upward. The sound of the bubbles and the hum in my ears was all I could hear as the heat and tension inside left my body and I stayed under until I couldn't stand it anymore. I came up, took a huge gulp of air and did it all over again. My whole body would be cool for hours.

To get shade during the hot days, Happy stayed under the house, which was up on cement blocks. She had a litter of puppies. They reminded me of tiny versions of Happy, squirmy little shepherd pups. We never did know who the puppies' father was. I wish I could say that they all found loving homes, but I don't remember them running around or playing before Dad took them away, and I am almost glad I don't know what he did with them, afraid of what that might be. It reminded me of when he drove off with Snoopy and I didn't want to think about that. When Happy's puppies left, a mother cat that had been hanging around had a litter of kittens and abandoned them. One day, I peeked under the trailer and there was Happy, nursing three little mewling kittens on her belly. I crawled under the trailer to pet them and I was instantly attacked by fleas. I had to crawl right back out. It haunted me to think about how Happy and the kittens must have been tormented by them.

Sometimes at night, lying in my hot room, I would close my eyes and see the barn fire on Taylor Road raging in my head. I couldn't sleep because I was afraid that I would dream about Cindy and hear her calling to me. But after seeing Happy and the kittens covered in fleas, that image replaced the fire in my nightly terrors. I imagined all sorts of scary things living under that crawl space with them. And I hoped they were safe. I hoped whatever was down there, like the boogeyman, wouldn't get us, either.

At home, inside the double-wide, Dad was becoming more and more irritable as the days grew hotter.

As long as we were doing something special, like going to the drive-in, Dad seemed like he was in a good mood, the "good" Dad. We took advantage of fun stuff Florida had to offer, like camping on the beach in our sandy van, or going to see the elephants at the Ringling Bros. and Barnum & Bailey Circus, or taking a trip to the Everglades to see alligators being wrestled. Dad loved those outings as much as any of his kids. Once, in a rare burst of extravagance, we went to Disney World.

Dad loved roller coasters and had been bouncing up and down like a kid in anticipation of Space Mountain. I was tall enough to ride it with him. I was less a fan of the queasy feeling every time a roller coaster plunged, but Dad looked back at me buckled into the hard seat behind him, and he grinned wide as the ride chugged up a hill. Then he lifted his hands. I wanted to be brave like him, but instead I held on tight and screamed my lungs out on the plunge down the other side.

Afterward, I was recovering with Mom and the rest of the family at an ice cream kiosk. Mom licked her standard—pistachio in a sugar cone. We kids had soft-serve chocolate vanilla swirl, without sprinkles because they were ten cents extra. I was noticing how sticky Jeannine's chin was and how even the napkin Mom was wiping it with was sticking to her when I realized I'd lost track of Dad. But I figured if I had Mom and my siblings in my sights, that would be good enough to keep us all together. And then Dad appeared, coming toward us through the crowd, looking frazzled.

"Time to go," he said to Mom. He hurried us along like he was herding sheep. He'd seen someone he knew from Doylestown and wasn't happy about it. And now we had to leave. He kept saying, "What are the odds . . . ?" Florida may have seemed far enough from Ohio to escape whatever we'd fled, but it wasn't.

It was toward the end of the school year that I noticed Curtis and Chris weren't on the bus. They stopped coming over to play. Dad would never let us go to their house, so when David wanted to visit them when Dad wasn't home, Mom wouldn't let him. She was unable to defy Dad.

Days passed and I began to worry that something bad might have happened to them. I asked Lucy if she knew anything, but she didn't know. I wondered if they had moved without telling us, which would have surprised me. Of course they would have told us, right? I suspected that we were about to move ourselves. Dad hadn't *said* anything about moving, but I could tell that he was getting restless. There had been a couple odd things that happened in a row, one being our abrupt departure from Disney World. Another was a visit from the police.

We had just returned from church with Lucy's family to find a police car pulled up to the double-wide.

After they left, I asked Dad, "Why were the police here?"

I expected him to say that they were there to ask him questions about a criminal he had snitched on or to help them in some case, like with the FBI men.

But instead, Dad said something that made no sense. "They wanted to question Mom about driving without a license."

I thought, *What? Mom doesn't even drive.* In fact, I'd never seen her behind the wheel of the van or the Winnebago. I suspected that the only true part of that explanation was that Mom still didn't have a driver's license. But I didn't challenge Dad. I knew better. Why *had* the police come?

Not long after that, Dad told us he had sold the house and we would be leaving as soon as the school year was over. In the meantime, I watched as Dad sold the furniture. He never had bought me that white canopy bed and matching dresser. He told me we couldn't afford it. I once asked Mom why we couldn't just put it on layaway like we had done the rest of the furniture. She'd said, well, we still owed money on the other furniture and didn't have more credit. So I knew that Dad was selling furniture we still owed money on.

I watched him take money from one person for the dining room table and before the buyer could return with a truck, Dad sold it again to another person who took it away. Then the original buyer would show up but the table was gone and an argument ensued. This happened more than once.

I was repulsed, too, to hear Dad use a sob story he'd tell people who came to our moving sale to get them to pay more. "These are tough times," he said over and over again. "It's getting hard to keep food on the table with so many kids." I hated that he was using his family, his children, to exact sympathy and a higher price. Even at ten years old, I thought, *Where's your pride? How could you embarrass us this way?* He was trying to make people pity us, and that was degrading. I had the sense that we were poor now, or that he was portraying us as poor, but I wanted to retain our dignity.

The day we up and left Florida in the Winnebago towing the van, Dad was in a hurry. Again, we were given the same reason. His research for his second book uncovered information about bad guys. And now we had to run. "You know," he said, "we've got to be smarter, stay one step ahead. We can't stay in one place too long." As we drove off, I thought of the angry people who'd paid him for furniture they never got to take home. Maybe they were the ones we were fleeing this time. Who had it been the last time? Who would it be the next time?

14

Verna

When my father was released from the Chillicothe prison in 1954, he was twenty-one years old. He decided that "there would be no more stupid, impulsive rip-offs." He wrote in his memoir, "I would plan every crime deliberately, patiently, and cold-bloodedly, whether it was forgery, burglary, or armed robbery." When the prison doors opened, he walked out a free man. A new chapter was beginning, but he was not seeking transformation.

First stop, as always, was Akron. He falsified an application and got a job at a department store. He proposed to a continual stream of women. Giving his "fiancées" free access to the department store inventory after hours. He personally accumulated two-thousand-dollars' worth of new clothes and accessories by helping himself as well.

With this loot, he headed off to Colorado, where he met Barbara, a young woman with an eight-month-old baby girl. He convinced her to run off with him to Dallas, Texas, assuring her that he loved kids. In Dallas, he enjoyed a double life, playing house with Barbara and her baby while dating several women at once, including one named Peggy. He liked Peggy's dark hair and thought she was pretty, but mostly he admired her bank account. With Peggy, he needed to play his cards right to get what he wanted from her, which wasn't sex. He got plenty of that elsewhere.

My father proposed to Peggy and actually went through with the wedding, but on their wedding night, before the marriage was consummated, he took off in her car (which was now technically his, too) and left town with Donna, a seventeen-year-old girl he'd just met. Their destination was Jacksonville, Florida.

In Florida, he got a job at, of all places, a private detective agency. He was given a camera and a client list. He quickly figured out how to scam the clients, convincing them to hire him freelance at a discount. But he never intended to do any actual investigating. This scheme brought in nearly two thousand dollars. He met an eighteen-year-old named Betty who had a three-year-old daughter. Betty was married to a man more than fifty years older than she was. With Betty and her daughter, the agency's camera, and his swindled cash, he lit out for Akron.

Back on his home turf, Dad was picked up on suspicion of burglary after he pulled a prank on an old friend. Once he was in custody, authorities realized he was the same man they had an arrest warrant out on, for kidnapping. Betty's husband had not taken the disappearance of his wife and daughter kindly. The police tried to tack a stolen car charge onto a growing list of offenses, but my father pointed out that the car was legally his and his wife's, back in Dallas, and he could prove it. A wife in Dallas, plus a young woman with a child who followed him from Jacksonville? "Who the hell do you think you are," the police sergeant asked, "Don Juan?"

While he was in custody pending a grand jury, my father committed his first jailbreak. The headline in the *Akron Beacon Journal* article from April 6, 1955, reads: CITY JAIL PRISONER DASHES TO FREEDOM. The article begins, "A speedy ex-private eye broke from City Jail late Tuesday by the simple expedient of shoving aside the jailer and running."

With nothing but the clothes on his back, he hitchhiked and begged for bus fare to Buffalo, New York. There he realized his only hope for fast money was, he wrote, to hook up with a "queer" to "pick up $5 or $10 and get a blow job as well."

He walked into a gay bar and met his John. This must have given him the idea to go into the sex trade, because the next day he met a woman named Martha and he had a proposition for her. It wasn't marriage. They hitchhiked to Wilmington, North Carolina. There, he set her up in a hotel and pimped her out to horny men in the military. She made $250 in one night, but Martha didn't stick around, and he found the prostitution business distasteful. Well, live and learn.

Next, he headed back to Florida under the alias of James Langley and met Laura, a nurse. He liked nurses for their mothering ways. He wrote that he was the first man Laura had ever had sex with. Like Peggy, he was careful with Laura. He was playing a longer game than a one-night stand. He asked her to marry him and suggested they buy a car, with her credit and his cash. They bought a 1955 Ford convertible.

Then "Jim" met Verna. According to my dad, he was always "partial to guileless girls." She didn't stay innocent for long. "Jim" left town with Verna in Laura's car. On the way out, they bought clothing and supplies on the joint charge accounts he shared with Laura.

He and Verna spent two months traveling around the country. When they needed money, he either cashed a bad check or he'd buy a thousand-dollars' worth of furniture for twenty dollars down and sell it fast for four hundred dollars.

In Idaho, he got a job at a potato farm. By this time, Verna was pregnant and he'd promised he would marry her, but in the meantime he needed to say she was his sister in order to con other women, which was proving to be a reliable scam. She went along with the deception for a while.

Everything changed when Dad, still aka James Langley, fell head over heels with a girl named Jeanette, the friend of the potato farmer's daughter. It was his first time in love. But now Verna no longer wanted to be known as just his sister. She'd become a problem that needed solving. As James Langley, he secretly married Jeanette and headed to Denver, Colorado, with both women. Verna was not only unhappy, she was afraid. He admits in his memoir that "she'd seen displays of my violent temper and was badly frightened of what I might do if she caused me trouble." So, he says he just left her in Denver and took off with Jeanette to begin his most impressive crime spree yet.

15

Westward Expansion

As soon as school was out, we said goodbye to our Florida lives, speeding off in the Winnebago, towing the van. We were headed out West.

It didn't feel like we were off on a grand adventure this time. Dad wasn't in the mood for Car Bingo. Mom tried to keep us occupied with games like the one where we tried to spot license plates for each of the fifty states. We got a point for every state we found, but Hawaii and Alaska were worth two points. Sometimes, within the cramped Winnebago, I would escape into a book, as my brothers bounced around me. I had graduated from my well-worn Disney book club picks. Now I'd disappear from my family and into a Nancy Drew mystery and my dog-eared copy of *Charlotte's Web.*

Dad said a man he'd met in Florida had told him that there was plenty of land for sale in Arizona, so that's where we were headed. But after we had traveled across the dusty plains of Texas and entered the state of Arizona, I thought that man must be an even better BSer than Dad was, because this place looked like the moon—the last place a person would want to live. We stayed in an arid, treeless campground for a week while we looked for property for sale. The towns we drove through were not much more than crossroads with abandoned shacks in the desert, surrounded by sand and rocks. Gas stations were few and far between. The van was hot, and we were thirsty and dusty from driving with the windows rolled down. The road shimmered with heat in the distance. Mom told us it was called a "mirage," something that looked like it was just ahead, but you could never get there.

"Like a pot of gold at the end of the rainbow," Dad said.

"I have to pee," I said.

"Hold it in." Dad kept driving.

I hoped I didn't have to hold it until we caught up to the mirage, because if what Mom said was true, I'd pee in my pants before we ever got there. When we did stop it was in Phoenix. We parked the van and got out in search of a bathroom and soda pop. The sun was so hot the bottom of Dad's shoe melted on a street grate while we waited for a light to change.

Dad looked around the city streets and told us he once lived here. I didn't see the appeal.

Finally, we gave up on Arizona and headed out of the hot desert and drove northeast through the Rockies. The Winnebago, towing the van, always struggled a bit on the hills, but one pass was so steep we slowed to a crawl. The road was narrow and switchbacked, with a drop-off on one side and a mountain rising on the other. It was clear we weren't going to make it. Cars passed our rig, giving us dirty looks. Finally, Dad pulled over at a scenic lookout spot and detached the van. This was going to require two drivers. Mom had no choice, he told her. She still didn't have a license, and the only time I could remember that she'd been behind the wheel of any car was back in Doylestown, when she'd pulled Dad's El Camino into a garage and she knocked the side mirror off. I could tell Mom was scared, but she couldn't say no. Dad didn't let us get out of the Winnebago. He wasn't risking any of us going in the van with Mom. With quaking hands, she got into the driver's seat, started the motor, and followed us up the mountain. I watched through the back window of the Winnebago, while keeping one eye on Jeannine, who was on the RV floor investigating a beetle carcass. Mom's face was frozen with fear. Her hands had a death grip on the steering wheel. There was no room for error. Cars kept passing us, risking head-on collisions in their impatience. At the top of the pass, at a pullover spot, we stopped. Mom nearly stumbled out of the van and took her seat in the Winnebago while Dad reconnected the van. I was flooded with relief that she was back safely in the passenger seat, but Mom's face was ashen.

We spent some time in a campground outside Denver while Dad looked for our next home. He found it in Brighton, Colorado, in the middle of a block of similar homes. Dad took us on a walk-through of a little brick three-bedroom ranch house, and I loved the fresh-paint smell of it. The house was unfurnished, and Dad bought a used dinette set from a woman, Denise, who lived nearby. We went to her house to pick up the table and chairs. She had bleached-blond hair, and I thought she looked glamorous. By Dad's sudden cheerful mood, I could tell he thought so too. I didn't like how he looked at her.

"So," he said. "What's your husband do?"

I didn't listen to her answer. I just rolled my eyes. Nothing new here. Just Dad chatting up a pretty woman. Denise had two boys close in age to John-John and Jeff, eight and almost five. Our family became instant friends with Denise and her husband and kids, or at least I thought we were friends. We joined their church and met other families with kids.

We had arrived in Brighton just in time for the school year. I entered fifth grade. David was in fourth, John-John was in third, Jeff was in first. On our first day, we all walked to school together. Jeff walked stiffly, trying to put a brave face on, but he was upset because he had to leave his pillow behind. My brothers carried their superhero-themed lunch boxes. Mine was old, pink, and had a peeling image of Cinderella. We all brought the same thing for lunch: a baloney-and-mustard sandwich on white bread. A few chips wrapped in plastic. A thermos of Kool-Aid. If we were lucky, a cookie or an apple. John announced when he came home from school that we could no longer call him John-John. He was just John now.

Across the street from our house was a big field, and just beyond the field was a strip mall. Mom got a job in the afternoons at a discount store in the mall. It sold inexpensive household items, clothes, school supplies, and trinkets. Other than the handful of times she worked as a substitute teacher in Florida, this was the first time she'd had a job outside the house since she'd met Dad. Mom could walk to work, which was a requirement after the trauma of the mountain pass, and she wasn't eager to practice for the driver's test. We rarely went into the store when Mom was working, but Dad would often visit her there. He sometimes brought a new shirt or other clothing items home with him after these visits, but I noticed there was never a receipt or a store bag. Once I even saw him remove a new shirt from under his coat.

Mom left for work when I got home from school and could babysit Jeannine and my brothers. She seemed cheerful as she left. This was a new side to Mom I hadn't seen before. Maybe she was glad not to be home when Dad came home. Or maybe she liked the job. I never heard her complain about it or her boss. She turned her paychecks over to Dad.

Dad got a job with a builder doing home construction, and he would sometimes take Jeannine on jobs with him. But his building job didn't last long. Unlike Mom, he usually complained about whoever had hired him, and when he stopped working there it was always the other guy's fault. Soon he was working "odd jobs," but whatever those were I never knew. Often when we got home from school, Dad would be sitting in his recliner watching TV. Jeff would hop on his lap, and they would watch TV together; Jeff, with his left thumb in his mouth, the old pillow gripped in his left fist, stroking Dad's stubbly cheeks with his right hand.

My fifth-grade homeroom teacher was Mrs. Thompson, who was grumpy and seemed like she'd rather be elsewhere doing something else, anything other than herding a bunch of rowdy, smelly kids. The classroom had an invisible fog of BO.

There was a girl in my class named Yvonne. She narrowed her eyes when I showed up as the new kid in class. I could tell that Yvonne was going to be trouble before I even took my assigned seat in front of her. Sure enough, she pulled my hair when no one was looking. Just a single strand of hair, so it stung. When I passed her in the hall between classes, she knocked my books out of my hand.

My first week at school, lunch was a trial. Every day I made sure not to sit near Yvonne. I picked a table that had a bunch of quiet kids. I didn't want to barge in on any groups of friends who didn't want me. Yvonne purposely walked by my table holding her tray and flicked a pea or a piece of lettuce at me. I pretended I didn't notice.

I opened my Cinderella lunch box carefully. One whiff would tell me if Mom had remembered to rinse it out. If it smelled bad, I closed it after extracting each item. I ate my baloney sandwich in silence while I eyed other kids' lunches. I tried to eat slowly so I wasn't finished before the other kids had barely started theirs. I wanted badly to buy my lunch instead of bringing it, especially on days when the school served hamburgers and french fries. I asked for lunch money and Dad exploded in a tirade about how expensive school lunches were, so I never asked again. Friday was pizza day; as I watched the other kids at the table bite into their rectangular pieces of pizza with little dry crumbles of sausage on top, my mouth watered. I just put a few potato chips in my sandwich to make it more interesting and took another bite. I sipped my watered-down Kool-Aid, wishing it was the creamy chocolate milk that would have come with a bought lunch.

The first time we lined up as a class for gym, Yvonne pushed me out of line and Mrs. Thompson told me to knock it off. Other kids saw Yvonne picking on me, but no one wanted to mess with her. She was big and loud and laughed like a fifty-year-old smoker. She had a group of a few girls who always followed her lead. At recess, on the playground, I tried to steer clear of them. I brought my Lemon Twist, which I'd gotten for my last birthday, to recess and played with it by myself. I felt self-conscious, but it was better to be lonely than laughed at.

One day my Lemon Twist wasn't in my cubby, and I knew Yvonne must have taken it. Instead of walking directly home after school that day, I followed Yvonne. I didn't want to get in a fight with her, I just wanted her to leave me alone and to realize that I wasn't a pushover. And I wanted my Lemon Twist back. Dad had not stopped his fight practice sessions, and I was not afraid of getting punched. But I hoped it wouldn't come to that.

Yvonne lived in the opposite direction from me, and I had been wondering if she would try to go out of her way to bully me after school. She hadn't, but I wanted to head it off at the pass. After just a few blocks, she heard footsteps and turned around and saw me. She looked surprised. This was definitely not what she expected of me.

We were not on school grounds, so there was no rule against fighting. If she went on the attack, I was, within Dad's rules, entitled to defend myself. In fact, it would be a requirement.

But instead of coming after me, she just looked alarmed. She wasn't used to being challenged. We just stared at each other for a few seconds. I didn't say anything. I didn't have to. She backed away and then turned around and kept walking. I turned to walk home, feeling relieved and triumphant.

Things at school got easier after that day. Yvonne stopped tormenting me. The Lemon Twist magically appeared in Mrs. Thompson's classroom closet where she kept the board games and craft supplies. Mrs. Thompson expressed surprise at seeing it and handed it to me, saying, "Well look what must have got lost and found."

One of the most thrilling aspects of being in fifth grade in Brighton was music class—each student had the opportunity to play an instrument. I had chosen the clarinet. I held the delicate black instrument with its shiny metal keys as if it were made of glass. We were supposed to buy the clarinet or rent it for the school year, but I never turned in the form or the money. Permission forms were often lost among the papers on the messy tabletop next to Dad's recliner.

One form that Dad never failed to sign was the Girl Scout membership form. Once again, I broke another state Girl Scout cookie record, selling more than seven hundred boxes of cookies. My brothers joined the wrestling team. John-John was showing serious athletic talent, and Dad wanted to develop it. Dad made me join the wrestling team too. Technically, it was a boys' team, but there was one other girl on the team who paved the way.

I was beginning to notice how different I was from the other girls at school. My clothes were boyish, my hair was long—the way Dad liked it—and unstyled. The girls in fifth grade all seemed older than me. I observed their smooth, hairless legs and was conscious of how hairy mine were. In the locker room before gym, I noticed they wore training bras, but I didn't have one and I was too afraid to ask my parents to get one for me. I didn't want to draw anyone's attention to my body, including Dad's. Especially Dad's. Other girls wore eye shadow and curled or straightened their hair. They were clearly spending more time in front of a mirror in the mornings. Secretly, I practiced using my giant Barbie head's makeup on myself, though I had to scrub it off before I left my room. There would have been hell to pay if Dad had seen me with blush on my cheeks or the stripe of sky-blue eyeshadow I was experimenting with.

In town, there was a local gym in an old building that taught kids classes in boxing and karate. Dad signed us up for those, too. We were becoming forces to be reckoned with. At home, Dad's mandatory fight sessions between me and David and John became more brutal as we became better at defending ourselves and landing blows. I was still bigger and I could still beat them up. But the stakes were higher. The dread I felt before every fight grew. And the resentment my brothers felt toward me grew, too.

When Dad and Mom went out at night, they no longer hired a babysitter. Now they left me in charge of my siblings. Dad always wanted Mom to look nicer than her usual plainness when they went out. She never wore jewelry other than her wedding band. Dad couldn't even get her to wear clip-on earrings, which she said hurt her earlobes. But he would tell her what to wear.

One night, they were going to a party at Denise's house. I could tell Mom didn't really want to go. On their way out, Dad handed me a list of chores that we had to complete before they returned. Or else. We knew what "or else" meant. The list was long. Cleaning toilets, sweeping floors, doing laundry, washing dishes, putting clothes and toys away—all the crap that accumulates in a house where no one cleans up after themselves, including the parents.

I delegated jobs. Jeff was assigned to gather dirty clothes. Jeannine was given the job of picking up the small toys like Legos and Matchbox cars and puzzle pieces, which littered the house. I told John to clean the bathrooms, I would tackle the kitchen, and I assigned David to sweep the floor.

Jeannine was willing to do her part. At three, she was probably just glad to have a job. I knew she'd get distracted in the middle and start playing with the toys instead of putting them away. I'd end up doing her job too. But David and John wouldn't buckle down to start a single chore. I was furious and screamed at them to get to work. Their resentment of me was already deep: for the fighting matches, for me being a bossy big sister. By this time, they no longer resented me for being Dad's favorite. Jeff had long ago replaced me as that.

Now, when we were under the gun to get the list of chores done, they resisted my instructions, which turned into orders. I could not accept insubordination. I was too afraid. They had never understood how much pressure I felt. Dad had drilled into me that my brothers were my responsibility, that I was in charge, that any failure by any one of them was my fault. Nothing had changed since they had stumbled around at the Kevin Drive construction site. I was still supposed to keep them in line. And they were still just as hard to corral.

"Get to work!" I yelled at David.

David screamed back at me, "You're not the boss of me!"

"Yes I am!" I shouted back. "Dad put me in charge!"

"Dad's not here, is he?" David shouted back.

"Yeah!" John said, partnering up with David, as usual.

"You guys better listen to me!" I screamed.

"Make us!" David screamed back. John grabbed the broom and started running around the kitchen table.

I knew things had escalated out of my control.

Then, as I was facing off David, trying to think of a comeback, *crack*, John brought the broom down hard on my back and nearly knocked me over.

"*Ouch!*" I yelled, and spun around to see John holding only half a broom handle. Apparently, the broom was not designed to be used as a weapon. My back stung, but that was nothing compared to what Dad would do to me when he got home. We three looked at each other in horror, transformed in that moment from adversaries to allies. What would Dad do when he found out we'd broken the broom?

I grabbed a roll of masking tape and we taped it back together. But it didn't work. We used half a broom as best we could. But we still had a problem with the broken broom.

"What do we do?" David said.

"Hide it!" I said.

We taped it back together—purely for the optics—and stuffed it in the back of the messy hall closet and got to work on the other chores in earnest. I got down on my hands and knees with towels to help David with the floors. We washed and dried dishes, hoping that Dad wouldn't find the broom and punish us.

A week later, Mom brought a new broom home from work without saying a word. I checked the back of the closet, and the broken broom was gone. Mom must have found it and thrown it away. I felt so relieved and hopeful. Was it possible that Mom was an ally? She definitely wasn't an adversary, the way I was beginning to see Dad, but would Mom actually step up to help me if I needed her?

One night after dinner, Mom and Dad were in the living room watching TV. He on his recliner, she on the sofa. I came in from playing outside and Dad looked up. "April, come here," he said. Mom looked up too, but then resumed her macrame project. She made a lot of hanging plant holders that year. I walked up to Dad reluctantly. What was he going to yell at me about? What chore had I forgotten to do?

"Come here," he said again, staring at my chest.

I stood in front of him.

"Looks like our little girl is growing up," he said. I almost asked for a training bra right then and there. But then he said, "Pull up your shirt. Let me take a look."

Horrified, I felt my face flush. I looked over at Mom for her to say something or at least acknowledge with her eyes what was happening, but she seemed intent on a knot she was tying. I did as Dad said, not wanting to defy him and face the consequences.

Dad examined my chest closely. Then he reached up and touched the area around my nipples, which had recently started to form small mounds. He pressed on my nipples, clinically, as if doing a medical exam. It hurt. I looked at Mom, silently imploring her to look up and say something, anything to make this humiliation stop, but she kept her eyes down on her handiwork. I guessed Mom could not be counted on to help me. I was on my own.

Finally, curiosity satisfied, Dad pulled my T-shirt down and went back to watching TV.

Crushed by shame, I walked to my room and closed the door as quietly as possible. If Dad knew that he'd upset me, he might do it again just to tease me. I could not let him know. But I also could not think of a way to make sure it did not happen again.

Up until now, Dad's behavior toward women and teenage girls was the extent of my sex education. We were sheltered in terms of what TV shows and movies we were allowed to watch, which was restricted to G-rated content that included nature documentaries, Disney movies, and *Little House on the Prairie*. But this was paired with the evening news and true crime shows, which were as unwholesome as you could get. Those shows flaunted deviant human behavior, mostly by men. Yet even by fifth grade, I didn't know the "facts of life," as the school's sex education class (or "Health," as it was known) referred to the topic in the permission form they sent home for our parents to sign. Mom had never talked to me about sex or menstruation or puberty or anything that might have prepared me for what was soon to come. Well, the school was about to let that cat out of the bag, and now one of my parents had to sign the form or cause me great embarrassment at school. I'd have to go sit in another room with the Jehovah Witnesses. I begged them to sign. Dad signed. Then he, not Mom, preemptively sat all his kids down, except for Jeannine. He wasn't going to leave this business to a lame gym teacher; he was going to make sure we had the facts straight. Dad explained in the most clinical terms how a man put his thing inside a woman and made a baby. I remember thinking, *eww*. But I still didn't know how that related to what I saw Dad do to women, like when he grabbed other ladies' butts and caressed them. Or how he had flirted with our babysitters. I suspected his behavior was connected to the birds and the bees, but I wasn't sure how.

• • •

Here in Brighton, we had the same contrast between inside and outside as we'd had everywhere we lived. Inside the house, Dad ruled his family with his fists and belt. Outdoors, he was known as the most fun dad in the neighborhood. He rallied the neighborhood kids—including older kids—to play hide-and-seek at night. Running around outside being pursued or being the pursuer takes on a much different feel in darkness than in broad daylight. Something about darkness triggers a visceral fear all on its own. The thrill increases tenfold.

Dad was the only adult player in these games. He hid himself by squeezing between the house and a row of bushes, and when the seeker passed him, he popped out with a "Boo!" and scared the kid. When it was John, he would fall to the ground in fear, curled into a fetal position, covering his head with his arms. But when he got up, he wanted to do it again. Dad also hid up on the roof. As the seekers crept by in the dark, on the lookout for hiders, he dropped a water balloon on their heads. They shrieked in surprise.

Dad taught us all a variation of hide-and-seek. When the seeker found someone, the person would be blindfolded and get in line behind the seeker, holding on to waist or shoulders, stumbling along. As the seeker found more, those kids would be blindfolded and join the end of the line, holding on to the person in front of them. Soon there would be a whole line of blindfolded kids, one behind another, moving like a massive, clumsy caterpillar. However, anyone hiding could sneak around if they could evade the seeker and tag the person at the end of the line, releasing them from the line and from being blindfolded. When Dad was the one to sneak up on the line and free blindfolded kids, he'd snatch the kids, putting one hand over their mouths and grab them hard by the arms. To be grabbed like that at night while blindfolded was terrifying enough to almost make you pee yourself. But we begged him to play with us.

The game was even more spooky when everyone's lawn was decorated for Halloween. Our neighborhood in Brighton was ideal for trick-or-treating. As in previous years, Dad controlled the choices we made for our Halloween costumes. Where other kids were witches and serial killers, we weren't allowed to pick those. We weren't allowed to have fake weapons while trick-or-treating, either. So a cowboy with a gun in a holster was out of the question. Ghosts were always a safe choice. A pirate without the sword was another easy "yes." Dad never allowed me to dress as anything he considered unsavory. Princesses were safe. I was still drawn to fairy tales and I used the occasion to play with makeup, the one time of year Dad wouldn't object. My giant Barbie head's makeup was the extent of my kit, but it was enough to make my cheeks rosy and my eyelids sky blue. One of the only advantages of moving so often was that I could be the same thing for Halloween every year without anyone knowing. This year I wore a princess dress that Mom got for free at the discount store because it had a small tear in the seam. David wore Bob's police shirt as a costume. Dad had a few useful props for disguises and let David wear his sheriff's badge and hat. Jeff and John went as ghouls with fake blood and bruises. I applied drawing charcoal to make them look like they had black eyes. Dad saved money by not buying candy. Our house stayed dark on Halloween. Jeannine and Mom went with us. Mom and Dad waited by the sidewalk, Dad on high alert, while we kids walked up the walkways and steps to knock on doors. When we got to Denise's house, Dad came up to the house with us and chatted with her.

"What are you dressed as?" he asked her in a husky voice. "A movie star?" She wasn't in costume. Dad helped himself to the candy basket and winked at her. We moved on to the next house.

Unlike on Halloween, when our house was one of the few on the block not participating, for Christmas Dad transformed our front yard in Brighton into a wonderland. In the past, he'd gone all out on the inside of our homes, but this year he made the outside of our house one that people stopped their cars at night to admire. The many close neighbors made for a sizable and appreciative audience. He set up a sleigh and reindeer on the roof, and strung lights on the roofline, the trees, and the bushes.

Aunt Lucille and Uncle Al arrived for Christmas, which they had funded, as usual. They'd made it to Florida the year before, too. Uncle Al was getting more feeble, but Aunt Lucille wanted to bear witness annually to her nephew's family as we grew. They slept in my room, and I had to bunk in with my brothers. I didn't mind, though, because Dad was always on his best behavior while they were visiting. And of course, Christmas was the time he was as happy as a little kid.

The Colorado house had a finished basement. We used it as a playroom. There was a little room in the basement with a door. A month before Christmas, the door to the basement room was locked. David and John looked through the crack in the door and saw piles of wrapped presents. They called me over. I peeked through the crack and saw the pile too. Then, come Christmas, the same gift-wrapped boxes appeared underneath the tree. My brothers recognized the gifts too.

Wait a minute, I thought. *Why had Santa stored the gifts in the basement?* I was in fifth grade and was still genuinely puzzled.

I realized all at once that Santa was a hoax. "Hey," I said. "We saw these in the playroom!"

Dad got mad. "No you didn't," he said. He swore up and down that the gifts were from Santa.

Jeannine started crying. We'd all seen the gifts in the basement, including her. Finally, Aunt Lucille couldn't stand the tension anymore. She said, "Wayne, the jig is up." Dad wanted to explode, I could tell, but because Aunt Lucille and Uncle Al were there, he wasn't able to express his fury. I felt confirmed and mildly satisfied that I'd been a good detective and figured out one of childhood's grand mysteries. But Dad was crushed, far more disappointed than my brothers and I were. Jeannine was just happy to start opening presents.

But then I had a terrible thought. After the triumph of being right about Santa, I realized this meant there was also no Easter Bunny, no Tooth Fairy. And this realization was crushing. I'd spoiled it for everyone. Now even poor Jeannine knew there was no such thing as these stealthy and generous omniscient gift givers. Dad was in a terrible mood for the rest of the day. The illusion of Santa was the highlight of his year, creating this magical world for his kids—and even more so for himself. It was the end of our collective innocence, in a way.

That Christmas there was a large box under the tree for Mom. I waited with great anticipation for her to open it. Dad had made an excellent Santa. He was always good at getting the right gift for everyone, but he'd had help from us. Normally, we would never ask for anything extra. Not sprinkles on ice cream that cost ten cents extra. Not even ice cream itself unless it was offered first. But for Christmas, we wrote Santa a letter with a wish list. For birthdays, we were allowed to make lists of all the things we wanted. No restrictions applied, thanks to the funds that had been sent in advance by Aunt Lucille and Uncle Al, and Mom's parents. We wouldn't get everything on the list, but we'd always get something from it. Of course, I always asked for a pony along with other more practical items like Barbies. My brothers would usually ask for trucks, BB guns, or anything related to cowboys and Indians. No toy that Jeff ever received replaced that old pillow as his favorite, though. Finally, Mom opened her box. It was a giant makeup set. I knew for sure she had not wished for it, but I was thrilled we now had one of these in the house. I had used up the giant Barbie head's kit. To demo the gift, I helped Mom apply foundation, eyeshadow, eyeliner, blush, but just as she had said it would, the final touch of mascara made her eyes water. It made her feel uncomfortable to be looked at and admired, but I thought she looked pretty. Later, as the family makeup expert, I would use my experience with foundation makeup to cover bruises on my face and arms. Hers too.

That Sunday, when I got ready for church, I put on one of two dresses that I had for services and then I helped Mom by doing her hair. I used a curling iron to give her hair more body. Using her new makeup kit, I put just a bit of blush on her cheekbones for church. That was all she'd let me do. But I was glad she let me do even that much. I didn't want her to be plain. I wanted her to be as beautiful as she could be so Dad would look at her the way he looked at Denise. He looked at other women, too, when we were out in public or socializing in the neighborhood. And I saw that they looked at him in the same way. He was like a magnet. Somehow there were always attractive women around him.

• • •

We got a ride to church with Denise's family in their big station wagon every Sunday morning. Mom sat in the back seat with Jeannine on her lap, and my brothers and I piled into the way back with Denise's sons. Dad never attended services with us. Denise's sister Celia's family also attended the same church. We became friends with Celia and her boys, too.

This gaggle of boys was a self-contained pack when they were together. Dad invited all the boys to go on weekend camping adventures with us. Not the parents, just the boys. We had a favorite place to camp, which wasn't in a commercial campground. It was off the highway, by a river, beneath big aspen trees. But sometimes, once we got the gear unloaded and set up the tents, Dad would leave us. Mom was left with nearly a dozen kids to supervise. She'd sit in a camp chair by the Winnebago with a pencil and a book of word searches, leaving us kids to our own devices. We would play hide-and-seek or collect firewood or splash in the icy river if the current wasn't too swift. Sometimes Dad was gone for hours. I wondered where he went. Sometimes he said he had business to attend to. Other times he left without saying why. A few times he didn't come back until we were already asleep. I found myself wondering if he was somewhere with Denise. I didn't want to think that, but I couldn't help it.

Dad sold our well-worn Winnebago when he heard from the German couple whom we had met in Florida. They'd agreed to let Dad sell their much bigger and nicer RV after they'd completed their American adventures and returned home. Once Dad collected the German's RV, he sent them the money he'd made selling our old Winnebago, telling them that was what he got for selling their much nicer rig.

Then he kept their RV. We camped with it a few times, but we didn't keep it for long. It was too valuable, so Dad sold it and kept the money. It must have been easy to fool people who lived so far away. It was harder to fool people living close to home, and it sometimes required fancy footwork.

Dad acted super friendly to Denise's sister Celia and her husband, and he showed them pictures of the peacock mural he had painted on Kevin Drive. Impressed, they hired him to paint a mural just as big in the rec room of their spacious, beautiful house. Celia and her husband made the mistake of paying Dad in advance, and shortly after starting it, we left town without any notice. It was just after the school year ended. Dad had packed up a U-Haul and hooked up the van to it during the night. This was the first time I could remember us leaving at night. This departure I hadn't seen coming.

We got up before daylight and fled. Jeff and I sat wedged into the front bench seat between Mom and Dad. Jeff sucked his thumb furiously and squeezed his old pillow. Mom had Jeannine on her lap and Happy at her feet. David and John stood sleepily behind the seat in the space so narrow they could not sit. As we drove through the night, I thought that we had all grown up a bit too much in Brighton. My own eyes had been opened to unsettling truths: There was no Santa. Babies were made in the grossest way. Dad might have been having an affair with Denise. And he definitely ripped off Celia and her husband.

We drove northeast and watched the sun rise over the vast cornfields of Nebraska. Was Dad intending to return to the Akron area again? Maybe. But if so, he must have changed his mind in Iowa because we kept going northeast until we stopped for the night in a campground in a farming town outside Watertown, Wisconsin. We stayed just for a few months, long enough to leave an indelible mark on the community. Long enough to inflict pain on two families for generations to come. In a way, it was the beginning of the end for our family, too.

PART TWO

PART TWO

16

The Concord House

1980

It was early summer when our family of seven barreled down the highway in a U-Haul leaving our life in Brighton, Colorado, headed to who knew where. This time, Dad didn't have a tantalizing promise of Florida beaches or a quest for cheap land out west. How Dad picked Watertown, Wisconsin, I'll never know. Maybe he just drove through the night and ended up there.

When we arrived at a campground in what seemed like the middle of nowhere, I climbed out of the cramped U-Haul and stretched my legs, grateful to be out of the cab, which reeked of Dad's unfiltered Camels and stale coffee. We checked out the lay of the land, then set up the two tents—one big one for sleeping in that fit all seven of us and the other screened tent for over the picnic table. We unloaded our bikes from the U-Haul and rode in loops that kept us within sight of the campsite. Dad didn't like us to wander too far away. I kept an eye out for other kids, but we didn't need other kids to have a good time—we were never at a loss for things to do. Adventure was under every leaf and in every body of water no matter how small. This place, we could see, had great potential. There was a pond not far from the campsite and we were determined to check it out the next day. And there was a large events venue across a field, called the Concord House.

Our first night camping, I was snuggled deep into my sleeping bag, which I had placed next to one of the tent sidewalls, so I didn't have to breathe anyone's breath or look at anyone sleeping, when the first drop of rain hit the side of the tent. We'd camped through many rainstorms in the last few years. I thought nothing of it, at first. It would mean more puddles to ride our bikes through in the morning. But the rain soon pelted the tent and the wind picked up and began pushing its sides in, shaking it, threatening to tear the whole thing down. A loud clap of thunder split the air.

"Everyone, get in the van," Dad instructed calmly.

A huge gust of wind came and ripped the tent fly off. A flash of lightning lit up the tent, followed almost immediately by another boom of thunder.

"Now!" Dad yelled.

We unzipped the tent, which was shaking wildly, and made a mad dash for the van, getting soaked through our pajamas to the skin. The ground was already a puddle, and I glanced at the U-Haul, where Happy was tied. She was probably getting wet even underneath it.

Once safely in the van, I watched through the fogged windows Dad running around in the pouring rain, grabbing tent lines and tying it to the U-Haul to keep it from flying away. Bolts flashed and thunder cracked, and I was scared he'd get struck by lightning. Finally, he joined us in the van. The air inside felt heavy with moisture. The rain smacked the roof and I tried to fall asleep next to Jeff, who carried his comfort wherever he went. Unless he lost his pillow, or his thumb, he'd be okay anywhere.

In the morning, we emerged from the van to a blue sky. We were one of the few tent campers in a field of RVs. Our tent lay in a wet heap, tied to the U-Haul, but none of the parts had blown away or ripped. And Happy survived the night. It would take days for the soggy sleeping bags to dry out. We strung lines between the U-Haul and trees to drape our wet tent and bags. Dad introduced himself to the neighboring campers, accepted a cup of coffee from one, and talked about the storm, which had everyone excited. Dad steered the conversation to jobs and places to stay.

Someone told him there was an opening for a job as a handyman at the Concord House, right across the field from the campground. It was a big reception hall used for weddings and concerts. The floors were wood planks, and the place had a down-home country feel. Sometimes we'd hear the twang of country music coming from its direction. Dad got a part-time job there.

At night, Dad frequented the local bar. Bars were a great word-of-mouth source for leads of all kinds. There he met a man named John Simon, who lived not far from the campground. Mr. Simon was a farmer—most people in the area were. The fields he leased had an old house on it that was for rent. We moved in right away.

This house was beautiful, old, and dilapidated with many little rooms and two spiral staircases—one leading upstairs and one leading down to the basement. There was an enormous stained glass window in the dining room, eight to ten feet tall. The pieces of colored glass depicted the scene of an island with a mountain in its center and a castle perched on top. The sky was blue and the surrounding ocean was blue-green. It felt like a glimpse of some faraway world. And it was right there in our dining room. I couldn't believe our luck. It caught the sun and cast bright colors over the table and chairs and onto the floor.

One of the rooms was like a secret room. From inside, its two doors were hidden because they had bookcases built into them. When closed, you couldn't see the doors at all. It must have been a real library at one time. It gave me the same feeling of tingly possibility as I got from reading the Disney book about Mickey and the Haunted House. It didn't feel spooky, only mysterious.

Upstairs, I had a bedroom to myself. After sharing a tent with my entire family, this felt like luxury. When I unpacked my box of belongings, I noticed that my clarinet in its little black case had made the move with us. Probably costing the Brighton elementary school quite a bit of money to the rental company. The little music stand and my music book had also been packed in the box. I felt a little guilty that we'd taken the instrument, but I pulled the clarinet out of its purple velour bed. I shined its keys with the silky rag and played the few songs I knew until my lips were numb. I thought if I practiced over the summer, I'd be able to play in my new school's band. It would be a good way to fit in, being a new kid for the third school year in a row.

Like the hidden doors in the library, my bedroom had a secret passage, a closet that connected to another room. It was the perfect private fort. In every house we lived, I found a quiet nook where I could hide away. This one had a pungent musty smell of mouse, but I didn't care. I piled blankets on the floor and put my pillow against the wall and I spent hours in there, and by the light of my flashlight I could read in blessed seclusion. I had already read my Nancy

Drews so many times the pages were falling out, so sometimes I dipped into my parents' boxes.

Dad had a box that was full of magazines called *True Detective*. I knew this was his favorite and had often seen him reading one. I took a stack of them into my closet and settled in to read.

I picked up one, and at first I thought the cover looked a little bit like my Nancy Drew paperbacks. Except the illustration was of a woman looking scared instead of a girl looking brave. Then I looked at all the covers. Every issue had an illustration of a woman in danger, tied up and afraid of a man holding a knife or a gun. The magazines had headlines like: RAPE IN A COFFIN! and MURDER ENDED THEIR LOVE TRYST! I didn't know what a tryst was, but it sounded bad. I opened one of the magazines and started reading it like a book, skipping words I didn't know but getting enough of the gist to follow the stories. The articles were filled with gory details about how people were killed and raped, mostly women. I was unable to stop reading even when the details terrified me. The last article was about the murder of a woman who had been raped and impaled on a stake through her vagina. I was eleven years old. I was horrified but also fascinated. I put the magazine down. Just reading it made me feel guilty for inviting those grotesque images into my mind. I was afraid that Dad and Mom might know I'd read it. When Dad wasn't home and Mom was busy, I put the magazines back into the box they came from.

That night, I couldn't get the article out of my head. Who would *choose* to read this stuff? I knew the answer was sitting in the recliner in the living room. And there were plenty of others like him. *True Detective* underscored for me that the world was not a safe place, that men could do terrible things to women, and other men would find it entertaining to read about it.

We had been living in this beautiful old house for just a few weeks. We kids had taken to gravitating to the dining room in the late afternoon to watch the light come dancing through the stained glass window. We heard Dad come home. We were looking at each other, wondering how fast we could make ourselves scarce, when Dad strode into the room holding a hunting rifle as carelessly as if it were a tennis racket. I wondered where he got it. Back in

Doylestown, I was too young to wonder where that shotgun had come from when he had me shoot it in the yard and nearly rip my shoulder off. Nor did I wonder about the handgun he'd shot over our heads. But now I wondered where this rifle had come from. It was big, with a scope. It looked like it meant business. My brothers and I gathered around Dad, staring at the impressive weapon in his hands. Without warning the gun went off. I screamed and covered my ears. David covered his as well. John collapsed to the ground in a fetal position. Dad's face went white. He dropped to the floor next to his son, saying "John. John. Where are you hit?!" He was in a panic. But John hadn't been struck. He'd fallen in terror.

Dad looked around to see where he'd actually fired the rifle. There, on the worn carpet, was the gash. The bullet had ripped through the floor and lodged in the ductwork.

"Well, I'll be damned," Dad said. "I didn't know the gun was loaded."

I was relieved that none of us had been shot, but I didn't think it was strange for him to bring a loaded gun into our house. This wasn't the first or last house to bear scars from our tenure.

Here, like everywhere, the outside of our house was often safer than the inside. Outside, there were fields worked by John Simon, the farmer. The best part of the farm itself was a dirt track that led from the back of the house to the edge of the property to a creek that ran swiftly through a dense thicket of trees. A rickety railroad tie bridge crossed the creek, and we played back there for hours, splashing in the creek, trying to catch fish with our bare hands.

Mr. Simon got Dad a job repairing the porch of his neighbors, the Uttechs. Dad sometimes brought me with him to that job because the Uttechs' daughter Nicole was my age. Her house overlooked a big field. We rode her bikes—she had one with a banana seat—up and down the street. Sometimes she came over to play in the creek by the bridge with me and my brothers.

Dad was still working for the Concord House, and sometimes he worked late. I noticed one morning, when Dad showed up at breakfast, his nose was messed up. It was swollen, cut, and bruised. I asked what happened. He told me he hurt it with the rifle scope while hunting. I had only ever known my dad to hunt elk once in Colorado. But it was August. I didn't think it was hunting season. I was curious, but I held my tongue. He was in the kind of mood that didn't invite questions. I had also seen his boots by the front door, covered in mud. Those boots were an iconic article of my childhood. So wide I could fit two of my feet in one boot. He wore them until even duct tape couldn't hold them together.

The next day, the Concord House was the center of police activity. Two Jefferson County kids—nineteen-year-old sweethearts named Timothy Hack and Kelly Drew—had gone missing after attending a wedding reception there.

As the days went by, Dad kept turning on the evening news, hoping for coverage of the missing kids. Despite the fact that his own kids ranged in age from four to eleven years old, he couldn't seem to stop talking out loud about the case. He was obsessed. "I bet they find those kids in a field," he speculated, as if once again he was playing amateur detective.

The whole town was upset by the news. I had heard my friend Nicole's mom saying how worried the kids' parents were. Dad had just finished work on her family's deck, and they invited us for dinner on it. Mr. Simon and his wife, Allie, were there too. The talk at dinner was of Tim and Kelly, the missing kids. This was a small town, and Tim's father was a local farmer. Everyone knew everyone. The town was still traumatized by the disappearance of a seventeen-year-old girl six years earlier after a prom party at the Concord House. How could it have happened again?

The Simons and the Uttechs were nice people, but I remember feeling awkward being there for dinner. We were outsiders. We didn't know the families of the missing kids like everyone else did. And Dad was trying to be his usual jovial self in company. Every time Dad told one of his loud stories to make other adults laugh, Nicole's mom would glance at her husband. I could tell she didn't like Dad.

On the way home that night, Dad resumed speculating about the two missing teens. He repeated, "I bet they find them in a field."

I sat in the back seat of the van with David, John, and Jeff. It was dark, and at a stoplight I stared at the back of Dad's illuminated head, and thought, *Huh. Why does he keep going on and on about that?* Images from the articles I'd read in Dad's magazines flickered through my head like gremlins flashing in the dark, and I shut them down.

A few weeks after school started, Dad told us to pack our belongings. He'd rented another U-Haul. He told us we were hitting the road the same day. There wasn't much to pack up this time. Each time we moved, it seemed like we had a little bit less to bring with us. Just a bag each of our clothes and a few boxes full of toys and books that we hadn't even fully unpacked yet. Dad had somehow acquired a new washer and dryer that he muscled up and into the big U-Haul along with a few pieces of furniture that had been in the old house when we'd moved in.

As I took my seat with Jeff in the U-Haul between Mom and Dad, I looked over at Mom, sitting ramrod straight. I couldn't read the expression on her face. Her eyes were locked on the road in front of her. What was she thinking? So many times in my childhood, I wondered what was going through her mind. I turned to look at Dad's face as he drove. Something about this departure felt different, yet familiar. We hadn't left before the end of a school year ever before. Why were we leaving like this? That was new and I didn't like it. But the familiar element wasn't only that we were leaving a place that had seemed briefly like home. It was the recent disturbing news of two missing teens. It reminded me of the missing kids in Doylestown, the ones I had heard about in second grade. It had happened again.

"Where are we going this time?" I asked Dad.

He snapped at me. "Watch your tone with me."

Mom said nothing. My brothers and Jeannine said nothing. The only sound was of Happy panting at Mom's feet. She was nervous too.

The tone Dad had noticed was real. It was not one of pure curiosity. It had an edge. I was angry. If there is a before and after moment in the story of my relationship with my dad, this is it. This was when the doubt broke through that membrane I'd stretched across my brain. The barrier that kept the concept of "Dad, who I loved," separate from "the man who we lived with who did bad things" had begun to fray. And I never thought of him in the same way again.

None of us asked my father *why* we were leaving this time. Each time we left a town, it was because we were fleeing someone bad. This time, I had a flash of insight. We weren't fleeing the bad people. But we might be fleeing the good ones.

17

Most Wanted

After Verna was out of the picture, Dad and his new wife, Jeanette, lived a life like Bonnie and Clyde, hitting up gas stations throughout Montana and Oregon, with her as the getaway driver and him as the armed robber. But in quick succession, she got pregnant and he got caught and arrested. An article in the *Akron Beacon Journal* on March 9, 1956, opens, "The fleet-footed burglary suspect who broke and ran from City Jail here last April 5 has been arrested at Billings, Montana." My father was sentenced to ten years in the notorious Deer Lodge Montana State Penitentiary. There would be no running past guards to escape this fortress.

Now he was incarcerated with violent men who had committed heinous crimes, who had murdered, maimed, and dismembered.

The worst part of prison for him was the idea that his wife might take off with their new baby. Jeanette rented a trailer near the prison, within the sightline of his cell window so he could monitor her comings and goings. She wrote letters to him daily, and he bribed guards to break the one-letter-per-week rule. But one day, a letter didn't come. Or the next. Jeanette had taken off with his son. He was so deranged with fury that he plotted his escape, which was soon made impossible by the famous Deer Lodge prison uprising of 1959, when the National Guard stormed the facility to take control. Soon after the riot, my father was released on parole and sent to Portland, where he was to stand trial for two armed robberies he had committed there back before his arrest in Montana. Jeanette had remarried and was living back in Idaho. Dad decided to break the terms of his parole, leave Portland, find Jeanette, and kill her. But when he was spying on her in her home, he saw his son and was unable to carry out his plan. He decided to come back another time to get revenge another way. According to him, he planned to return to "at least maul her face enough so that people would throw her peanuts if she happened to be at a zoo." But he didn't. Maybe because he soon found a new wife.

He returned to Portland and embarked on a career that he was very good at: sales. He became a top Kirby vacuum cleaner salesman, though he developed a sideline stealing vacuum parts and selling them that turned out to be even more lucrative.

He developed another scam, orchestrating car crashes in which he was the victim to collect insurance money. This was a very profitable con, but it was hard on the body.

About this time, he met Marlene, a fair-haired beauty who had just graduated high school and was gullible as a baby. She believed him when he told her that he worked undercover for the CIA. She was spellbound by tales of his dangerous work. She was perfect. He married her. She even bought his excuse for dating many other women at the same time, even after they were married. He told her the women were spies that he was setting up for capture. Marlene and my father had a friend named Johnny, and the three of them shared fun times in Portland, dancing and drinking and driving around the city.

In November of that year, 1960, he and Johnny were caught trespassing on the crime scene of a highly publicized Portland double murder on a lover's lane. The site was crawling with gawkers. The murders of nineteen-year-olds Larry Peyton and Beverly Allan had been all over the news. It was considered by some journalists to be Portland's "most talked-about and written-about double murder." Larry was found dead in his car, stabbed twenty-three times. (Beverly's body would be found over a month later, partially nude, raped, and strangled.) There was a bullet hole in the car windshield, a shot from the back seat. No gun was found at the scene.

A week later, just for fun, Dad convinced Marlene and Johnny to pull fire alarm boxes throughout town with him one evening. He never had outgrown his big childhood thrill. But the fire alarm prank backfired, and my father was caught and arrested for it, and now he faced another long spell behind bars. He had a list of reasons he could be convicted again. He was not only in trouble for pulling fire alarms, he was also questioned about the Portland double homicide in the lovers' lane. On the night of his arrest, my father had a stitched-up bullet wound in his arm that was hard to explain. Things weren't looking good for him, and he panicked about being sent back to prison. He convinced a jailer to let him use the phone to call his probation officer, but he called Johnny and asked his friend to call the prison impersonating a parole officer. Johnny did, and it worked to get my father out on bail. Then he bolted. The article about his jailbreak in the *Akron Beacon Journal* referred to him as "Slippery Edward Wayne Edwards, 28-year-old bandit."

This is how my father finally made the FBI's most wanted list. He and Marlene lit out as fugitives.

18

Veil Lifted

1980

We drove from Wisconsin to Pennsylvania, for what reason we didn't ask and never knew, and Dad found a house for us to rent in Pittsburgh on a dead-end road in a run-down neighborhood just outside downtown. The street was steep and our house was the next to last one on the bottom of the road. The last house had a large brown dog chained outside on the front porch. It barked and growled and foamed at the mouth as we unpacked our boxes from the U-Haul. We all eyed the dog with caution as we made each trip to the house, hoping it wouldn't get loose and fight with Happy.

I already missed that beautiful farmhouse with its sublime stained glass window. This place felt devoid of any magic at all. The house had a little fenced-in backyard, and Happy would live there, so she'd probably be safe from the dog next door. Inside, smelly shag carpeting covered the floors of every room. My bedroom was barely big enough for a twin bed. There was a window over my bed, and on its sill, I placed the little treasure chest, which held my happy grams from my teachers in Doylestown.

Our new neighborhood was littered with hunks of soft white stone that were perfect for using as chalk. When the neighbor's dog was not on the porch, or when it was sleeping under its bench, my brothers and I played in the street. There was no danger of anyone coming down the road as far as us, other than the neighbor with the dog and his wife, and they hardly ever went anywhere. With the chalky rocks, I drew a blueprint of a house in the middle of the street. The house I drew had a living room, three bedrooms, two bathrooms, and even a laundry room. I drew beds in the bedrooms, and chairs and tables in the dining room and my brothers and Jeannine and I lay down on the beds and sat cross-legged in the chairs and played house. I drew plates and forks and knives. This felt way safer than playing house in our actual house.

The best thing about our actual house was the basement. It had a linoleum floor which was nice and smooth to roller-skate around on. I had received a pair of sneaker-style roller skates for my last birthday and spent a lot of time perfecting my stops and turns in that basement.

The steep road looked perfect for roller-skating, too. I tried my skates out on our street as soon as I felt confident enough. And I flew! I was half-thrilled, half-terrified. When I finally, barely, came to a stop at the bottom of the road in front of the neighbor's house, the brown dog exploded from the porch, coming up hard against his chain. The chain held fast. The man came out of his house and told his dog to be quiet. I learned to do a 180 at top speed to avoid skating in front of that mean dog's house.

Dad got a job remodeling a drug store at night. Every evening when Dad got in the van to go to work, we could hear the dog snarling and barking at him.

In the morning, when we trudged up the steep hill to walk to school, we heard the dog's barks all the way to the end of the street. He was outraged at our existence, angry at the world.

I had a lot of trepidation going to school. I had never started at a new school mid-year before, and this middle school was huge, way bigger than any other school I'd ever attended. Every morning, kids poured out of the buses like ants and filed into the giant school building. When I walked into my homeroom class, I noticed that the sixth graders in Pittsburgh talked fast. No southern or midwestern drawls here. I seemed to be the only country bumpkin. This was worse than I feared.

It was immediately clear to me that my wardrobe was going to be a problem. I didn't own a pair of blue jeans. My pants were polyester with elastic waists, and I wore them with flowered or polka-dotted shirts. My clothes were atrocious—announcing that I either had no sense of style or was dressed by my mother who had no sense of style. Neither was true. I was dressed by my father who wanted to keep his little girl little and unnoticed by the boys.

Maybe it worked because the boys didn't seem to notice me, but the attention I feared wasn't from the boys—it was from the girls.

One girl in particular seemed to be waiting for a false move to pounce. When she passed me in the halls, she wrinkled her nose. I didn't know why she disliked me, but I wasn't surprised when she dropped a note at my feet at my locker, challenging me to meet her in the bathroom after lunch.

I thought I needed to get this over with. Face her like I did Yvonne in Brighton, so we could both move on, otherwise, I knew she would keep tormenting me. When I got to the bathroom, no one else was there. I looked at myself in the mirror, scrutinizing my black hair, which hung wild and loose, and my eyes, which looked plain. I imagined taking tweezers to my eyebrows. The girl walked in and interrupted my reverie. I think she was surprised I had shown up. Still, she got up in my face.

"I'm not going to hit you first," I said.

She looked at me like I was crazy, wondering why I was so calm. I think she had expected me to tremble in fear. She looked slightly less confident now.

I had to make sure she took the first swing. That was Dad's rule. And besides, I didn't want to fight. If she had walked out then and there, I would have been relieved, but she didn't. Instead, she hit me, and I was upon her in a flash, straddling her and punching her in the face the way Dad had taught me to punch my brothers. Other girls came into the bathroom only to run back out. After a few punches, I asked her if she had had enough. She said yes, so we got up, dusted ourselves off, and returned to our classrooms. Later, we were both called to the principal's office. The penalty for fighting on school property was three days of suspension. The penalty at home would be worse. My parents were called, and Dad took a long time to come get me (Mom still didn't have her driver's license). On the drive home, Dad was seething. I was silent.

When we pulled into our driveway, I had to say something. "She started it," I said. I had played by his rules. I had to make this clear to him.

He slammed his hands on the steering wheel. "You're just as much to blame," he said.

"Why? She challenged me! I didn't start it!"

"You met her in the bathroom!" he shouted. "That makes *you* responsible! Why did you meet her in the bathroom? To fight! That's why!"

He looked at me with disgust. "Get out of the car."

I was afraid to get out of the van. But I didn't want to be dragged into the house, so I got out and walked fast to the door. The minute we were inside he took off his belt. No one else was home.

"Drop your pants," he said.

I was too old to drop my pants in front of him, but I could not disobey. He beat me again and again with his belt until I felt like my backside was on fire. Afterward, I looked in the bathroom mirror. The welts were red and angry and had nearly broken through the skin in places where the belt had come close to cutting even through my underwear. I wished he had drawn blood. Then he would know he had gone too far. At least I didn't have to deal with trying to sit down in school, as I was on suspension for the rest of the week.

Other than this rough start, school in Pittsburgh wasn't all bad. I'd never been to one with so many sports teams. A bonus of playing any sport was that after-school practices would delay my going home until just before dinner. I joined the swim team, a sport that I didn't need to buy expensive shoes or equipment for. The school provided the swimsuit.

I was always conscious of not shaming Dad for not having money. Even expensive Christmas gifts had begun to make me uncomfortable. Without the funding from relatives, they wouldn't have been possible. The previous Christmas, I'd received a Barbie town house and as soon as we had moved in, I set it up on the smelly shag carpet in my bedroom. There was barely room for the glorious cardboard structure that towered over me when I sat on the floor next to it. Often, for birthdays and Christmases, I would get a Barbie-like doll, a knockoff. I had one honest-to-God Barbie with blond hair and blue eyes. She had bendy legs that almost felt like real skin. The others had hard plastic legs that didn't bend. There was no comparison to the real thing. But I didn't mind. I had enough dolls to make a real family out of them. David sometimes popped the heads off the dolls. But they were easy enough to pop back on.

I was aware that I was possibly getting too old for dolls, but I still loved them. I was pleased when I met a girl in the neighborhood who openly admitted to loving her Barbies, too. Sally attended a private school but lived just a block from me. I never went to her larger house, but she would come over to my house and bring her Barbies. She had real Barbies and Barbie suitcases filled with Barbie clothes and accessories. She even had the Barbie pink convertible. I thought she must be very rich to have so many real Barbie dolls and such a wealth of actual Barbie paraphernalia. My Barbie-like dolls wore clothes that Mom or I had sewn. I was becoming a competent seamstress, but there was no way I could compete with Mattel.

One day, Sally left her Barbie suitcases and car and dolls at my house when she went home. I thought it was incredibly generous of her to let me play with them without her. I don't remember if she'd planned on coming over the next day or if she was just feeling sorry for me, but I do recall that late that afternoon we received a knock at the door. Dad hollered for me downstairs. Sally's mother was standing in our living room. She had long blond hair and wore jeans like a teenager. She'd come to get her daughter's Barbies. Why? I wondered. Did she think I would steal Sally's Barbie gear? I would never have taken as much as the tiny pink comb. I felt slapped by the suggestion, which is what this mom's unexpected arrival at my house made clear. I went up to my room, where I had been playing with Sally's Barbies and gathered the articles of clothing, packing them neatly in the pink suitcases along with the dolls and accoutrements and the car that Sally had entrusted me with. On my way downstairs I could hear Dad's flirting voice, the one he used when he wanted to impress women. Mom was in the kitchen, in her plain slacks, her back to the visitor. I felt embarrassed for her.

I handed Sally's mom the suitcases and she thanked me and left quickly, not lingering to flirt back with Dad. I took notice of this too. She wasn't interested in being in our living room one second longer than necessary.

Sally's mom's abrupt departure left Dad in a terrible mood. That night we were going to have meatloaf. Mom was cooking more now that she didn't have a job and my swim practice kept me after school. Dad took his seat at the head of the dining room table, like he did every night, but tonight he glowered. Mom set the food on the table. It smelled good and I was hungry. My stomach had been growling all afternoon. I was looking forward to making a little gravy pond in my mashed potatoes for my corn. We all took our seats at the table and served ourselves. I had helped make the mashed potatoes so I knew they would be perfect, and the gravy was from a packet. It was good, since Mom's gravy was always lumpy. Dad lifted his fork and knife and stared at the meatloaf and then he got very still. I looked up at him, hoping we'd get through whatever this was without anyone getting hurt and without dinner being ruined.

"God damn it, Kay!" he roared. "The meatloaf is burnt!"

We all sat up straight and looked at Dad. *Please don't*, I thought. *Please don't.* I held my breath.

And then Dad stood, and with a roar flipped the table, sending meatloaf and mashed potatoes and corn and gravy into our laps and all over the walls and the floor and an open bottle of ketchup hit the ceiling, spraying red everywhere, like blood.

Jeannine cried out. She was covered in warm gravy. Dad ranted at Mom as I dabbed Jeannine's shirt with napkins, which only made the gravy seep through her shirt.

As Dad continued to yell, Mom got on her hands and knees and started picking up plates and pieces of broken glasses that had smashed into each other. Her expression was blank, almost robotic. I got to work scraping pieces of meatloaf off the shag carpet, scooping up sticky mashed potatoes with my fingers, and wiping them on a plate. I wasn't hungry anymore. My brothers picked up food from the floor, too.

I thought Dad was going to grab Mom and punch her. We were all scared, bracing ourselves for violence. But finally, Dad stopped shouting. He got a can of beer from the fridge and took himself to his living room recliner. We could hear the snick of the can opening and then the TV being turned on. We kept cleaning until there was almost no sign of meatloaf or potatoes stuck in the carpet. The relief I felt that he hadn't hit Mom overwhelmed every other thought. But over the next few days, every time I found corn kernels under cabinets or stuck to my socks, I felt an ache in my belly.

As repulsed as I was at Dad's bad behavior, I was always desperate to wipe the slate clean, welcoming with a flush of happiness any night that was peaceful or fun. A good night was when we all got to eat dinner and we didn't go to bed hungry. An even better night was when Dad was in the mood to play board games. Dad loved family board game sessions. He'd smoke his Camels and drink his cream sodas while we played. Can't Stop was one of our favorite games. When we lost, we had to drink huge tumblers of water. The winner would get to pick a prize from a grab bag filled with lip gloss, baseball cards, bubblegum, and Matchbox cars. I was fiercely competitive and coveted every trinket I won.

Monopoly was another favorite of ours. We had to play to the bitter end. If anyone went bankrupt, they still had to sit there until the game was over. Mom was usually the first one to lose. She was always the banker, so she still had a job to do. Dad played with cutthroat intensity, wheeling and dealing with us to get properties. I realize now that he taught me how to negotiate, how to not be taken advantage of, and how to assess and assign value to what I was buying or selling. Because Dad was always changing the rules to suit him, I developed a reputation of being a stickler, consulting the game directions in the box to call him out on infractions. Like Car Bingo, playing board games was a safety zone.

Sometime during that year, I visited the store Dad was remodeling at night. I noticed that the shelves sold all the same goodies that we had in the prize bag. I was shocked at how much the Matchbox cars and lip gloss cost. I calculated the value of that bottomless goodie bag at home. A terrible question occurred to me: Had he stolen these things from the store? Had he stolen them so he could give us treats for winning? Was that less bad than stealing for yourself? I wasn't sure, but I didn't think so. After that, I wasn't as keen when I picked out my prize for winning a board game, but I couldn't let Dad know what I suspected. So I always picked the smallest thing. Usually a square of Bazooka bubble gum. The comic that came with it wasn't as fun to read as it had been before.

Dad seemed to be on to me, even though I hadn't said anything, hadn't challenged him about the goodie bag at all. Maybe I imagined it, but I thought he looked for excuses to rattle me, to catch me off guard. Family time that wasn't spent playing board games was spent watching movies together. The scarier the better. In the living room in the little house in Pittsburgh, we watched the movie *Halloween*. During a commercial break, Dad sent me outside to get his cigarettes out of the van. It was dark, and the street didn't have streetlamps. The only light was cast from the windows of our house and the other houses on the road. I kept an eye on the house next to ours to see if the dog was on the porch, but he wasn't. I slowly walked out to Dad's van parked in the driveway, looking right and left.

My dead-end street was as secluded as the campground in *Halloween*. Before I opened the driver's door, I looked around again, nervous to expose my back to a murderer. I ducked in quickly, scanning for the cigarettes. I heard something in the woods beyond our yard. I yanked my head out of the van to scan the vicinity. Nothing stirred. I spotted the pack of Camels on the dashboard, grabbed them, and bolted toward the house. Dad jumped out at me from behind the house and I screamed and hit the ground, nearly peeing in my pants in terror.

Dad laughed and laughed. It was just like the drive-in movie night during *Jaws*. I had found it funny then, but not now. Dad was still chuckling when he settled back into his recliner to continue watching the movie.

When we watched movies, bedtimes were not strictly enforced, and my brothers and I would often fall asleep on the living room floor. This was the perfect setup for a prank Dad liked to perform. He pulled one of my brothers to a standing position while he was sleeping and led him around the house. He couldn't do this to me because I always woke up, but my brothers were sound sleepers.

Dad would sleepwalk my brothers around the house and make them do things, like tell them they were in the bathroom. "Okay," he'd whisper. "You're in the bathroom. Time to pee." And sometimes they'd start pulling their pants down. Other times they'd just start peeing in their pants. "Stop!" Dad would say, sometimes failing to stop them in time. This was less of a problem when he sleepwalked them outside.

Jeff was the easiest sleepwalking target. That Christmas, Aunt Lucille and Uncle Al visited us in Pittsburgh. Dad let us stay up late watching Christmas movies, and sure enough Jeff fell asleep, clutching his pillow. Dad stood him up, showing off for Aunt Lucille and Uncle Al.

"Hurry up!" Dad whispered in Jeff's ear. "The house is on fire!" Then Dad walked Jeff outside in his bare feet. Jeff just stood there in a stupor while Dad put a lit cigarette in Jeff's mouth and came back into the house. He watched through the window to see when his son would wake up. On Jeff's behalf, I wanted to crawl under a bed and hide in embarrassment.

Aunt Lucille said, "Wayne, that's not nice! It's freezing! Don't do that to him."

Aunt Lucille was the only person who could say what was really on her mind to Dad. She'd been the one who visited him with her parents in the orphanage, bringing candy. She had no illusions about his past, she had lived through his wild, uncontrollable youth, she knew all about his crimes, and yet she had never given up on him.

Jeff woke up choking and the cigarette fell from his lips onto his naked toe, and Dad brought him back inside, laughing, and told him to go back to sleep.

My brothers were usually quick to recover from these stunts. And this was Christmas after all, and everyone had presents to look forward to. My gifts this year included a beautiful doll with shiny black hair.

"She looks just like you, April," Aunt Lucille said when I opened the box. I loved her even more for this. She had seemed so excited about me opening it that I suspected it had been from her. Though we knew Santa wasn't real anymore, we still pretended he was.

That Christmas night, I put the black-haired doll on my windowsill next to the chest with my happy grams. While I was happy for the doll, I had hoped to get a pair of jeans and other fashionable clothes like the other girls in my class wore. I'd put them on my wish list, but Dad must have nixed that idea. He did say I could get my ears pierced, though—another item on my list. One of my gifts had been a festive pair of earrings that had silver-colored posts and gold-painted Christmas bells with a green speck of holly and a tiny red bow.

The night before the Christmas break ended, Dad said he was going to pierce my ears himself. This, I had not expected. "Why pay to do it in a mall when I can do it for nothing," he said.

I watched as he held a sewing needle under the flame of his cigarette lighter to sterilize it. Then he told me to stand next to him. He took hold of my ear and put the needle point on my earlobe and began to push it through. Slowly. There had been no numbing with an ice cube beforehand like I had seen done in movies. I clenched my teeth so hard I thought they would break. I could hear a crunching sound as the needle passed through the flesh of my earlobe with a nauseating pain. I started to pass out. Dad caught me as I started to faint. The needle was still in my ear, so he propped me up against the living room wall paneling to finish the ear.

For the second ear, he sat me down. When he was done, he inserted those new Christmas earrings through my earlobes. One of the holes was at an angle and the holes frequently became red and pus-filled. So much for having fashionably pierced ears. Even this I couldn't do right. I was not passing for a normal girl.

During that year's swim season, I was also prone to inner ear infections. Dad treated them at home by pouring peroxide in my ears after practice and meets. Dad said it was essential that I wear a hat to protect my ears from the cold and he made me wear a bulky black knit cap. On the coldest days, Dad would drive us to school. One morning he dropped me off in front of our school, and I was wearing the hideous black cap. Other girls getting off the bus, or out of their parents' car, or strolling into the building were wearing hats too, but theirs were cute, colorful, with pom poms and matching scarves and mittens. Mine was mannish and ugly, like something a bank robber would wear. As soon as Dad drove away, I took the cap off. Before I went through the front doors, I turned around and saw Dad sitting in the van at the drop-off area looking at me. He had come back just to see if I was wearing the hat. I immediately put it back on and was sick to my stomach the whole day at school because I was afraid of what was going to happen to me when I got home. By late afternoon, he had simmered down enough to merely yell at me. I got no beating this time for my show of defiance.

I went to the backyard to be with Happy. She never judged me for what I wore, never judged me for defying Dad in whatever small ways I tried. She was just happy for attention. Plus, she'd had another litter of puppies a few weeks earlier and nothing was more fun than playing with her puppies. It was cold, and she snuggled with them in the doghouse in the small yard. She had seven this time, and she was such a good mom to them. But when I arrived, she was walking the fence line, whining, with a limp puppy in her mouth. I felt so sorry for her when she lay it on the ground and nudged it with her nose, licking it. Another limp puppy lay in the yard. She tried to nudge that puppy awake, too. Dad came into the yard and reached down, picked up both puppies.

"Are they dead?" I asked.

"Yeah. It happens sometimes," Dad said as he left the yard with them. Happy followed him to the gate, whining, and then went back to the doghouse to nurse the others.

The five surviving puppies grew strong, and we all played with them every day after school. We begged Dad to let us keep them, or at least one, but one day after school they were gone, and Dad said he had given them away to good homes. I believed him. I wanted to. Happy seemed lonely when they were gone.

Maybe as a consolation prize, since he didn't let us keep a puppy, Dad brought home three kittens. I claimed a gorgeous white fluffy kitten, who I named Snowball. David claimed a black one he named Midnight. John had an orange tabby, who ran away.

Snowball slept in my bed each night and snuggled under my covers. I hadn't had her for long when one night, while the rest of the family was in the living room watching TV, I was in the kitchen doing dishes with only

Snowball keeping me company. Dad came in and found me at the sink with Snowball next to me on the kitchen counter.

"What's she doing on the counter!?" Dad screamed, and picked up Snowball in one hand. Time slowed down as I watched with horror. I knew that he was not simply going to lift her off the counter to put her down. With the kitten in his hand, he pulled back as if to hurl a stick. I clapped my hand over my mouth to stifle my scream as I watched Snowball fly across the room. She hit the wall with a sickening thud. A sound left my throat, a strangled roar of sorrow and rage.

I trembled as I ran to her. The kitten was knocked unconscious, but when I stroked her soft fur she opened her eyes. I set her on her feet, but she didn't seem to be able to walk right. She staggered around for a few steps and collapsed.

Dad was saying something, but I ignored him. Without looking at him, I carried Snowball up to my room and wrapped her in a baby blanket and put her in my bed. That night, as she lay next to me, the memory came to me of the time I had been the one to be thrown across the room and knocked out. I had called Dad a liar. What had Snowball done to deserve this? It was my fault for letting her be on the counter. I should have known better. Maybe Snowball would recover, like I had. I prayed for this to be so.

In the morning, she still wasn't able to walk. I carried her back downstairs and showed her to Dad. I wanted to scream, "Look what you did!" but instead I asked meekly, "Can I stay home from school to take care of her?"

I was already late for school, and Dad wouldn't let me stay home. I ran sobbing up the hill, my lunchbox hitting my legs hard as I ran, my breath ragged as I struggled to weep and run at the same time. All day at school I prayed for Snowball. But when I got home, Dad was in the living room, watching TV.

"How is Snowball?" I asked him, looking around the living room for the box I had left her in.

"Snowball died," he said.

He told me he'd given her some medicine to put her out of her pain. "It was the right thing to do, not to let her suffer," he said.

He made it sound like he'd done her a favor. He didn't admit that he was the cause of her suffering. He didn't apologize. I ran to my room and threw myself on my bed and wept. Midnight jumped up and cuddled with me, and I bawled into her sleek black coat.

At that moment I hated Dad. And I hated myself for hating him, but I had started to feel that nothing was safe in my father's hands. I thought of the ponies Cindy and Max that he said had been "put down" after the barn fire. What was sacred to him? He didn't go to church with us. He didn't ever pray. He let precious things die and sometimes he was the cause.

That year, a kid in Jeff's class was bullying him. The kid was Black, which wasn't remarkable. There were lots of Black kids at our school. But the reason I remember him is that the boy mysteriously disappeared. Much later, we heard the shocking news that he had been murdered, and a young man went to jail for it. I thought of Curtis and Chris, our friends in Florida. And the missing boy and girl we heard about in Doylestown. Then the missing teens in Watertown. And now this boy. Was the whole world really such a dangerous place? Or did it just seem to follow us?

After swim practice, I always took the same route home. I'd daydream as I passed the same houses and lawns I did every day. But I had developed a crush on a boy on the team and he also walked home from school, though in a different direction. One day after practice, we left the building together talking. When he turned to begin his walk home, I didn't want to break up this easy conversation, so I walked with him. I paid attention to our route, so I could reverse it after we parted ways.

At some point, it became awkward that I'd come so far out of my way, and I said, "I'll see you tomorrow." I set off down a road that I had never been on. I planned to loop around to familiar territory. On this strange road, an old man approached me in a black trench coat. He stopped me on the sidewalk, "Are you lost?" he asked.

I scanned the houses on the block and didn't see another person.

"No, I'm fine," I said. It was true, I wasn't lost. I knew the direction of home.

He nodded and kept walking, and several times I looked behind me nervously, but the man hadn't followed. I picked up my pace.

When I got home, Dad was fuming. I was late. If I'd told him that I'd been speaking to a boy and had taken a longer route to do it, I knew I would be in huge trouble. Instead I told him that I'd been stopped by a stranger on my way home, even though that really hadn't been the reason for my delay. I assured Dad that the man was harmless, but Dad was outraged.

He asked me to describe the man, and I was able to, to a tee: long black coat, older man, dark-black shaggy hair, pasty complexion with a scruffy beard. Dad ran upstairs. He came running back downstairs, pistol in hand, and then ran out the door, jumped in the van, and took off.

A cold sweat prickled my back. This man had done nothing to me, but I used him as an excuse to save myself a beating from Dad. And now Dad was after him with a gun. *What had I done?!*

I paced the living room for an hour until Dad returned, and police officers were with him. They wanted to question me about the man, and I could tell by their questions that Dad had told them that the man had grabbed me, even though I had said no such thing. If I had contradicted Dad by saying, "What? No. The man didn't grab me. He only asked if I was lost." Dad would have been made a fool of, or looked like a liar. And I didn't want to think what he would do to me. I tried to figure out by their questions what Dad had told them and I confirmed it.

The next thing I knew, the man had been arrested and we were to appear in court.

Dad coached me in what to say beforehand. He made me memorize his version of events. In a crowded courtroom in downtown Pittsburgh, I was called up in front of a judge and asked what had happened. I was too scared to speak. When the judge repeated his question, I parroted what Dad had told me to say, that the man had grabbed me and I had wrestled free and run home. I was too afraid to say anything else. The old man was there, and he shouted, "No! I didn't do that!" I couldn't look at him. Before we left the courthouse, a lawyer informed us that he would contact us when a date was set for the trial.

I kept waiting for news of the trial date with dread, but it never seemed to come. And then one day Dad reassured me that I would never have to worry about the man again. He told me that I wouldn't have to go back to court, either. I didn't understand why but was afraid to ask him. Much later, after we moved away, I realized that the trial date never came. Why had my father been so sure this would be the outcome? Had something bad happened to the man? Was my father responsible? If something had happened, it was entirely my fault. It was like Snowball. The man had done nothing wrong, but I had put him in harm's way.

Living with that lie day after day made my stomach hurt every time I ate. I wanted us to move again. I wanted to never see anyone here again. In fact, our time in Pittsburgh was coming to an end, but I didn't know that yet.

Near the end of the school year, something else happened that was unprecedented. My brothers and I liked to skate in the basement and play jacks on the smooth floor. But one Saturday, I found the basement door was locked.

"Why's the door locked?" I asked Dad. I recalled the wrapped Christmas presents in our basement in Colorado. Maybe there was a surprise for us, like new bikes. Mine was getting too small for me. It didn't seem likely, though.

"Stay out of the basement," was all Dad said.

David and John and I were not so easily put off, though. Now we had to know why the basement door was locked. When Dad left the house, we took turns looking in through the keyhole. David looked through and gasped. When it was John's turn, he recoiled and let out a cry. I looked next and instantly regretted it. There, through the hole, we could just see the dangling hind legs of the big brown dog.

My brothers and I looked at each other in horror. We would never be able to unsee that graphic image. We had all been afraid of the dog, but we never wanted the dog to be killed. Dad must have taken matters into his own hands to protect us, we rationalized. We figured he must have somehow drugged the dog, dragged him into the basement, and hung him. We never let Dad know we knew what he had done, and we would never talk about it between us again, but it was branded into our minds forever.

The next day I saw the neighbors in front of their house, yelling at Dad as he was about to drive off in the van. They didn't come onto our yard, but just yelled from theirs. They shouted, "What did you do to him?"

Dad stood his ground, and his voice rang out loud and clear, "I don't know what the hell you're talking about."

As soon as the school year was over, we left the city. Dad had lost his job and said it was too hard to find work here. In the days before we left, he paced like a tiger at the zoo, shouting at us to pack our things.

We set out the morning after the last day of school. Another U-Haul. Another tight squeeze, but as we pulled away, I breathed a sigh of relief to be out of that house, away from the memory of the hanging dog, the broken kitten, and the red stain on the ceiling. We left Midnight behind. Dad wouldn't let us take her with us. He said she'd be fine, that cats always land on their feet. I wondered if we would land on our feet. As we drove off, I dragged along my doubts. I didn't for a minute consider that we were running from bad guys. This time, there was a clear question in my mind. What had Dad done this time?

19

Catch Me If You Can

1960

Life on the lam meant constantly being on the move. Dad and Marlene would swoop into a town, Dad would carry out a few scams for quick cash, and then they'd head out to another city in another state on a Greyhound bus. They assumed the aliases Ed and Cynthia Martin in Louisville, Kentucky. After Louisville came New York City, where Dad bought two round-trip plane tickets to California with a bad check. He quickly cashed the tickets out, which funded the next leg of the journey, by bus to Chicago. He pulled the same scam at O'Hare before they lit out for Indianapolis.

There, my father bought a marine uniform with sergeant stripes at a church basement thrift shop and impersonated a retired military officer wherever he went, which got him and Marlene free meals and drinks and a bucket load of goodwill from strangers. This goodwill got him hired as an assistant night manager at a theater. Marlene didn't like his hours. She enjoyed going out on the town at night. When the kindly, trusting theater manager took a week's vacation, leaving my father in charge, it was like leaving the fox to guard the henhouse. Dad pocketed all the theater's earnings for the week and then told Marlene he'd been reassigned and had to immediately move to Houston. Marlene seemed to still buy his story that he was working undercover as a special agent fighting communist subversives.

In Houston they assumed the names Gene and Ricki Starr. Dad found a letter in Marlene's pocket addressed to another man. Clearly, she hadn't been whiling away the evening hours in Indianapolis by herself while he was hard at work earning the trust of the theater manager so he could swindle him. The letter apologized for having to leave on short notice, but it was also an indirect cry for help. In it, Marlene expressed doubt that her husband was actually an agent of the U.S. government and suspected that he was, in fact, a dangerous criminal. Dad flipped out, and, by his own admission, savagely beat Marlene, calling her a whore and threatening to cut off her breasts and flush them down the toilet. He convinced her that her infidelity may have jeopardized national security. She didn't leave him after the beating. She was probably too afraid of what he would do if she tried and failed.

Of all the scams that my father pulled during the thirteen months he was on the lam with Marlene, the most outrageous was posing as a psychologist in Minneapolis. He was like the guy in the movie *Catch Me If You Can*, fooling everyone, everywhere he went. His alias was Dr. Jerry Love, and women seemed to be extremely receptive to an off-duty psychologist who offered to analyze them over drinks, for free.

Whenever he saw FBI wanted posters of himself in post offices or bus stops, he would stealthily take them down and throw them away. Once he even saw his face on a poster on a park bench while he was talking to a police officer. At night, he left Marlene at home and went out by himself to bars to pick up women or hang out with the local guys, playing pool, or shooting the breeze. He felt pretty satisfied with the success of Dr. Love. On the night his luck began to turn, he was cueing up a game of pool at a tavern when he noticed a man at the bar watching him too intently. He knew the look. This guy was a lawman of some variety. It was time to hightail it out of town.

He and Marlene managed to sneak out of town on a Greyhound bus to Akron, back to the hub of his wheel. They needed money, and there was no point in risking capture for small change. This time, he'd go big. He decided to rob a bank. At gunpoint. He told the teller, "I'm wanted all over the country, so I'd as soon kill you as not." No one was hurt, and he left the bank with a paper bag filled with about seven thousand dollars. They escaped in a stolen car.

Dad never fled directly from one city to another. There was always a detour to stop in another city or two as a deception. He had always outsmarted his pursuers. After the bank robbery, he and Marlene flew to New York City, and while waiting in Penn Station for a train to Atlanta, something caught

Marlene's eye. She pointed out a man seated near them reading *True Detective* magazine, my father's favorite. The magazine was open to a full-page article on Edward Wayne Edwards with mugshots. It called him "cunning," with "an incredible criminal career and an ego to match." It described him as a "go-for-broke" fugitive who needed to be approached with extreme caution. Dad must have really felt like he'd arrived. He couldn't have been more pleased if he'd made the cover of *Life* magazine. New York City was a great place for anonymity. The man didn't recognize him, and they hopped on their train with no interference.

But the feds were on his trail.

20

Grifter

1981

We drove away from that smelly house with the dirty shag carpet in Pittsburgh and into the fresh air of wide-open spaces just an hour northwest of the city. Dad had met someone in a bar in Pittsburgh who had a house to rent in the middle of nowhere—a little town called Portersville near Moraine State Park, in the township of Slippery Rock, with a population of around three hundred. As we drove through the town, we passed a church and a small mom-and-pop grocery store. The house we rented was a stately two-story brick farmhouse that sat high on a hill surrounded by woods. It had no visible neighbors and a long, steep tree-lined dirt driveway.

When we walked inside, it was as if we had walked into someone else's beautiful home when they weren't there. It was fully furnished with polished wood floors. Its big living room had a fireplace and heavy wood furniture and plush couches and chairs.

I walked slowly upstairs to my bedroom, admiring the ornate stair rail and banisters. After the little room in Pittsburgh my new bedroom seemed huge. It had two twin beds with sturdy wooden bed frames and matching pastel comforters. The same fabric was used to make curtains on the big window between the beds. I put my doll with black hair and my little happy gram treasure chest on the windowsill. A little wooden nightstand next to one of the beds had a clock radio. It was like the room was just waiting for a girl to come live in it. I thought, *This is the ninth bedroom I've lived in. And it's the best.* I stood at the window and looked out onto the sloping driveway and front yard. I took out my clarinet and music stand and, there, before the open window, with the sunlight illuminating the sheet music and the summer breezes blowing in, I played my music directly out into the world.

That summer, Mom and us kids began attending the little church every Sunday morning. Dad dropped us off. I never knew where he went while we were in church, but he picked us up after services. And as a family, we explored the state park right next to us. It had hiking trails and a big lake for swimming. I practiced my back and breast and butterfly strokes.

Dad got a job doing construction work at a fancy office building in Pittsburgh, so he was gone during the day. The only music he allowed us to listen to was his music, which was Elvis Presley and Frank Sinatra. The alarm clock radio in my room got staticky AM stations. When Dad wasn't around, I sat on my bed and fiddled with the dial until I got it lined up perfectly to the station that played Casey Kasem's American Top 40. It was an act of rebellion. Casey's familiar singsongy voice made him seem like a kindly uncle. The songs filled me with vague images of romance and heartbreak and a delicious longing and I sang my heart out.

Dad began bringing supplies home from work in the van, including beautiful teak boards and saws and wrenches and a drill. One day he came home with rusted metal scaffolding.

He wrangled the scaffolding poles out of the van with difficulty. They were heavy.

"What's that for?" I asked.

"We're going to clean this up and sell it," Dad said.

"Where'd you get it?" I asked.

"Oh, they were throwing it out in the dumpster," he said. I believed it.

The scaffolding poles were big, and there must have been dozens of them. They were so heavy we could not flip them. Dad laid them on the grass in front of the house under the hot summer sun. For most of the summer, David, John, and I worked on that scaffolding while Dad was at work. Our job was to get the rust off with wire brushes. By the end of every day we would be covered with bits of rust stuck to our aching sweaty arms and sunburned faces.

We had no shade. The metal pieces were hot to handle. When I reached up to touch my black hair, it was hot, too. When Dad got home from work each day, he would check to see how much rust we had removed. I worried each day he would think I hadn't gotten enough rust off. I knew most kids my age got to play in summer. They went to camp or they rode their bikes and played with friends. But not us.

My arms and legs and back ached. I went to sleep sore and woke up sore. One day, I broke down sobbing when Dad got home. "*It's too much!*" I wanted to say. I hated for him to see me break under pressure. I never wanted to show weakness, but now I felt too tired to be ashamed. I wept openly.

At the end of the summer, Dad gave up on the scaffolding restoration project. His band of child laborers lost the battle with the rusty scaffolding. So much of the summer wasted. I don't know which was worse—knowing that it had all been for nothing or doing it in the first place.

When the school year started, my brothers and I hiked down our driveway, where David and I waited for our bus to make the long trip to Slippery Rock Middle School. I didn't know what to expect from seventh grade. Whether it would have a swim team, or band, whether I would make friends, or not. I worried I wouldn't fit in any better than I had in Pittsburgh.

On my first day it was obvious that my classmates had known each other all their lives. They had formed their cliques and friendships, and, once again, I was an outsider. Even here in the country, my clothes weren't cool enough.

In gym class we wore short red gym shorts and white T-shirts. I had gotten a bra over the summer, so at least I didn't need to worry about stripping naked and revealing my breasts to other girls in the locker room, but it was harder to hide the black hair that had begun to cover my legs. By now, nearly all the girls in my class shaved their legs and they looked at mine with raised plucked eyebrows. I pulled up my tube socks as high as they would go over my knees.

There were other reasons to cover myself sometimes. Once Dad made Mom write me a note to excuse me from gym for a week so no one could see the black and blue marks across the back of my legs from one of his beatings.

The bleachers were hard, and it hurt my butt and legs as I sat on my hands, watching the other kids play volleyball. But no one knew. There was a lot they didn't know.

I realized something else no one knew about me. In fifth grade, in Brighton, Colorado, I had gotten braces because I had an overbite. Maybe Denise had recommended their orthodontist, but for some reason, my parents were suddenly motivated to have my teeth fixed. At the time, I had no idea how expensive braces were or that my parents had elected to pay in install- ments, which no doubt they couldn't make. Since we left soon after I got the braces, I never went back to the orthodontist. Not once. I'd noticed in sixth grade, in Pittsburgh, kids getting called out of class for orthodontist appoint- ments, and I didn't think much of it, but it was happening here in seventh grade, in Slippery Rock, too. It occurred to me that I had no orthodontist. No professional was checking my braces and adjusting them. From the outside it looked like I was having a normal childhood and that I was a normal girl. But if anyone had bothered to look inside, I knew they would see that my family was not doing things right. But no one bothered to pry.

No one was more surprised than I was when a boy in my class, Derrick, asked me to a school dance. I had no idea he'd had a crush on me. I was so flattered! But it made me nervous because I knew Dad wouldn't allow it. How- ever, this dance was in the middle of the school day, so Dad didn't even need to know.

On the day of the dance, Derrick and I and all the rest of the class filed into the gym. The light had been dimmed and Kool and the Gang's "Celebra- tion" blasted from speakers.

I was out of my element, but most of the seventh graders stood at the edge of the dance floor, drinking punch and trying hard not to look awk- ward. I hardly appeared more ill at ease than they were. Derrick and I bopped to Michael Jackson and the Bee Gees. He had an impressive pointer finger disco move. Thanks to Casey Kasem, I was able to sing along. I felt so normal, so wonderfully normal. We would stop when we got too out of breath and take a punch break, but we'd jump back as soon as a new song came on unless it was a slow dance. I didn't have a crush on Derrick before he asked me to the dance, but I did now. I wouldn't have minded swaying to Air Supply in his arms.

When the bell rang to signal the dance was over and we all had to go back to our last class of the day, Derrick dashed off. It was just as well. I knew I'd never be allowed to have a boyfriend. After the dance, when Derrick passed me in the hall, it was back to exchanging a short, "Hey," except now it gave me a small ache every time, wishing it could be more.

I was changing both in my body and in my mind. I was less interested in playing with dolls. I let Jeannine play with my Barbie town house. David and John were spending a lot of their free time in the woods that stretched from our house to the main road. My days of playing house or making forts with them in the woods were over. They played with their BB guns, shooting at trees and squirrels and at cars that drove by on the road at the wood's edge.

One of my after-school activities for a while was helping Dad organize all the building materials and tools he'd accumulated from the job site. When I asked him where he'd gotten all of it and again, he said, "Oh, I pulled this from the dumpster. You wouldn't believe what people throw out." I believed it when it came to the rusty scaffolding, but I didn't think people would be careless enough to throw away a perfectly good saw or good lumber. I kept this to myself.

One day a man stopped by the house to look at the stacks of teak boards, hand tools, drills, circular saw, and two sawhorses, and bought everything all at once. Dad told the man he could get more. And he did.

Dad brought home bigger items, too. One was a tow-behind camper in need of work. I believed him that someone had been willing to give this away. I spent hours sweeping and cleaning out the mouse nests in the cabinets. Dad patched the leaky roof and replaced missing sections of the floor. We took it with us when we went camping in the nearby state park.

Dad made another unexpected acquisition as the days were getting shorter and colder. This one was so impractical, it thrilled me. David and I walked up our driveway after school to find a small brown horse in our yard, hungrily snatching at the long grass on our neglected lawn. The whole family was in the yard watching him. Mom had on one of her blanker-than-a-board expressions, which meant she wasn't happy. But I was hopeful.

"Where did he come from?" I asked Dad.

"Oh, a guy I work with needed to get rid of him. I thought you might like another horse," he said. I smiled big at Dad.

"Thank you!" I said, truly grateful. *Another horse in my life!*

I named him Brownie—since Dad didn't know his name. And as happy as I was about having him, Brownie had no interest in having a kid in his life. He was crabby and strongly opposed to being ridden. If I so much as thought about climbing on his back, he'd start to buck. I did manage to get him to let me comb out the matted tangles in his mane and forelock. After that, I could brush him and braid his mane and tail.

I didn't think about how impractical having a horse was. I didn't wonder how the horse would manage in the winter. As the fall days grew shorter, Dad's fuse was getting shorter too.

I was in the dining room setting the table for dinner one night. I could see Mom pulling the tuna casserole out of the oven and it smelled good. Dad walked in through the kitchen's back door and began to yell at her.

"Get over here!" he said.

I paused, a fork suspended in the air. My siblings' heads swung away from the TV and their wide eyes sought mine.

We braced ourselves for the sounds of her body hitting the wall and his fist hitting her body, but instead, in a move that was unheard of in our family, Mom did not obey.

She bolted fast out the kitchen door. Dad followed with long strides.

"Kay! Get back in here! Get back in this house or I'm going to kill you!" he yelled.

That's when I noticed the handgun he held in his right hand. Before he got to the door, he lifted his arm to chest level and then walked out after her. This had never happened either.

I looked over to my siblings. We had all frozen. I wanted to gather my brothers and sister and run out the front door and keep running. But we did not move. We did not rush to the window to watch what was unfolding outside. We did not speak. We just waited, suspended like the fork I hadn't yet put down.

Then we heard a shot. Jeannine burst out crying. I considered calling the police. But before I could make up my mind, Mom came back in, slinking like a punished dog, shaking from head to toe. Dad was no longer holding the gun. And it seemed the rage had left him. I was disgusted. I realized I hadn't believed he was actually going to shoot her. I had seen him punch her and throw her, but I didn't believe he would ever truly threaten her life. He needed her too badly.

When winter came, I worried about Brownie. Dad nailed a few metal roofing panels to tree branches as shelter for him. His water bucket would freeze overnight so I had to lug fresh water before I went to school, which he would thirstily guzzle. Sometimes icicles would hang from his mane and his whiskers would be rimmed in frost. He looked forlorn and I felt sorry for him.

On a January night, the temperature dropped below zero and the wind blew hard. I didn't really want to go outside to bring Brownie water and grain while everyone was warm and cozy by the fire in the living room, but the horse depended on me.

As I carried the bucket, the water that sloshed on my legs froze instantly. When I got to Brownie, he didn't even want a sip. He didn't eat his grain. He was shivering violently. I ran back to the house and told Dad.

Dad went out to check on him and returned with the horse, bringing him right into the house through the back kitchen door and into the dining room.

Mom said, "Well, I've never seen a horse in a house." Jeannine giggled and my brothers looked amazed. *What was Dad up to now?*

"We need to get this guy warm," Dad said. "Got no choice."

There, standing on the wood floor in the dining room, Brownie's tremors subsided as Dad rubbed a blanket in circular motions along his rough coat. As I watched Dad, I was flooded by a memory of sitting on his lap in the hospital after I'd had the first surgery on my burned mouth, his arms wrapped around me, telling me everything would be okay. I grabbed another blanket and started rubbing Brownie's other side. As Dad and I worked together to warm our horse, I remembered then that I loved my dad. But it was different than when I was little. Now I no longer believed he could make everything okay. I was overwhelmed by nostalgia and grief. I had such conflicting emotions I didn't know how to reconcile them. Not only did I think he could not make things better for me, but now I understood he would make things worse. He could take away my summer. He could take away my radio if he knew what I'd been listening to. And if I made any friends, he could take those away too by making us move again.

When the snow melted enough for a horse trailer to get up the driveway, Dad gave Brownie away. He said we could no longer afford to keep him. This was all too familiar and heartbreaking. What would become of that poor old horse? It might have been better for Brownie if he'd never come to live with us at all. But I told myself that maybe Brownie had found a more responsible owner who would take better care of him. For me and my siblings, however, we were stuck here.

21

Arsonist

1982

One night that winter, Dad didn't come home. I didn't realize it until the next morning because he sometimes came home late if he went to a bar after work. That morning, eating breakfast, I watched Mom as she stood at the sink. She was standing differently, more relaxed. She took a seat at the kitchen table with a plate of toast and a glass of milk. She was never a coffee drinker.

"Where's Dad?" I asked her.

She didn't look at me while she buttered her toast. She said, "He's traveling for work for a few days."

At dinner that night, David and John laughed and told stories. We all were different. No one feared the table would be overturned. No one tiptoed around the house, worrying that someone would make a wrong move and unleash a maniac upon us all.

When Dad wasn't home the following morning, I didn't ask Mom for more information about where he was because I felt a sense of lightness that I didn't want to let slip away. I reveled in the calm that filled me with him gone.

That night, we did our homework on the kitchen table and then we watched what *we* wanted to watch on TV—not the news. I could tell everyone felt the lightness inside them.

But the next day Dad returned, and we were all back to walking on egg-shells whenever he was in the house. His impatience had grown even worse—with his family, but also everyone else he encountered, including the landlord, who he complained was a liar.

Soon after Dad's return, a man came to the house and Dad sold him the dining room table and two beautiful chairs, the coffee table, and end tables from the living room. I knew this wasn't right. What would the owners say if they found out Dad was selling their furniture?

But he was about to do much worse.

The next night Dad was out late. Mom, Jeannine, and my brothers had fallen asleep while watching a movie in the living room, which was always the warmest place in the house, and I was upstairs asleep in my bed. I preferred to sleep upstairs snuggled beneath my thick pastel comforter even on the coldest nights.

I half woke up, when I heard Dad shouting and banging downstairs. Then I fully awoke when I heard his heavy boots pounding up the stairs. My stomach clenched. I was afraid he was going to grab me and pull me out of bed and beat me.

But instead he said, "Get up. I'm taking Mom to the hospital." He told me to get downstairs to take care of my siblings. "You're in charge," he said.

"What's wrong with Mom?" I said, but he had already left my room. "What's wrong with Mom!" I called after him.

I came downstairs in time to see the door closing behind my parents. I heard the sound of tires spin on gravel as the van tore off down the driveway.

I looked at the couch and there were my siblings, Jeannine sobbing quietly, and Jeff sucking on his thumb wide-eyed, his pillow pressed against his stomach.

"What happened to Mom!" I yelled. *Why did I still not know!?*

"David," I turned to him more gently. "What happened?"

Through hiccupping sobs, he told me that they had been asleep on the floor and Mom asleep on the couch and Dad came home, hungry. He woke them up, yelling about an empty potato chip bag.

"We finished the bag," John filled in, wiping his eyes. "We didn't mean to!"

"What about Mom!?"

In turns they told me that in his rage over the empty chip bag, Dad had stabbed her in the hand with a knife. It must have been a deep wound. Not something he could stitch up by himself. We all knew it was serious if he had taken her to the hospital. The bile rose in my throat. I choked it down.

I joined my siblings on the couch, pulling a blanket over us all. Like the old days on Kevin Drive and hoped that in the morning, everything would be okay. I didn't sleep, waiting for the sound of the van outside, expecting Dad to bring Mom back home with a bandage on her hand.

But he didn't come home until the early morning hours, and he didn't have Mom with him.

I sat up and said, "Where's Mom?" My brothers were awake too.

Dad said, "She's in the hospital. Grab your stuff. We're going to the campground today."

"Without Mom?" I asked. We'd never gone camping without her. "When will she be back?"

"Soon," he said.

"But is she okay?" I asked, unable to control my trembling lower lip. I put my hands over my mouth to cover it.

He told us she was having an operation on her hand. How serious an operation, or how long she would be there, I was afraid to ask, and he didn't offer.

"Start packing up. We're going to be leaving," he said.

What?! I wanted to say. *Again?!* I hoped we would at least stay a few more months to finish out the school year. Instead I asked, "What about school?" trying to keep the tremor from my voice.

"We'll just move to the campground," Dad said. It was March. I was pretty sure living in the camper for months was going to be cold, cramped, and miserable.

Jeannine was awake now. "Where's Mom?" she asked. She was five, and there was no time in her life that Mom had not been home when she woke up. I had experienced Mom's hospitalizations a few times by now. There was the time Jeannine was born. And there were two times that Dad had broken Mom's jaw by hitting her. Another time, she got a concussion when she fell off the back of the El Camino. Dad was transporting a mattress in the back and had told Mom to lie on top of it to weigh it down. But he hadn't strapped it down well enough and it had blown off, taking Mom with it.

I brought Jeannine upstairs with me and reluctantly started packing up my things in my favorite-ever room. I packed my doll with the black hair, my treasure chest, and my clothes, but I wasn't in a big hurry, thinking we had at least a few days. I loved this room. I wanted to savor every minute in it. Then I helped Jeannine put her clothes and toys in a box.

Dad walked by the open doorway with a bag of Mom's clothes. I hugged Jeannine as I watched him. I wanted to scream, *He stabbed our mother! He is a horrible person!* But instead I just whispered to Jeannine that we should go downstairs and I'd make her breakfast and tell her all about the camping adventure we were going to have.

Later that day, when Dad put our boxes and bags in the camper, we hadn't finished packing up and were under the impression that we'd be back to get the rest of our things. But we didn't dare ask when Dad told us to pile in the van with Happy. I was so furious that I couldn't look at him, afraid I would not be able to hide my disgust and rage. To distance myself from my father I sat in the third row of seats as far away as I could get from him, and even the others. When he caught my eye in the rearview mirror, I made myself give him a blank stare, to show him nothing. I wanted to seal him out so he couldn't get inside my head. As the van and camper bumped down the road, I imagined that I was riding Cindy, galloping along the roadside, jumping over guardrails and mile marker signs.

Once we arrived at the campground, Dad unhooked the camper and told me to stay behind with Jeannine and he drove off in the van with my brothers.

Several hours later, the van pulled into the campsite. My brothers got out, dirty, and dazed. Dad brought them into the camper. They smelled like a just-lit charcoal grill.

"They're hungry," he said. And then he left in the van again.

The only food in the camper was a case of instant mac and cheese. As I set a pot of water on the stove to boil, I asked them where they had been.

They didn't answer. They were silent. Their eyes were red-rimmed, and they reeked of acrid smoke. Something very bad had happened to them. It was a while before they could speak. I had to coax the story out of them. Bit by bit. And what they told me shook me to my core.

Dad had taken them back to the house, that beautiful old house at the top of the hill, the one with my favorite room that I had ever had. And he had made my little brothers help him set fire to it. Then when the fire wasn't burning fast enough, he made them run back *into the house* and open windows. *He made his sons run into a burning house.* That might not even have been the worst of it. He then made them run down the hill to a neighbor and, with rehearsed lines, tell them that the house was on fire, that it had been an accident, that a log had fallen out of the fireplace.

When they finished their story, I looked into their eyes. The terror I saw there made me hate my father with a frightening intensity. Physical abuse is something we all endured and recovered from, but this was a wound that must have cut deeper than any lash with a belt. How would they ever recover from this? How could he have done this to his own children? It was like he had shattered their spirits. It dawned to me then why Dad had packed us up so quickly. He wanted to make it look like we were expecting to come back. He thought it was a good cover to avoid being accused of arson. My fury felt bottomless, infinite, like an inferno. I wanted to kill him. I was afraid for the first time of my own uncontrollable rage.

The next evening, we hooked up the camper and picked up Mom, who emerged with her bandaged hand in a sling. With no explanation from Dad about where we were headed, we hit the highway. None of us was brave enough to ask Dad where we were going. Mom sat in the front seat cradling her arm, her eyes closed, saying nothing. None of us said anything, just listened to our own thoughts and the rattle of the camper behind us as we tore down the highway.

We stopped in Akron, and Dad canvassed the relatives asking for money, but he didn't want to stick around, so we drove all through the night. In the morning, when I woke, I was amazed to see that we were pulling up to the beautiful home of Grandma Lucille's niece, Sandy, and her husband, Bob, the policeman. I had fond memories of playing in their pool years earlier. Their Atlanta house looked like a palace to me. We parked the camper in their driveway and set ourselves up as if we were in a campground. I wanted to ask Dad how long we were staying, but didn't dare. It was Bob who came out of the house with Sandy to greet us in the driveway, who asked Dad, "So, Wayne, how long you here for?" Dad shrugged and said, "I don't know yet, Bob. Just for a bit."

Sandy looked at the camper, which was much shabbier and smaller than the Winnebago we were towing last time we were here. "Come on, y'all. Let's get you some real beds tonight." I think she really felt sorry for Mom, who must have been in so much pain.

Sandy escorted us into the house and to the finished basement, which had a bathroom and a big space with sofas and beds and that's where Mom and Dad and the boys and Jeannine would sleep.

"April, you can have the guest room upstairs," she said. "A young lady needs her privacy."

The room was fit for a princess, with a comfortable queen-size four-poster bed and an oversize dresser, into which I put my few items of clothing. I couldn't even fill one drawer.

That night, we had burgers on the patio by the pool and we all ate heartily. March in Atlanta was a lot warmer than it was back "home." I now vaguely considered home to be somewhere between Akron and Pittsburgh. But the word "home" conjured no particular house.

After dinner, while I was helping Sandy with dishes, I overheard Bob asking Dad in the living room, in a more serious tone, how long he planned to stay. But Dad was still vague. "I just don't know, Bob. Right now, we don't have anywhere else to go."

I thought that wasn't exactly true. Couldn't we go to Aunt Lucille's? Or camping, like we had last time? Why not go back to Florida? But Dad seemed to have no intention of moving on.

In just a few days it would be my birthday. I would officially be a teenager. *Thirteen!* That felt like a major milestone. I couldn't believe it was occurring while we were essentially homeless, dependent on other people. *Will Mom even remember?* I wondered, or is she just not up for it? Dad usually was the king of birthday parties, but I was expecting nothing from him this year.

I knew back in Slippery Rock Middle School classes would be in full swing. School had been the constant in our lives wherever we had lived and now I felt adrift. That night over a spaghetti and meatball dinner around Bob and Sandy's dining room table, I asked, "What about school?"

All heads turned to Dad.

Bob said, "That's a good question. Wayne, how long *are* you planning to stay in Atlanta?"

Dad said, "I'm looking for a place, Bob, and I think we'll stay a while. Probably the kids should start going to school here."

Bob got up and left the table.

Sandy looked at me and each of my brothers as we forked spaghetti into our mouths. She looked at Mom, who was focused on her plate. Sandy cleared her throat and said, "The bus stops on our street. Let's make arrangements tomorrow."

On the morning of my birthday, I came downstairs and Sandy was making pancakes. The smell of bacon was heavenly. By what had quickly become my seat at the dining room table, was a stack of brightly wrapped gift boxes. My family was gathered at the table with big grins, eager for me to unwrap my birthday haul.

My favorite gift this year might have been from Sandy—my first pair of jeans. They had elastic and a zipper at the ankles. I also got a pair of aqua-colored cotton parachute pants. At the time, I only had two other pairs of pants that fit me, so these were a godsend, considering we were starting school that week.

The camper hadn't moved from the driveway, and Happy, on a chain attached to the hitch, wagged her tail at me on my first day heading to the waiting bus. Wearing my new jeans was an instant boost to my confidence. But there was no getting around the fact that I'd come to a new school in a new state with the school year nearly over. If it had been hard to make friends in Slippery Rock, it was impossible here, so close to the end of the school year. I didn't even try.

One day in gym class, while I was still getting my bearings at the new school, I was struck with terrible stomach cramps. At first I thought I was just hungry, but this pain doubled me over. I was sent to the nurse's office, and she called home. "Home" being Sandy and Bob's house. Mom came to pick me up, driven by Rick, Bob and Sandy's adult son who lived nearby. Back at the house, up in the bedroom fit for a princess, I clutched my belly and rocked back and forth on the bed.

Sandy knocked on the door. "April, can I come in?"

Between moans, I said, "Uh-huh."

She pushed open the door and I felt better just knowing she was there. She sat on my bed and handed me a heating pad.

"This will help," she said as she plugged it in for me. Then she gave me a Tylenol.

"Do you know what's happening, April?" she asked.

I shook my head. I assumed I had eaten something bad.

She gave a big sigh. Then she explained to me that I was getting my period. I was shocked. I only vaguely remembered what I'd learned about it in health class in Brighton. Why had my mother never told me anything about what to expect? Sandy gave me Kotex pads and explained how to use them. When she told me that I would see blood in my underwear soon, I began to cry. I felt ill-equipped to become a woman. My own mother was a mystery to me, and she made no effort to be anything else.

Back at school, I was even more self-conscious, afraid everyone would see blood leaking through my pants. I carried around a purse with pads and ducked into the bathroom to check my pad between classes. I hadn't known this was part of being a woman, that it would be so painful or so messy. Being a woman definitely had drawbacks. Even beyond the terrifying things that could happen to you, which I had read about in Dad's book and his magazines.

After living for two weeks with Sandy and Bob, it was obvious that we had outstayed our welcome. After dinner, I heard Bob ask Dad to leave, and Dad just said that we couldn't. He repeated that we had nowhere else to go.

By the three-week mark, our family was still sleeping in the house, but we were not welcome to eat dinner with Bob and Sandy, which I could tell was as awkward for Sandy as it was for us. In the cramped camper, we ate macaroni and cheese on paper plates night after night. The directions on the box called for milk and butter, and when we didn't have either, I just added extra water. Often Dad was not with us. Sometimes both Mom and Dad would go out. Once I put green food coloring in the mac and cheese to try to make it fun for my siblings. And we couldn't eat it. It turns out that green mac and cheese is even less appetizing when you're sick of it to begin with.

Every afternoon, coming home to Sandy and Bob's house after being dropped off at the bus stop was a reminder that we were unwanted guests, and it was all Dad's fault. Why wasn't he finding us another place to live, like he'd done every other time we'd moved?

And then everything changed. About a month after my birthday, in late April, I came back to the house after school and Mom met me in the driveway. She was acting strange. "April," she said. "I have something to tell you."

That alone was a new development. She rarely shared news. But what she said next was a game changer. She said, "Your father has been arrested."

"For what?" I asked, though I knew, because six weeks earlier, on that awful night, my brothers, reeking of smoke, had told me what he had done.

Mom said that back in Portersville, fire investigators had been looking for Dad, but no one knew where he'd gone. Unfortunately (for Dad), he'd accidentally left a clue in the house. Much of the contents of the closets had not burned. Investigators found an old Atlanta police department shirt hanging in a closet. They traced the name and number on it to the station where Bob worked and called him. When asked how his shirt came to be in a house rented by Edward Wayne Edwards, and did he happen to know where that suspected arsonist had fled, Bob said, "He's right here at my house. Come and get 'im."

And that's how, just a little over a month after we had arrived in Atlanta, Dad was arrested on April 29, 1982, for arson and extradited to Butler County, Pennsylvania, where he would be held until his trial, which might not occur for months. But Mom told me, as reassurance, that there was a possibility of getting him out on bail, where he could live with us until the trial date. That wasn't reassuring to me, but I didn't tell her that.

"It's happened before," Mom told me. She explained that he'd been arrested before and she'd bailed him out. Quite recently, in fact. Those two days of peaceful calm in Portersville? He had been in jail for shoplifting from the little grocery store in town.

"And we bailed him out," she said. She'd collected money at the church we attended. She would work on doing that again.

My first thought was, *Please don't.* My second thought took me straight into the bathroom, where I shaved my legs, now that Dad wouldn't be around to say a darn thing about it.

22

Rebirth

1962–1967

On January 20, 1962, Dad's long string of luck ended in Atlanta. He and Marlene were arrested and escorted out of their apartment by federal agents. He was already known in the press as an "escape artist" and a "near genius." He felt like a celebrity. It seemed like every cop in Atlanta was out front, with rifles trained on him, as gawkers looked on in amazement.

At the police station, Marlene was interrogated separately. She astonished police with her story—which she stuck to—that she believed her husband was a secret government agent and that all his actions were at the request of his superiors. She also had another story that was tough to swallow. Dad had had a gunshot wound that the police in Portland had asked him about. Both then and now, Marlene explained his injury this way: he had told her—she claimed—to shoot him in the shoulder. Bail was set for Marlene at fifty thousand dollars. She was nineteen years old and, you guessed it, pregnant.

Bail for my father was set at one hundred thousand dollars and he was put in the county jail to await extradition to Ohio. He had done hard time in Montana. He wasn't about to do it again. He convinced an orderly he'd trade his watch and ring for a hacksaw blade and toothbrush holder. The man agreed. My father broke the saw blade in half, hid it in the toothbrush holder, and inserted it into his rectum. Later, to avoid being caught in a cavity search, he hollowed out the sole of his shoe to hide the blade. Once he was transferred to the Cuyahoga County Jail, near Akron, he planned with other prisoners to use the blade on the steel prison bars, but the plan was discovered and the charge of attempted jailbreak was added to his list of crimes. According to the *Akron Beacon Journal*, fourteen bed sheets were found tied together to form an escape chain.

Marlene had a miscarriage and didn't serve time. Dad, however, was sentenced to sixteen years in Leavenworth Federal Penitentiary in Kansas, the notorious prison that housed reviled and (by some) admired criminals and gangsters, including Machine Gun Kelly, Baby Face Nelson, would-be presidential assassins, and Mafia dons.

He had escaped from other jails, but once the doors of Leavenworth clanged behind him, he was surrounded by high barbed-wire fencing, as you would expect from an institution housing prisoners serving multiple life sentences.

He was given a prison number and informed that he would be eligible for parole in five and a half years if he behaved himself. He got a job in the carpentry shop and then on a construction crew that was remodeling the prison offices. His boss, Mr. Alexander, was impressed by Dad's hard work. He encouraged him to study construction in the prison school. Being the object of praise and support for Dad was like a man dying of thirst being brought to a clear stream to drink. This was the sustenance he'd always needed. He had never finished sixth grade. Now, with Mr. Alexander cheering him on, he enrolled in prison school and got his elementary and then his high school diploma, then he got his associate's degree. He became highly trained in first aid.

Because it held the promise of earlier parole, Dad requested transfer to Lewisburg Federal Penitentiary, in Pennsylvania, which once housed Roy Gardner, a far more notorious bank robber than my father. There, Dad continued to get training in first aid and self-defense—people in the prison system trusted him, and he seemed earnest and honestly devoted to self-improvement. He received Red Cross certification and even taught courses to other inmates.

In Lewisburg, he met and became friends with Jimmy Hoffa. They played basketball together. Hoffa got him a guaranteed job driving a truck for the Teamsters upon his release, which greased the wheels of his parole. When Dad left Lewisburg's walls, Jimmy Hoffa wished him well.

In his memoir, Dad wrote of being overwhelmed with gratitude and emotion upon his release. Everything made him cry. He wrote, "Never again would I put myself even remotely in jeopardy of having to return to prison." He was elated to return to his hometown of Akron a free man. He wrote, "Life is beautiful, and I would see to it that it stayed beautiful for the rest of the time God gave me."

One year after leaving Lewisburg Federal Penitentiary, he and Mom were married. Fifteen years after promising himself he had changed, he was back in prison. But this time he had a wife and five kids.

23

This Is Who You Are

1982

Soon after Dad's arrest at Sandy and Bob's house, Mom, my brothers, Jeannine and I, and Happy returned to Slippery Rock, delivered by their son, Rick, who drove the van, towing the camper. Mom still did not have her driver's license. She was fully at the mercy of other people now.

The church that we had attended in Slippery Rock stepped up to do what Dad could not: find yet another new home for his family. A couple we knew from church, Gary and Kathy, were building a house, and they offered to let us stay there with them while it was still under construction. It was a lot farther along than our house on Kevin Drive had been when we moved in. Gary and Kathy's had plumbing and electricity and walls. They offered us the living room, and also offered sanctuary for Happy, where she slept under their deck.

The living room had one couch, which Mom slept on, and the rest of us slept on the floor. I made a little fort for myself in a corner behind an armchair by draping a blanket over it. I knew I would need a refuge for reading and doing homework in privacy.

There wasn't much left of the school year, less than a month, but we had to go back to finish so we wouldn't have to repeat our grades. I returned to Slippery Rock Middle School a different girl than I had been when I left. Now I had a pair of jeans and my legs were shaved smooth. Now my father wasn't in the van lurking in the school parking lot to make sure I was wearing what he wanted me to wear. He was in prison awaiting trial, and a deep shame settled on my shoulders as I walked into the school building for the last month of seventh grade. Everyone seemed to know all about my troubles. Teachers greeted me with false cheer, but students looked at me like I had fallen into a deep crevice and crawled back out as a bug. Even Derrick, who had asked me to the dance just a few months earlier, barely said hi to me. He walked down the halls holding hands with another girl from our class. A lot had happened here while we were gone, and I felt like I had missed everything important while nothing at all had happened to me. But in fact, it was the other way around. The teenage world in Slippery Rock Middle School remained the same, while my world had been turned upside down. This was worse than being the new kid. I was humiliated. I knew people were talking about me and about what Dad had done. But they didn't even know the worst that he'd done. And I realized that I didn't know his worst, either. I wanted to be anywhere but school. Anywhere but in my own life, really. I escaped into books and daydreamed of an alternate reality where my father wasn't a criminal, where my family wasn't poor, where I could carry my head high and not be always full of shame.

At the end of the school year, I had good grades in all my classes except for English. The final exam was on diagramming sentences, but that unit had been covered after I left, and it wasn't what was being taught while I was at the school in Atlanta. I failed the test completely. I couldn't even answer a single question. My English teacher, Mr. Smith, looked at me with pity when I explained that I'd never learned any of it. He told me he'd disregard my final exam grade and gave me an A in the class. I didn't like that he felt sorry for me, but I wasn't going to argue with the A. My education was suffering from all this moving around. But I had bigger worries.

I had found a copy of Dad's memoir, *Metamorphosis of a Criminal*. It was in the van, which was parked on the street with the camper, and we stored our things there because Gary and Kathy's house didn't have room for us *and* our belongings. I brought the book inside to read. Mom saw it in my hand and said, "Put that back, April. That's not for you to read."

Now I have to read it, I thought, but I said, "Okay."

I didn't put it back. Instead, in my blanket fort, I began to read all about Dad's life. The book took me a few weeks to get through, reading in stolen moments.

There was a lot I didn't understand in the book. I didn't even know what the word "virgin" meant. I had to look it up. My father's book seemed to be all about sex. I was shocked, reading his own accounts of how he treated women. Some of them just a few years older than me! I recognized some of this behavior from our own lives, like when he fondled babysitters. But I was surprised at how freely he wrote about beating a woman named Linda in Houston and another woman Marlene, and then there was poor pregnant Verna! What had he done to her? In the book, he just leaves her behind in Denver. I could almost hear Dad reading this part out loud in his "lying voice." I thought of Snoopy. Where did Dad take him? Where did he take Verna?

In his own words, I read how Dad beat and cheated on women just the way he did to Mom. That part wasn't a surprise. It was a disgusting affirmation of what I already knew. Now I saw that how he treated Mom was how he had been treating women all his life. And she had helped him write this book. What did she think when she heard these stories? Had they made her feel sick, like they were making me feel? Of course, I couldn't ask Mom about any of this. She'd told me not to read it. I understood why now, but I couldn't stop.

I had already known that Dad had the capacity to be a con man, I just didn't realize how bad he had been before he'd met Mom. Was he just as bad now? I began to recall shop owners refusing to add items to our large, unpaid credit tabs. Was an unpaid tab reason enough to leave town and uproot your children every single year? Had he done this in every town we'd lived in? After reading his book, I decided that yes, he probably had. And he probably had done much worse.

As I read, I couldn't help but think, *So this is who you are.* I knew he had intentionally set fire to the house in Portersville, but had he also done this on Taylor Road? Had he burned the barn on purpose? Had he burned down that wonderful old farmhouse? I didn't understand yet about insurance fraud, but I understood that my father had no respect for other people's property. He would scam landlords any way he could. These houses we'd lived in and briefly identified as "home" were not ours. The ones he burned, the ones he shot holes through, the ones he stained and damaged, were not his and were not ours, they were someone else's, and someone else had to pay the price for his destruction.

Maybe the most earth-shattering revelation for me was that Mom was his fourth wife, and that I might have other siblings. I was haunted by the revelations that he had fathered other children. Where were they? Why didn't I know them? Did Verna have a boy or girl? Where was the son he'd had with Jeanette—my half brother? They would be nearly grown by now.

I learned that Dad had briefly lived in many of the places he had taken us to live. I had no idea he had such a long criminal history, beginning as a child. Even as a kid not much older than me, he was obsessed with women and sex. And fire.

When I read that he had been arrested in Atlanta twenty years earlier, it felt like an eerie foreshadowing.

I knew I would never see Dad in the same way. I didn't want him looking at me ever again. Just the idea made my skin crawl.

Unfortunately, I had to see him. While Dad was in the Butler County Jail awaiting trial, we had to visit him regularly. I hated it, but Dad insisted that we come. Sometimes we had to wait outside the building on the hot, shadeless sidewalk. Then we would sit in the visiting room across the table from him. I knew he wanted us to look lovingly at him, but I couldn't look at him at all.

My whole family knew Dad was guilty, but Gary and Kathy were not only kind and generous in housing us, they believed in giving people the benefit of the doubt. They were willing to believe Dad was innocent, because surely someone they knew, with a family like ours, could not have done this awful crime. I thought that they must not have read his book. Gary and Kathy were not done being generous. They gave Dad funds to hire a hotshot young defense lawyer. And to my grave disappointment, they posted my father's bail.

I knew that once he was released, the sense of freedom I'd felt would be gone, chased away by his oppressive presence. When Dad got out of jail on bail it was September. Dad knew someone who knew someone who had an empty house, and we moved out of Gary and Kathy's living room to a place way out in the country, at the edge of McConnells Mill State Park.

As we pulled up to a house with surrounding fields bright with yellow goldenrod and unmown hay, I had to squint to imagine what the house had once looked like. In its present state, it looked abandoned, but you could tell it had once been beautiful. Dad backed the van and camper into a large outbuilding next to the house, which might have once been a barn or a farm equipment shed. It had a large storage loft above, and pigeons roosted in the rafters and some of the roofing shingles were missing, letting in shafts of light that shone on cobwebs and striped the dusty floor.

We unpacked what few things we had and moved into the house. It smelled stale and had scarred, sloping, wide-planked wood floors. Cool mold-scented air seeped from beneath the cellar door. The kitchen was big, with old appliances that didn't work. The water coming out of the kitchen sink's cold-water faucet sputtered and then ran gray. The hot-water faucet didn't disgorge anything at all. This took the prize as the worst house so far.

A narrow staircase led upstairs, which had two small bedrooms and an open area. Jeannine and I got one of the small bedrooms, and my brothers got the other.

That night, lying on a thin, dusty mattress on the floor, listening to Jeannine breathing quietly beside me as the wind whistled through the crack in the window, I thought back to all the bedrooms I had slept in, in all the homes I had lived in, and tried to conjure the happy memories in each. I had recently seen the movie *Pollyanna*, about the orphan girl who always thinks positively no matter what happens, and I was inspired by her. I attempted to make myself feel better by remembering happy times in the places I'd lived, but at this moment I felt defeated. My life was not moving in a positive direction. Everything seemed to be getting worse, not better.

The next morning, I looked around, hoping that the morning light would make the house feel cheerful. But no sunshine could change my opinion that this house was ready for the wrecking ball. We couldn't even take a bath in it. We had to bathe in a tiny spring-fed pond behind the house in the weeds or shower with ice-cold water in a moldy shower stall. But Dad informed us that we were there rent-free because he'd agreed to paint and repair the house.

Repair *this* house? I would have laughed if I hadn't been afraid to get smacked for it.

Dad came home with supplies he'd picked up. There were ladders and paintbrushes and cans of paint. He also had several five-gallon glass carboys.

"What are those for?" I asked.

He announced proudly that he was going to make wine in the cellar.

Seriously? I thought to myself. *That trial can't come soon enough.*

The best thing by far about living there was walking past McConnells Mill State Park to get to the bus stop each day. Deer watched us go by early in the morning, their ears alert, their bright eyes trained on us. One morning I was daydreaming and heard a loud, sharp, rasping sound. I looked around alarmed, only to see a buck staring at me and blowing through his nose, snorting his warning.

I was now in eighth grade, a new student in another new school—Laurel High School in nearby New Castle. This was a small rural school, grades seven through twelve in one building. I joined the band and walked home each day with the black clarinet swinging.

After school, David would take the shorter way home from the bus stop, but I would take as long a route as possible, detouring into the park for a walk through the woods. The park was named after the McConnells Mill, an old water wheel, on a Class 4 white water rafting river, named Slippery Rock Creek—which was notorious for drownings—and a roaring waterfall. I'd sit on the banks and watch kayakers shooting the rapids. The river had carved a deep, tranquil gorge. The soothing sound of the trickling water slowed my breath and my heart rate. I would take my shoes off and walk through the creek. Once I stepped on a mossy rock and fell, knocking my head against a rock so hard I saw stars. I lay in the shallow stream, wondering if I had cracked my head open. I eventually got up, soaked through, checked myself for blood, and gingerly crossed the stream, not at all deterred from walking on the slippery rocks. Discovering this magical wild place gave me hope. The world was bigger than the one back home.

When I got back to the house, there was Dad, outside, waiting for me.

When he said that he'd agreed to repair and paint the house, what this really meant was that he would make us do it for him. Dad didn't get up on the ladders himself. He just watched from below, shouting that we'd missed a spot here and a spot there.

The first day, after a couple of hours of being up on the ladder, scraping, I felt a sharp stab in my side. I flinched and grabbed the ladder for balance. I leaned over, looked at my side, and saw a hole in my shirt with a small red welt peeking through. I looked down and saw Dad staring up at me, pointing a BB gun at me. His grin was wide.

"Stop it!" I yelled.

He laughed and said, "Better run, honey."

I scampered down the ladder and sprinted away, feeling the sting of the BBs hitting my back and legs as I ran. Dad was out of shape—probably from all those years of delegating chores from the comfort of his recliner, shouting for coffee, his cigarettes, a glass of water. I was faster than he was and he knew it, so he only made a show of chasing me. I bolted around the house, easily outrunning him, and hid in the tall weeds at the edge of the yard. I didn't come out until the "game" was over. I didn't want to play Dad's games anymore. I had no patience for him now. My brothers were targets too, but they didn't consider running away and finding a place to lay low until Dad got bored and went in. One of my brothers ran into the house and emerged with his own BB gun and shot at Dad. But this wasn't a game with more than one player, and Dad beat the crap out of him. He may have grown fat and lazy, but his reflexes were still lightning-fast. When Dad grabbed you, you barely saw it coming until it was too late.

Waiting for his trial felt like we were trapped in a bubble of absurdity, painting a house that should have been torn down, while Dad shot his kids with BBs and attempted to make wine that no one would ever drink. The most pointless activity was Dad's new obsession with Pac-Man. Right down the road from us was a bar. Dad spent hours in the bar, bringing rolls of quarters to play the Pac-Man and poker arcade machines. During the day, he became a pro at Pac-Man and often brought us with him and challenged us kids to beat him. We never could.

Meanwhile we were hungry. It had been a while since Dad had had a job that provided us with chicken and meat, and I found myself even wistful for liver and onions. Dad brought home crates of apples along with large tubs of peanut butter and big blocks of cheese. This was our mainstay.

We didn't sleep inside the house for long. It was too cold and drafty, and the heating system was defunct. Instead, we moved into the camper that was parked in the shed, which had a wood-burning stove. The camper was too cramped for me, though, so I moved into the big loft above. It was full of rusted coffee cans, old nails, inches of dirt, bird droppings, and bird feathers. In a dry space between missing roofing shingles, I swept an area clean as best I could. I found a place to hang my clothes and set up my "room." I found a cracked mirror that I perched on top of planks that I laid flat on stacked milk crates to use as a desk. I ran an extension cord up to the loft for a desk lamp and for my curling iron, which I used before going to school in the morning. I laid my sleeping bag down. *It's just another version of camping*, I told myself. And I liked camping, right?

I would lie in my makeshift bedroom in the loft as my stomach growled and think about those rolls of quarters Dad brought with him to the bar down the road. Why was he wasting his money on Pac-Man when we were hungry? And then the morning sun would come streaming in the places where the roof shingles were missing, and I'd eagerly get out of bed. There was always free milk in the school cafeteria in the morning.

Before school I would take either a cold bath in the pond or a cold shower in the moldy shower stall in the house before the long walk to the bus stop. I may be living in a barn, but I still wanted my hair to look good.

My new school had a cheerleading team, and a girl I had become friendly with named Michelle told me she was going to try out. I decided to try out too. It would be a good use of my gymnastics skills as well as my loud voice. At home, in the wonderful acoustics of the living room of that old house, I made up a cheer. I went to Michelle's house after school to practice a few times and I taught it to her.

Once, I spent the night at Michelle's house so we could work on our cheerleading jumps and the new cheer for the approaching tryouts. The next day her mom drove me home. I didn't want to let on that we were actually living in the barn, so when she stopped in front of the house, I got out and acted like I was just going to go in. I did still use the house for two things: the moldy shower and the living room's acoustics. When I practiced the clarinet there, the sound carried through the empty rooms, rich and clear.

But now, hoping to walk in as if I actually lived there, I was foiled because the front door was locked. Michelle's mom wanted to wait with me until my parents got home. I assured her they'd be home soon and I'd be fine waiting by myself as I sat on the step leading to the side door. After she reluctantly left, I practiced my cheer in the yard a few times, and then went to my room in the loft of the shed.

I was gung-ho on making the cheerleading team and I was excited that, as a special treat, the eighth-grade band members got to march in a big upcoming football game. We also got to help them out with a pie-selling fundraiser for new uniforms. I had been happy to dust off my champion Girl Scout cookie salesmanship skills for the cause.

The night after the football game—which we *won!*—there was a bonfire event where awards would be given out. I had showered beforehand in our freezing water and got all dressed up. I'd taken extra care, drying and curling my hair up in my loft. Dad drove me to the bonfire and stayed for the awards ceremony.

It was still daylight when we arrived, but the bonfire was already big and hot and it seemed like the whole field was filled with kids from the high school and middle school. Parents were there, too, eager to see their kids get awards. I hung out with my fellow eighth-grade band members, but I kept an eye on Dad as he chatted in his animated way with the other parents. I hoped he wasn't saying anything embarrassing. As darkness fell, it was hard to see beyond the circle of light cast by the fire. When the awards ceremony began, my band friends and I sat down in the grass to watch. I got called up to receive an award for selling the most number of pies—a gift certificate for a local ice cream shop. I stood there, thanking the band teacher for the gift certificate, and then looked out at the assembled crowd. With disbelief, I saw Dad was six feet away, running toward me with a paper plate piled high with whipped cream. To a collective gasp, he smacked the paper plate in my face. He rubbed it all over my head and down the front of my shirt. I tried to wipe the whipped cream from my eyes, unable to stop the tears from leaking out of them. I heard nervous laughter from the kids. Dad was laughing the loudest of all, enjoying his prank. Enjoying being the center of attention. But I knew that this was about more than attracting attention to himself. This was his retaliation. He felt my churning resentment, my growing disappointment in him, my rejection of him. I had lost respect for him since the fire. My waning belief in him had begun before that, but the fire was like a coffin lid slammed down on my childhood innocence. He was not the center of the universe. He was not the hero in my story. He was the villain. We were on opposing sides now.

I turned away from the crowd, and one of the chaperone band mothers came up to me holding out a towel. I wiped my face, and she helped me scrape the whipped cream out of my hair. On the silent car ride home, I fumed. Dad ruined everything. Any time I tried to pretend to be normal, he had to go and wreck it. What had his excuse been for the buttermilk days on Kevin Drive? What childish impulse had made him do that? I didn't want to take another cold shower that night or jump in the freezing pond in the dark. I got a washcloth and tried to clean myself up, but I went to bed all sticky in my loft. I realized that in the commotion Dad had caused, I had lost my ice cream gift certificate. My stomach growled in protest. Ice cream would have cheered me up. Even better would have been a roast beef sandwich.

24

Trial

1982

Finally, the first day of the trial came, and we had to arrive in the courtroom as a family, to show our support, Dad told us. He made all of us sit behind him and instructed us kids to cry as hard as we could every time he turned around to look at us. That was our cue. But there was a woman in the jury who looked at us—his five children ranging from ages seven to thirteen—weeping throughout the trial. The whole thing was so sad. *Look at this man—a family man who has done this terrible thing . . . What will become of these poor children?* Seeing how sad she and some of the other members of the jury looked made me feel twisted up inside. I cried, but not because Dad wanted me to. I wept nearly through the entire trial. Mom wasn't crying. She just looked miserable.

When a police officer was called to the stand to testify that Dad had started the fire, I was supposed to shout from my seat, "My dad would never do that!" But I didn't say anything when the moment came. Dad turned around and glared at me for missing my cue. I turned away, lifted my chin, and looked elsewhere, imagining myself not sitting in a courtroom behind my father, but walking through the woods in McConnells Mill, taking my mind through the trails I had walked the day before.

When I wasn't crying, I was listening to our stomachs rumble. One day during the trial, to distract myself, I went through my multiplication tables. Another day it was my spelling words. During the break, we didn't have money for lunch. We bought one bagel at the courthouse concession stand to share between all seven of us.

I don't remember how long the trial lasted, but we attended every day. When the verdict was finally read, the juror who had been in the first row and wept quietly through the whole trial, began to bawl. The jury of his peers had found my father guilty of arson. He was handcuffed and taken out of the courtroom. We saw him again in the hallway near a stairwell so that we could say goodbye to him.

We took turns hugging him. I went last. After we began walking away, he called me back. "April," he said, "I want to say goodbye. I can't go back to prison. I wanted you to know I love you."

Then I watched as he pulled out a square of bubblegum from his pocket. It was studded with small yellow pills. He looked at me and said, "Don't tell anyone about this," while giving me a meaningful gaze. I watched him put the gum in his mouth. *Go ahead*, I wanted to say. *Die.* But he knew what I would do. I would tell the first person I saw.

I followed my family, who had hung back, and walked down the hall.

Facing serious jail time—five to twelve years—as a convicted arsonist, Dad was pulling out his best con moves. If he had to go to jail, he was determined to do it on his own terms. He orchestrated those terms as if he were directing a movie, starring himself, with me as his co-star. We both should have been nominated for Oscars. I'm not proud of my performance and what it granted him, but I was not in control of my destiny. He was. Still. Even as he was about to be put away behind bars for possibly the rest of my childhood. I *hoped* for the rest of my childhood.

I strode to the first police officer I saw in the courthouse.

"Excuse me," I said with an unnatural calm. "Um, my dad just took a bunch of pills."

The officer said, "What!?"

I added, "I just saw him do it."

He turned to speak rapidly into his radio. Then he said to me, "Don't worry, hon. We'll take good care of your dad. You're a good daughter. He's lucky to have you."

They took Dad to the hospital, pumped out his stomach, and put him on a suicide watch. His transition was cushioned because his suicide attempt kept him from being thrown immediately into the general prison population.

With Dad in jail, we left that wreck of a house and moved into an apartment in the projects in a cluster of buildings named Neshannock Village in downtown New Castle, called by the residents "The Village." It was infested with cockroaches, but at least we now had hot water and a bathroom with a shower and a toilet that flushed reliably. But the apartments did not allow dogs. The church pastor, who had young children, offered to take Happy and find a good home for her. Mom was in no position to object. I was devastated to say goodbye to her. She had been so faithful since we first found her in the woods in Doylestown. She'd traveled with us through every campground, lived tied outside every house, bore witness to every crisis, and through it all, was always willing to cheer us up with a lick on the cheek and to roll over and let us pet her belly.

We now lived in a different school district. I had to leave Laurel School, just as I was settling into it. I learned that Michelle made the cheerleading team, using the cheer I had made up and taught her. My new school was within walking distance of downtown New Castle. Ben Franklin Middle School was huge. I was back in an urban environment, but this was not my first rodeo, and I was not the same person I was when we had lived in Pittsburgh. I had become more confident sewing in Slippery Rock Middle School's seventh grade home ec class. Mom had a sewing machine, and I was making many of my own clothes. I was not the drably dressed country girl anymore. On my first day I wore a bright yellow miniskirt that I had sewn myself, a white shirt, sandals, and big yellow plastic disk earrings. And Dad wasn't around to comment on my transformation.

Everything was different now. Our father was in jail, and we were on public assistance. We shopped with food stamps, which actually looked like tickets, not real money, so there was no hiding the fact that we were using them. When we were checking out at a grocery store, handing a stack of tickets to the cashier, I tried to imagine I was somewhere else, like in a field of daisies back at the farm on Taylor Road.

But at least now we could buy food, and at school we qualified for free lunches. The process of getting free lunches, though, was humiliating. I had to go up to the register and turn in a red ticket. Everyone knew the red ticket meant your parents couldn't afford to feed you. All my siblings and I now had red tickets. Sometimes I was too self-conscious to use mine and went without lunch.

I joined the school band and made a friend, a boy with sandy hair named Richard, who didn't seem to care that I'd started at his school late in the year, lived in the Village, or had a red ticket for lunch. Something about him made me feel safe and at ease. Not judged. He played the trumpet in the school band, so we had practice together. We also had all our classes together. I was always relieved to catch sight of him when I walked into a classroom.

With all her kids in school during the day, Mom started working again, at a discount store a few blocks away, like the one in Brighton. And we joined a new church called the New Castle First Assembly of God, which was of the Pentecostal denomination, a new one for us. The church van would pick us up for services, which were held three times a week. The church was enormous. At our first service attendance, a woman in the pew next to me stood and threw her hands up in the air and began to tremble and speak rapidly in a language I didn't understand. I turned around, looking for someone to step in to help her. I thought she might be having a seizure. Why was no one else alarmed? Instead, everyone swayed and clapped, and when she snapped out of it, with glazed eyes and a shy smile, the people around her nodded and touched her arms and said amen.

The church and its community quickly became a lifeline for us all. That Christmas we did not have a tree, and we did not display our family ornaments. We did not have piles of wrapped gifts. Instead, the church congregants brought us casseroles and gift bags filled with toys and clothes. Many of the bags were full of out-of-style hand-me-downs. My awareness of style was so hard-won, I was not about to release my grip on it. One bag included brand-new boots that laced up like moccasins. But they were intended for indoor wear, and as I walked to school, I could feel the stones pressing right up through the soles.

I signed up to join the church youth group, led by Pastor Jimmy, mostly to get out of our crowded apartment. The church van was to pick me up in front of my apartment building for my first Wednesday night youth group meeting. I was nervous and excited. I'd styled my hair and applied makeup carefully. I was ready early and standing outside our apartment building waiting for the van, when I heard someone say, "Hey! White girl!"

I wheeled around to face a Black girl who looked boiling mad. She jumped me, and my instincts kicked in. I wasn't the daughter of Edward Wayne Edwards for nothing. I grabbed her around the waist, picked her up and slammed her back onto the ground and placed my knee on her chest and pulled back my right arm and punched her in the mouth. Her lip split open, and she started crying.

"What's your problem?" I hissed at her. Adrenaline coursed through me. I had just moved to the neighborhood. What could she possibly have against me already? When I let her up, she stared daggers at me, but she covered her mouth and backed away as the van pulled up. I got in the van, still shaking. The driver asked if I was okay. I said I was. But I felt like an impostor. Was I a fighter? Or a Christian? Can a person be both? *Do I really belong in a church youth group?* I wondered. Do I need to be a good person to join? Was it possible to be my father's daughter and still be a good person?

The next week it happened again while waiting for the church van. Only it was a different girl. Sometimes I got jumped in front of my apartment. Sometimes it was around the corner. Sometimes it was when I got home from school. The results were always the same. I never knew when and where it would happen, so I was in a constant state of vigilance. After several weeks of this, one morning there was a group of a dozen girls waiting for me in front of my building. They surrounded me and, finally, one older girl stepped into the circle with me. I took my fighter's stance and waited for her to make the first move. She stood there with her hands on her hips and examined me. "White girl," she finally said. "You can hold your own."

Her name was Puffy. And I had passed some sort of initiation. I was now a part of her gang, whether I wanted to be or not. Gang membership was not what I envisioned for my teen résumé. How this would sit with Pastor Jimmy, I hoped to never know, because I had no intention of telling him.

I was at a crossroads. I needed to decide which path my life would take. With my father confirmed as a bad man in society's eyes, I knew he would be out of the picture for years, but not forever. I would be out of the house by the time he got out of prison. This idea filled me with hope. What I made of my life now was entirely up to me.

25

Freedom

While Dad was in prison, I began to relax. My stomach didn't clench in knots every time I heard tires on a gravel driveway. I packed my schedule with activities. I joined the Neshannock Village softball league, where I played first base on the girls' team, and joined the school band. I got fully involved with the church youth group, I kept up with my schoolwork, I started a successful babysitting business, and I was somehow a member of a neighborhood gang. Exactly what the neighborhood gang did, I still wasn't sure. It seemed a bit like the church youth group in that mostly it involved recruitment and social activities, but with alcohol present, and since I didn't drink, my attendance record in the gang was poor.

The only time I felt the old anxiety return was when we had to go visit Dad in jail. I hated visiting him, but not going was not an option—he was still in control.

Mom still didn't drive, but there was a woman who lived in the Village who had a husband in the same prison and so we got a ride with her every other Saturday. It was a long drive, and as we got closer, my sense of dread increased.

The Western Pennsylvania Penitentiary was a two-hundred-year-old building made of stone blocks that looked like some kind of castle in a vampire movie. Upon entering, you gave the guard your name and took a seat in a waiting room. When they called your name, you walked through a metal detector.

The first time we went, I wore a bra with metal clasps, and it set an alarm off. I was told to take off my bra right then and there and put it in a container, where they held it for me while I was visiting. It made me feel like a criminal. Getting to the visiting room required being escorted through a maze of halls with bars on all sides. I crossed my arms over my chest, feeling vulnerable.

We entered a room full of tables, with a prisoner and his visitors at each. There was Dad at one, waiting for us with a big smile on his face. We took our seats and I looked around at all the fidgety families and strained couples at the other tables. There was no privacy. This was okay with me because I knew Dad couldn't do anything to us with the guard standing there.

He had never let me cut my hair, but with him gone I decided to crop it to shoulder-length. It was the era of the Breck girl, and I wasn't going to miss out on that. I didn't want him to notice, so I had worn my hair in a ponytail. I just didn't want to hear his judgment. I didn't want his opinions about my clothing, my hair, or my body.

"You cut your hair," he said when we sat down. "It looks nice."

This was a surprise, but I know he was putting on a show for the guards and all the other prisoners sitting at tables with families in the room. He spoke in a loud voice, asking David, John, Jeff, and Jeannine how school was going.

I had also cut Jeannine's hair, but Dad didn't notice. He didn't scrutinize her in the same way. I had taken over cutting Mom's hair and my brothers' as well. He didn't comment on Mom's either, but Dad saw more of her than he saw of us. She sometimes went to visit him without us during the week while we were in school.

When we left, he told us to keep an eye out for letters from him and that he'd see us in two weeks. The first letter to me came soon after. He wanted to play chess and he proposed his first move. I was supposed to make his move and write him back with mine. I cooperated in the beginning, but the game was too slow, and I was never any good at chess and I wrote to him less and less often. After a few months, I stopped playing the game completely.

Mom seemed much happier without Dad. She had government assistance, she had a generous support system in the church community. I thought we were all way better off without him. I didn't understand why she visited him so often. It would have been a great opportunity for her to leave Dad, but Mom was steadfast. Did she actually miss him? I could not bring myself to ask her. For whatever reason, she did not leave him. Was it fear of his retaliation? That would have been a valid fear, if his accounts in his memoir were true. But I think she didn't leave him for another reason. I think she truly loved him—or whatever her sense of dependence upon him could be called. Despite his violence, his infidelity, his inability to hold down a job, his constant moving, his crimes, she preferred to hold on to him rather than let him go.

I wanted her to file for divorce. It was against the church's teachings, but exceptions existed for exceptional situations. This was definitely a situation where loyalty was not called for. But I understood that Mom was powerless to make a decision without Dad, especially the decision to leave him. And I would never have made the suggestion. It would have hurt her so much if she thought I wanted her and his children to leave him. After all, we were still a family.

Without Dad to demand liver and onions or criticize Mom's cooking, I became braver in the kitchen. Home ec inspired me. And thanks to food stamps, I had the raw ingredients. I pored through Mom's tattered Betty Crocker cookbook for recipes we would all enjoy. The pages with the pie crust recipe were so sticky they could no longer be separated. I learned to make homemade pizza dough and Italian meat sauce from scratch. The apartment filled with the aroma of oregano and thyme and garlic. My brothers piled as much spaghetti as they wanted onto their plates. And they often came back for seconds. No one insulted my cooking or overturned the table. Cleaning up after dinner never involved picking corn out of the carpet. Mom was more relaxed than I could ever remember. She seemed to be making good friends in church.

The church was so big it had more than one pastor. One of them, Pastor Jimmy, was in his late twenties or early thirties. He was handsome, gregarious, and single. All the girls in youth group had crushes on him. He had a great rapport with kids. He'd organize games and he got everyone into a party mood. And when it came time to talk about the Bible, he made it accessible and entertaining. He seemed to live the life he preached. Goodness, compassion, faithfulness. It was the first time I spent any length of time with a man who I didn't have to fear. David joined youth group too, and Pastor Jimmy became a male authority figure who David could joke around with and not fear it would turn into a humiliating experience for him.

The church had a lot of well-to-do congregants. We were the poorest among the flock. Mom was barely making our subsidized housing rent. Pastor Jimmy understood this, but welcomed us as if we were just like anyone else.

Jeff and John joined Rangers, which was like being a Boy Scout. Jeannine eventually joined the Missionettes, the Girl Scout equivalent.

My social life revolved around youth group. At home I started tuning my radio to Christian rock stations. I'd found my anchor. I made friends with a girl named Jennifer. She and I had made plans for her to spend the night at my place after a youth group bonfire. I had told Pastor Jimmy, who had given me a ride to the bonfire that evening, that Jennifer would be sleeping over. "That's great, April," he said. I knew he was happy that I was developing close friendships within the church. But that night, as the kids all talked around the fire, ate s'mores, prayed, sang songs, played games like twenty questions, Jennifer didn't sit with me. When the evening ended and we all stood up to go home, I walked over to her and she told me she'd made arrangements to spend the night with other girls. They didn't invite me to join them. I didn't let on that I felt betrayed or sad. I didn't blame her for not wanting to sleep over at my crappy little apartment with the cockroaches. But they could have invited me to come along with them. None of the teenage girl friendship dynamics were lost on Pastor Jimmy, who at the end of the evening dropped me off at home. He hugged me. "You're a wonderful person, April," he said. "You are strong. It's the trials we go through that make us stronger." *If so*, I thought, *I should be pretty strong by now.*

Even my friends were not truly my friends. I kept up with Jennifer so she wouldn't realize how much she'd hurt me. At school, Richard's face lit up whenever I walked into the classroom, and I could tell he wanted to be closer to me but I kept him at arm's length. Something held me back from letting anyone become really close to me. I didn't like how exclusive female friendships in school were. I didn't want to be in a clique, even if they would have had me. I went out of my way to include the outcasts, sticking up for them whenever they were teased. I knew only too well how being a pariah felt. People who needed help were like projects to me. Still, I wondered if there was ever a place I'd feel like I fit in.

In sports, I didn't have to worry about fitting in. I just played my position and that was good enough to be part of a team. The Village softball league had kids of all ages—and of all sizes. In one practice session, an enormous kid hit a long, low drive straight to right field. I was the first baseman and caught the ball right as the big guy came pounding into first base. I was thrown to the ground. The guy had come in like a freight train and landed on my ankle. I was in an itchy cast from foot to knee for six weeks and I had to walk to school with crutches, making my armpits more sore than my ankle. If Dad had been around, I caught myself thinking, he'd give me a ride. But Dad wasn't around. He wasn't where a dad should be, there to take care of his family. But *my* dad wasn't like other dads. *My* dad was exactly where he should be. Behind bars.

Having a father in prison made me different from the other kids in school and church, but not in the Villages. I had this in common with many of the girls in Puffy's gang. In other ways, I couldn't be more different. I didn't look like them or dress like them. I didn't drink or have any interest in doing anything illegal. Some of Puffy's friends were well on their way to a life that was likely to end up in prison as well. I wanted no part of that.

Many families in the Village were multigenerational, with children, mothers, and grandmothers, but rarely fathers. I tried to imagine what our lives would have been like if Mom had left Dad and moved in with her parents. It wasn't worth pondering, though. I just could not conjure the images of what that life would have looked like.

I wasn't much interested in attending any of the parties Puffy kept inviting me to, but I felt I had to accept an invitation, otherwise it might give her the impression that I was either rude or racist like Dad. My ankle was still in a cast, and I hobbled into the party on crutches. It was at the apartment of one of Puffy's friends. Most of her friends had graduated from high school or had dropped out. I was still in eighth grade. At the party, I sat on the sofa and was plied with some kind of punch. I lost track of how many I had. I began to feel sick and limped to the bathroom to vomit. And then I passed out on the sofa. I woke up in the morning with a terrible headache. I grabbed my crutches and hobbled back to my apartment building a half a block away. Luckily, I had told Mom that I would be spending the night at a friend's house, so when I came home in the morning, she wasn't suspicious. I just crawled into my bed and slept off my terrible hangover.

Later that day, Puffy told me I'd tried to do back flips down the stairs with my cast the night before. She and her friends had grabbed me and saved me from breaking my neck. I decided that drinking wasn't for me. I didn't smoke. I didn't do weed. I didn't even swear. I knew I was going to be a great disappointment to Puffy. But Puffy and her friends never teased me about my convictions. Maybe my fighting skills trumped my partying skills in their book. But they accepted me for who I was without judging me. And though I didn't want their lifestyle for myself, I didn't judge them for it, either.

I went to one last party at the end of the school year. This time, I knew to be careful to avoid the punch. I sat on a couch, listening to music and conversation, and watched Puffy and her friends dance in the smoky room. My cast was off, but I didn't feel comfortable dancing. The party was loud and hot and crowded. There were men and women of all ages. I was getting sleepy sipping my can of pop, and then the room began to spin. The next thing I knew, I was in a bed with a large grown man on top of me, crushing me. I panicked. I couldn't breathe. He stank of sweat. And there was a stabbing between my legs that was unbearable. I tried to cry out, but I felt like I was under water. I had never had sex before. I had no idea who he was, but I knew what he was doing to me. I was so terrified that I froze, unable to move because he pinned me down and because I could not make my body move. I must have passed out because I don't remember anything else until I woke up at dawn in this strange bedroom alone. My skirt was bunched up around my waist, my underwear was gone, I was sore between my legs, and my head ached.

I stumbled out of the bed and found my underwear on the carpet. I found the bathroom and sat on the toilet, catching my reflection in the mirror as I did—a wide-eyed, frightened stranger. There was blood when I wiped myself with my shaking hand.

I walked past sleeping forms in chairs and couches. I stepped over the empty bottles and cups on the floor and let myself out. As I walked home to my apartment building I was trembling, sick to my stomach. I vomited in the grass in front of someone's house. I was able to let myself into my apartment without waking anyone. I crawled into my bed and pulled the covers over me and sobbed.

As I lay in bed, I thought of my father's memoir and the section he included with advice for people to avoid becoming victims of crimes. In one section called "Woman! Protect Thyself from Evil" he had written: "A woman who behaves foolishly in public, however innocently meant, often finds herself in serious trouble." Had I behaved foolishly in public? Was what happened to me at the party my own fault? I felt a deep shame and prayed that I would be forgiven. I didn't think I deserved to be forgiven, but Pastor Jimmy was always telling us that God was merciful and that there was nothing so bad that it was beyond forgiveness if we prayed and asked the Lord to come into our hearts. I asked and I prayed for my salvation. I prayed for my whole family. And I even prayed for my father.

When the school year was over, Mom found a new place to live, a duplex up a hill outside the Village. Moving extracted me from Puffy and her gang. I don't know why Mom moved us. It wasn't because she knew what had happened to me. I had told no one about what happened that night at the party. I didn't even tell myself what happened that night. "Rape" was a word I had heard before, but I thought it didn't apply to me.

After that party, I moved closer to the kids in youth group and Pastor Jimmy and the New Castle First Assembly of God. The youth group had adult chaperones who functioned as surrogate parents. Jennifer became my best friend despite the previous year's sleepover "misunderstanding." She had a wild streak that complemented my strict adherence to the church teachings. She didn't seem afraid to act out a little bit. She wasn't controlled by her dad in the way I had been controlled by mine. Jennifer's father, Mr. Barber, was the Ranger leader, and took my brothers under his wing.

During one day at Sunday school, I was weepy. Jennifer asked me what was wrong, and I honestly didn't know. She recognized that I needed help, even though I didn't realize it myself. Church services were going on and Jennifer slipped into the sanctuary and emerged with a woman a moment later. Wendy was a social worker at the Bair Foundation, a Christian organization that places children at risk in foster care. Wendy invited me to go into an empty Sunday school room. Jennifer came with me. As I took a seat, I focused on the posters on the walls depicting scenes from the Bible. Mom and my siblings had gone to see Wendy, who also provided counseling for families whose parents were in prison or in trouble. So she knew my dad was in prison without me needing to tell her. But this was the first time I had met her.

"What are you feeling, April?" Wendy asked me. I noticed her beaded necklace and the way she wore a little red rouge on her cheeks. She exuded kindness and patience.

I didn't say anything for a while. I thought about what had happened the night of the party, but I couldn't talk about it. I would never, ever tell a soul.

There was something I could talk about, though, and I shared that I was afraid that Dad would come home early. I couldn't tell her why I was dreading his return. Even from prison, he had control over me. I wanted to tell her what it was like living with him, that I would flinch at the sound of his belt buckle hitting the floor when he undressed. The way he hit Mom for no reason at all. The way dinner was a daily torture to get through, waiting for him to explode. It wasn't always like this, but this was the only way I could remember it being. I didn't tell her any of that. Wendy listened to what I told her and also seemed to be hearing what I wasn't saying. She counseled me, "April, don't ever forget what you have gone through, because God is going to use you one day to help others."

Her words stayed with me. I wanted to help others. It gave me hope that what I had gone through was not for nothing.

Before the start of ninth grade, Mom took me to a dentist and my braces were removed. Not once since I got the braces in fifth grade had a professional looked into my mouth. Getting them taken off felt significant, like some of the shackles in my life were being removed. I was able to begin New Castle High School confident at least in the way I looked, even if in other ways I still felt like I didn't belong. Some of the kids were the same ones I knew from middle school, including Richard, so it was not really like starting over. But I was not the same. By now, I had a booming babysitting business among the families in the congregation, and I used my earnings to buy makeup, clothing, and all of my own hygiene products like tampons, deodorant, and shampoo and body wash that smelled like flowers.

In my father's absence, I began thinking about ways I could create a life that was nothing like my mother's. I saw my mother as weak, as a victim. I felt sorry for her that she was never able to stand up to Dad, but I understood that it was impossible for her to do so safely. She had no voice. She had lost it long ago when she married him. I was angry at her for getting herself—and her children—into this situation to begin with. I realized that without my father, I wouldn't exist, but I didn't like to think that I had come from him. That I was *of* him. I knew that I needed a plan so I didn't end up like my parents, on the move constantly, unable to properly feed and clothe and house their children. I wasn't going to be a victim. I was going to use my voice.

The life I wanted required independence and that required money. My babysitting business expanded by word of mouth among church families and spread to teachers at school. I started stockpiling my earnings. I figured I'd have four years of high school without Dad and calculated that I could save a sizable chunk during that time.

The Lawrence County School District had an excellent vocational program, which I switched to for tenth grade, hoping to graduate high school with the training and certification to go straight into a well-paid job as a medical secretary. My friend Jennifer from youth group attended the same program. The vocational branch had a separate campus and a separate school bus, and that's where I met Mark, a boy in the welding program. He was so shy at first, it took me a few weeks to realize that he was funny. He seemed older than a lot of the other boys. His own dad didn't work much, and Mark had to help keep his family afloat. With him, I felt like I could be honestly myself. He had a sweetness about him. I was smitten. And the amazing thing to me was that the feeling was mutual.

Soon Mark began picking me up at the bus stop in his restored light green 1974 Oldsmobile Cutlass Supreme. We'd arrive at school each morning in style. He'd head off to the welding school and I headed off to the classrooms.

My main teacher, Mrs. Houk, transformed her classroom into our future workplace. We wore white scrubs, like we were working in a doctor's office. We had to keep our nails short with no nail polish. We were expected to behave like professionals. She had a kind of faith in me that my own mother never expressed. "You'll go far, April," she told me often.

Mrs. Houk was an adviser for the school's chapter of the FBLA, Future Business Leaders of America. FBLA was a huge national organization, and her students held offices in regional, state, and national positions. Her students won competitions at every level. With her encouragement, I joined the club, ran for secretary, and was elected. Jennifer and I competed in the category of Parliamentary Procedures and our team won events in the regional and state level competitions two years in a row.

My competitive salesmanship prowess came in handy in fundraising my travel to FBLA conferences. I went door-to-door with a cardboard suitcase, selling the heck out of candy bars, notepads, pens, and trinkets. My fundraising was so successful that once I'd raised enough for my hotel and meal expenses, I gave the rest to Mrs. Houk, who allotted it to other FBLA members who were short on funds. "April, you have a gift!" she'd said.

Once I headed up a fundraising campaign to help a student get a heart and lung transplant. I realized that I'd learned how to be a good salesman from Dad. And I also realized that with his drive he could have been a successful man, if he hadn't been a criminal. I felt a glimmer of hope for my future. If I had his talent for sales, maybe I could be successful in life, because I was 99.9 percent sure that I did not share his criminal nature. If I was a criminal, I would already know it. I had always wanted to be a good girl. Maybe I had what it took to be good *and* successful as an adult.

• • •

My high school years are divided in my mind into two eras. *Light* and *Darkness*. In the Light era, Dad was in prison, I had a boyfriend. I was thriving in school and kicking butt as a Future Business Leader of America club member. I was finding my way to God and finally making good friends. Maybe we lived with cockroaches, but Mom and us five kids felt safe in our home.

We woke up in the morning and had breakfast before school, slurping up whatever cereal we wanted to have. There were no special foods or drinks off-limits. Mom smiled. We all laughed more and fought less. I slept in my bed at night without fear that someone in my family would come home and stab one of us in a fit of rage.

The summer before tenth grade, we moved out of the duplex on the hill to a three-bedroom house on Court Street. It was just shy of being condemned. It had a washer and dryer in the basement, which was so cobwebbed, dark, and smelly—with scuttling, invisible creatures—that I tried to stretch out laundry day as much as possible. That winter was cold, and my brothers and I would sit on the dining room floor around the heater grate as if it were a campfire. They begged me to tell them scary stories the way Dad did when we were younger. I always used an abandoned house in Doylestown as the setting; with each new telling, the details became more frightening. There was the story about the claw hand that reached up from the floorboards, and the mysterious cries the people heard only to discover that they were coming from a locked closet. Inside the closet was a bloodstain that grew bigger and bigger. And then I'd grab one of my brother's arms and he would scream and jump, causing us all to jump and then collapse in peals of relieved laughter. I had learned the jump scare from a master. Once, right at the most suspenseful point in my story, a clank came from the heater grate, and we all jumped out of our skins. The adrenalin rush of fright was familiar to us, but here, in the safe space of our dining room floor, on our own terms, it was fun again.

But the fun came to an end when Dad was released on parole after only two years in prison. I had figured I'd be out of high school when he was released. I had only gotten through tenth grade when the *Darkness* era came.

26

Darkness

None of us kids were excited about this news. Dad had been telling us on collect calls from the prison that there was a good chance he'd be coming home early, but I hadn't believed him.

Apparently, it was true. Dad was going to be released early because he had exposed* the crimes some of the incarcerated men had committed that the police hadn't known about. He was a prison snitch, and his reward was shortened prison time.*

His reward was my punishment. It was almost summer, and I'd been looking forward to time with Mark and my friends from church. But now I was only full of dread.

"April," Mom said to me when we learned that indeed Dad would be coming home any day. "Things will be different now." I wondered how long things would be "different." Probably only as long as it took for him to plant himself in the recliner and demand that someone get him his cigarettes. But Mom also believed that my brothers needed their father. She was afraid that they were getting into trouble, and knew that Dad would keep them in line.

And sure enough, one day when we got home from school, there he was in the living room, standing with arms wide and a smile so big I thought it might crack his face in two.

He moved into the house on Court Street with us. As shabby and unsuitable for human habitation as it was, it had been preferable to living anywhere with Dad. But now that he was back, there was nothing any of us could do

---

* He lied and was later sued by the person he "snitched" on.

about it. There were behaviors of his that I didn't question before he was arrested. Now that he was back, I began to notice them and wonder why, for example, he never closed the door to the bathroom when he used the toilet. And he thought nothing of walking in on us when we were using the bathroom or in the shower. There were no boundaries. This was not new—he'd always been like this. But what had never seemed strange before, now seemed like assaults on my privacy. It was like he was saying, *When you think you're alone, you're not alone. I'm back. I'm here. I will always be here.*

Dad went to church with us. I couldn't recall him ever doing that before. New Castle First Assembly of God's sanctuary held over six hundred people. He stood in front of the congregation and thanked the people in the church and declared himself a changed person. He spoke like a preacher, getting emotional, his deep voice resonating through the sanctuary. The congregation clapped wildly. I looked around at the smiles on every face. Forgiveness was at the heart of our church. We humbled ourselves before God. But I knew that humbling himself was not in Dad's bag of tricks. I knew he was not sincere. He was using his lying voice. He was putting on a show. The crowd loved it and he ate up their praise.

After services, people came up to Dad, hugging him, welcoming him with open arms. Mom was hopeful that he had changed, too. Just like he'd had a metamorphosis before she'd met him, she believed he had done it again—been reformed. She was glad to have him back.

I was not. Now that Dad was back, he wouldn't let me wear makeup. The first time I left the house to meet up with Jennifer, he stopped me at the door. In the two years Dad had been gone, I had perfected my makeup routine, meticulously applying foundation and mascara, eyeshadow and lipstick each morning.

But now Dad said, "You can't leave this house looking like a whore!"

He made me scrub it off before I left. I felt naked and vulnerable without my makeup.

He didn't like the way I styled my hair and ordered me to stop cutting it. He also had problems with the clothes I wore.

If a skirt was too short, pants too tight, shirt too clingy, he'd make me change. One night a church parent—a father—came by to pick me up to babysit. Dad stopped me when I came downstairs, and said right in front of him, "Get back up there and change into something decent!" Dressing provocatively was the last thing I wanted to do and was careful to dress modestly but fashionably. But Dad didn't even want me looking attractive in any way.

My appearance wasn't the only thing about me that Dad disapproved of. He didn't like that I went out with friends. In fact, he didn't like that I *had* friends. He especially didn't like that I had a boyfriend. I was now not allowed to call Mark, and we were never able to go out alone together. Instead, Mark would come over and Dad would put him to work.

Dad got a gig fixing up an old house with the plan that we'd move into it. This house had a big garden, and he gave the responsibility of the garden to me. He had ambitious plans for it, and, when school was out for summer, I had to execute them. Planting in June involved hot, backbreaking work with a hoe. One day, when Dad was inside the house working on wiring, Mark came over as I was hacking a semi straight line to plant green beans. Sweat was pouring down my face. I stood up and wiped my brow on my sleeve and stopped when I saw him staring at me.

"What?" I asked.

"Nothing," he said. "You just look really pretty without makeup."

I blushed and got back to hacking away at the dirt, and Mark picked up the bag of beans and started planting. Jeannine and her friend Sarah had come over to the house to play in the big yard, and Sarah brought a doll that had dark skin, like her. Mark and I toiled in the garden while the girls played nearby. We were jolted by a bloodcurdling scream. It was Sarah, and she was staring in horror at the house. I looked up, expecting to see Dad falling out a window or something like that. Instead, I saw in one of the bedroom windows, Sarah's doll, hanging by a noose around her neck, swinging.

I ran into the house, shaking with rage, wishing it had been my father hanging in the window. I didn't know what to do with my fury.

"She's just a little kid!" I screamed at him.

"Come on, April. It was a joke!" Dad said, getting mad at me. I knew that if Mark hadn't been there, I would have been backhanded, but Mark was a buffer. Dad might humiliate me in front of other people, but he wouldn't physically harm me in public.

I ran to the window and rescued the doll, cradling her in my arms as I returned her to Sarah in the yard.

Sarah cried as she took her doll. Jeannine tried to comfort her friend, but I knew Sarah would never come play with Jeannine again. Mark and I just looked at each other, and I shook my head. *Now you know. Welcome to my world.*

One Saturday, Dad and I were alone at the house, caulking the tiles in the downstairs bathroom. I was planning to go to the county fair with Mark that night. The rest of my family was going to the fair, too. Dad started asking me questions about what Mark and I did sexually. I was a devout Christian girl and sex was off-limits by my own set of rules. But Dad didn't believe me. He asked me if Mark had put his hand down my pants yet. He asked if we had done anything in the back seat of Mark's car. I objected, indignant, and said that Mark and I had only kissed. Then Dad asked me if Mark gave me hickeys.

"What's a hickey?" I said.

"You don't know what a hickey is?" Dad asked as if I was lying.

I shook my head, afraid of the gleam in his eye.

"I'll show you," he said, and he grabbed me and started sucking on my neck. I froze. What was happening? I wanted him to hit me, punch me, kick me, anything but what he was doing. Finally, he stopped and threw me down on the cold tiles. "You can show that to Mark," he spat, and left me curled in on myself in shame on the bathroom floor.

I felt like throwing up. I didn't know if I could look at Dad again.

That night, as we drove to the fair, Mark noticed. He said, "What's that?"

Until then, I hadn't realized that there was a mark on my neck, but now I understood that Dad had wanted Mark to see the fresh hickey. He thought it would provoke a fight, that Mark would think I was cheating and leave me.

I looked in the visor mirror and felt bile rise in my throat. I began sputtering and ranting. When Mark understood that my father had given me the hickey, he grew silent. He didn't know what to say, but I could tell he was worried for me. *Save your worries for yourself,* I wanted to say.

Mark and I managed to have a fun night at the fair. I avoided my family, which was easy in the big crowd. When Mark dropped me off, we lingered on the porch. Then he surprised me with a gift of gold teddy bear earrings. We kissed.

Then came the crunch of the van's tires on gravel. The family piled out of the van. Dad was seething.

His voice was flat and all the more frightening because he didn't raise it.

"You better leave," he said to Mark. That was all. He said nothing to me until I was in the house.

I didn't go inside until I saw Mark safely behind the wheel of his car. Then I entered the house and held my breath, bracing myself. I got the rebuke I expected, full of profanity. I was a slut and I would end up a pregnant whore.

That night, I wrote a Dear John letter. I didn't trust myself to break up with Mark in person. If I'd had to look into his kind eyes, I would have broken down sobbing. Here, in the privacy of my dark bedroom where no one could see my tears, I wrote to Mark advising him that he would be better off dating someone else. Someone who had more freedom. I wrote that trying to talk me out of the breakup was a waste of breath. I could not tell him that my father was too much, too powerful, too frightening, and that I liked Mark too much to risk his life. He wrote me two letters and I didn't respond to either. Finally, he got the message, but I knew he was as heartbroken as I was.

I now felt such revulsion for Dad that it pained me to be in the same room with him. But the church community had bought his story of redemption and welcomed him back as a reformed man, and a good-hearted one. He volunteered to drive the church van and pick up people who needed rides to services every Sunday and he even attended some services himself. But he was fooling all of them.

When the lease was up on the Court Street house, we couldn't move as planned to the house with the vegetable garden I'd planted, because Dad had a falling-out with the owner. That was okay with me because that house already held terrible memories and we hadn't even spent a single night in it. Thanks to the hickey, the entire house represented Dad's control over me, and I seethed within the grip of his control. But once again, we were without a place to live.

My Sunday school teacher was an older woman named Nellie Montgomery, and she and her husband, Don, lived in a two-bedroom cinderblock house with their twenty-two-year-old son Jerry, the youngest of their four children and the only one still living at home. Don was a car mechanic and Nellie worked at Goodwill. Dad befriended Nellie and Don. He must have made a good impression because when we moved out of the house on Court Street we moved into the Montgomerys' house. We all slept in the living room. Mom and Dad shared one pullout sofa, Jeannine and I shared another, and my brothers slept on the floor in between. I couldn't believe this was happening again. Ten people shared one bathroom. Somehow, Dad had come back into our lives and plunged us right back into the cramped living conditions that we were forced into when he first went to jail awaiting trial. We had taken a giant step backward. Once again, a church member took pity on him and his family and took us in like lost sheep. But I didn't feel lost. I was mad. I didn't want to be squeezed into a small house with another family. It was bad enough to be squeezed into a small house with my own.

The Montgomerys' house was on a patch of farmland, surrounded by woods and other rural parcels. Dad acquired a school bus like the one we'd had on Kevin Drive and parked it in the Montgomerys' yard. It contained all our belongings—books, dolls, toys, keepsakes, furniture. We strung curtain rods in the bus to hang our clothes. I would go to the bus the night before school and select what I was going to wear the next day. We all shared one bathroom. Mornings were an exercise in speed grooming and dressing. I was glad to see that Dad at least had the decency to close the door when he used the bathroom in someone else's house, but he would still barge in when it was one of his own family using it.

Nellie got Mom a job at the Goodwill store, and she got Dad a job driving the Goodwill truck to pick up donations. He would often bring my brothers with him when he did pickup rounds, and I overheard Nellie telling Don that some of the people who had donated furniture complained that the driver just sat there while he made the boys do all the work.

As repayment for living there, Dad told Nellie and Don he would put a new roof on the house. Don supplied all the materials and Dad supplied the labor: his three eldest children. David, John, and I would go up ladders in the blazing afternoon summer sun to lay out the chalk lines, line up shingles, and drive in nails.

Meanwhile, the bus sat on the lawn, weeds growing thick beneath and around it, reminding me every day how long we had been there.

But the plan was to eventually move to an old wreck of a farmhouse nearby. That fall, we kids were the weekend demolition crew, tasked with ripping out all the plaster walls of the old farmhouse. We got covered with black dust as we carted pieces of lath outside to a burn pile. One day, as we were hard at work, Grandpa Hedderly's car pulled up to the farmhouse. He'd driven over an hour from Akron. He stepped out along with my cousin Todd, whom we hadn't seen in years. I looked down at my sweat-stained, blackened T-shirt. I looked like a chimney sweep. I was embarrassed, but I was also exhausted and would have loved nothing more than to visit with Grandpa and Todd. But Dad had given us a tight deadline that we had to finish tearing out the plaster in the downstairs by the end of the day, and we were afraid to stop working. I didn't know where Dad was. He would often give us orders and then leave the site. I was so frightened of the consequences if we didn't complete our task that I couldn't stop to talk to Grandpa and Todd. They soon got back in the car and left.

Nellie and Don's son Jerry felt so sorry for us that, while we were in school, he and a friend finished tearing out the remaining walls.

Junior prom was coming up. My best friends from school and I made a plan to go to prom together without dates. It was going to be an awesome girls' night, and it didn't stop there. The next day we were all going to the Future Business Leaders of America conference.

"You're not going to prom with your friends, April," Dad said. "Jerry is going to take you."

"What are you talking about?" I said. "Jerry's a grown man." He was at least five years older than me. I had just turned seventeen. He was a sweet guy, and I know Dad trusted him, but what would a grown man do at a junior prom?

Nevertheless, I couldn't argue with Dad. He'd asked Jerry to take me to the prom, and for whatever reason, Jerry didn't feel like he could say no. Maybe Dad didn't trust that I wasn't meeting a guy at prom and sent Jerry as his spy. I had nothing against Jerry personally. I was just so disappointed not to go with my girlfriends. We were all supposed to gather at Lori's house to get ready for prom together, do each other's hair and makeup. To bond. We'd planned to go in Jennifer's car. Unlike Dad, Mr. Barber had allowed—even encouraged—his daughter to take driver's ed and get her license. But now I wasn't going to drive with them, singing along to whatever was on the radio.

Now I had to get ready for prom with my father scrutinizing my dress and my hair, making sure I hadn't used too much blush or lipstick. Jerry wore a black suit and I wore a floor-length, bright pink satin dress with ruffles on the sleeves that I'd bought from Goodwill. I accessorized with white gloves and white high-heel pumps. Jerry drove, and in the car we didn't sing or even listen to the radio on the way. When we walked into the reception hall, he made a beeline for the teachers standing around the punch table, many of whom he knew from his high school days, and that's where he stayed all evening. I made a beeline for the bathroom to add a touch more makeup. My friends arrived, looking glamorous and perfectly groomed. I danced with them that night, understanding that those pre-prom hours of sisterhood I had missed were something I wouldn't be able to get back. It was just one more way my dad was robbing me of what remained of my childhood. He was choking off memories before they could be formed. They were lost opportunities that could never be re-created. Boyfriends, friends, and even, it turned out, college.

27

On My Own

I returned one late afternoon after school to find police cars and a fire truck in the driveway. I felt a flash of panic.

As soon as Dad saw me, he called me over. I'd never seen him so agitated.

"April," he looked me in the eye and hissed. "Go find your brother. If he doesn't come back, I'm going to send him to juvenile detention. And you better find him."

The police were there because David had run away. He and my father had argued. Dad was forcing my brother to work, and David had had enough. Dad had threatened to beat him, so David ran off. Nellie had called the police. There were two ponds on the property and a fire rescue truck was on the scene with a crew to drag the ponds. I wondered what had been said to the police to make them think they should take this extreme action. Did they think David was dead?

I had to find David. I couldn't bear him getting sent away to juvenile detention. The stakes were high for my father. Not finding David would mean scrutiny by the police, exposure, revelations of abuse and forced labor. Dad wasn't going to chance that and I knew his threat to send him away was not idle. I took off running through the tall grasses of the field, crying as I called my brother's name over and over again, pleading with him to show himself. I heard John and Jeff calling his name from a far field. I entered the strip of darkening woods between fields and kept calling, telling him that he had to come out or Dad would send him away to a juvenile detention center.

Finally, I gave up and walked back to the house. It was getting dark. The police were still milling around when David crawled out from beneath the school bus. Its weeds had offered the perfect hiding place. He had been there the whole time. Dad rushed to him and made a show of affection, wrapping him in a crushing hug. Then the officers gathered around David, taking him off to the side while my father looked on. Dad had good reason to worry. He gathered Jeff and John and me around him.

"David had better keep his mouth shut," he said. "If he doesn't, they can take him away."

He stared at us as if this was all our fault. He put the blame for whatever David said and whatever was about to happen squarely on our shoulders as if we could communicate telepathically to David to say nothing incriminating.

But whatever David said to the police, they did not take him away. I expected each of us kids to be questioned by police. In fact, I wanted them to ask me about my father's behavior, but they left after talking to David.

I wondered what David had told the police. Whatever he'd said, it had not blown Dad's cover. But I still thought David was heroic. He was the only one of us to overtly defy my father. I had defied him plenty of times in my mind, but never to his face.

Dad was quiet. He couldn't unleash himself on David because Nellie and Don were watching. Nellie had been getting on Dad's nerves lately. Tensions had risen between them when some of the items he picked up for Goodwill never made it to the Goodwill store. Very likely he'd sold them along the way. It also turned out that Dad had been using the church van to run his own errands. Church members had noticed it in parking lots all over town. More than once, he kept it overnight. Both those volunteer driving jobs ended abruptly. The Montgomerys were way too close for comfort. They knew too much about us. It was high time to move out of their living room and into the farmhouse we were still renovating, which was just far enough away through woods and fields as to be out of sight.

The farmhouse had a chicken coop and a big enough field to acquire a young bull named Willy. This was not the same as the dairy cow that we had in Florida that I milked twice a day. Willy was being raised for meat. I wasn't a vegetarian, but I didn't want any part of taking care of Willy. I knew I'd get too attached to him.

We moved into that house before the drywall had been put up. The walls were down to studs when we carried the furniture inside and up the stairs into our bedrooms. But we were living in the lap of luxury compared to Jonathan, the guy to whom Dad rented out the chicken coop as lodgings. This poor kid—eighteen years old—had fallen on hard times. He had a job, but no place to live. Dad offered him the chicken coop for a low rent—but hard cash nonetheless. It had no plumbing other than a bucket of water and a bucket for waste. A cot with a dirty blanket were all that the coop had in the way of amenities.

It was winter, and Jonathan reminded me of that poor horse in Portersville. I wanted to bring him into the house to warm him up. Dad never offered. He liked to tell people the "hilarious" story about the kid in his chicken coop who had to crap in a bucket. The level Dad had sunk to make a few bucks truly shocked me. Where was his humanity? Was he really this depraved? I wanted to alert someone to Jonathan's living conditions, but I was afraid that Dad would find out and then what would Dad do to me? Jonathan had come from an abusive home, so his sense of alarm wasn't raised about the danger my father presented. He just listened and nodded when Dad told him that if he ever caught Jonathan in the house while I was at home, he would kill him.

But luckily Jonathan had a friend, Michelle, who had no idea of the squalor he endured until she and her grandmother came to check on him one night. They found him in a state of hypothermia. Michelle's grandmother brought him home with her, where he lived until he went away to Bible college.

As eleventh grade came to a close, I was offered a summer job as the school receptionist. I'm sure Mrs. Houk had played a role in this wonderful turn of events. The pay was great. It still left me time to babysit in the evenings and weekends. This also meant I was hardly ever home. I would ride my bike to and from work rain or shine—sometimes arriving a sweaty mess or drenched from torrential downpours. I got home each evening in time to grab something to eat, change my clothes, and go out to youth group, or get picked up by a parent who had hired me to babysit that night. I did everything I could to make myself scarce.

I knew that Willy the bull was destined for the freezer, but I tried not to think about it until the night I came to the table for dinner and saw that we were having steak. I was immediately suspicious. This must be Willy. I ate the mashed potatoes on my plate and then the corn and didn't touch the steak. Dad got angry. We were still required to eat everything that had been put on our plate. That's how he had always raised us. If we'd gone to hell in a hand-basket while he was gone, that wasn't his fault. We had to toe the line now that he was back and that's all there was to it.

"April," he said to me in a low voice. The controlled rage in his tone made me wish he was yelling and throwing things. "You're not getting up from the table until you finish that steak."

I didn't see how I was going to get out of this. Mom and even Jeannine had finished their steaks. The boys of course had wolfed theirs down first thing. I began to cut into the meat and my knife and fork slipped, causing the slab to jump off my plate. My brothers snickered. David said, "Oops, there goes Willy kicking!"

I didn't think this was funny, but I cut a piece of steak and put it into my mouth. As soon as I began to chew, Dad said, "Mooo."

Tears streamed down my face as I continued to chew. I cut that steak into small pieces and chewed and swallowed and repeated until my plate was empty. With each bite that I got down my gullet, I hated my father more. I was counting the days until I could graduate from high school and leave home forever.

Jennifer and I were looking forward to our senior year together. We were going to be senior officers in Future Business Leaders of America. Jennifer was going to serve as president of the state district. I was looking forward to serving as Western district president. But Dad had other plans. He announced just a few days before school started that we were moving back to Ohio. On my last day of my summer job at the school, Mrs. Houk gave me a charm bracelet with three charms. One was a lighthouse, which she told me was to remind me to "Let my light shine." She said, "Don't let anyone dampen your bright light, April." She had been helping me decide which colleges to apply to. Mrs. Houk's last bit of advice to me was to request the applications be sent to my new address, whenever I knew it. In the past, Dad didn't tell us where we were moving next. This time, however, he had told us but forbade us to tell anyone else. I didn't even tell Mrs. Houk. Both she and I wept, saying goodbye. Her brow was furrowed in concern and sorrow.

One more time, my family packed up the van—we'd had to sell the camper when Dad was in jail—and off we drove to the small village of Burton, Ohio, to a new church, a new school, a new life. Moving back to the state of Ohio was symbolic for Dad. It was his home, the place he felt most connected to, and it was a new start for our family. Dad had arranged for us to live in yet another dilapidated house, this one owned, ironically, by his nemesis, the Catholic church.

The house was run-down, with an attached garage that had been converted into an apartment. The apartment had a tenant. Dad was not nice to the man, and he gave all of us kids instructions not to talk to him. The house itself had an odor of dirty socks that permeated every room. But there were no fleas or cockroaches. I shared a room upstairs with Jeannine, and my brothers shared another. The highlight of this house was the river behind it and a cabin set beside the running water. The cabin had once been quaint, you could tell. Across from the river, was a bar, a place where Dad could go in the evenings.

The school we would attend went from grades seven to twelve. For the first time, I'd be going to the same school with all three of my brothers. I learned quickly that this school was not going to be anything like the Lawrence County vocational high school I'd just come from. For starters, there were no class options for vocational training. There was no Future Business Leaders of America. There was, however, Future Farmers of America. The FFA was a club I was not interested in. I later learned that my FBLA team went to nationals that year, and I missed it.

Where I had received thoughtful advice about college from Mrs. Houk, here the guidance counselor looked at me like she was surprised at my question when I poked my head into her office. She just handed me financial aid forms.

I took the forms home that day and gave them to Dad. I spoke excitedly about colleges at the dinner table that night. I couldn't help myself. I told Dad that I was hoping to go to college in Pittsburgh to major in business administration. Dad didn't appear to be listening to anything that I was saying. A couple days later, I passed by his recliner in the living room. He always had a cluttered TV table next to his chair, containing an ashtray stuffed with Camel butts, coffee cups—he drank coffee morning, noon, and night—medicine bottles, unpaid bills and paperwork, and always a bag of candy. We were not allowed to touch his candy. If we were all watching TV, he might throw a piece at each of us, like a gift bestowed, while he ate piece after piece of candy throughout the whole movie. He had a trash can next to the table usually filled with candy wrappers. Tonight, I saw that there, in the trash, lying among the wrappers, was the application for financial aid ripped in half. I ran upstairs to my room and broke down and wept. *How would I ever get to college? How would I escape?*

The next day, I went to the guidance counselor's office and asked for another set of financial aid forms. Once again I took them home, but this time I filled out as much information as I could myself. I presented them to my father, showing him the parts I couldn't fill out and asking him to fill in those lines himself and sign the forms. I told him it wouldn't cost him anything. And that I could go to one of the local colleges instead of the one in Pittsburgh. He said he'd look the forms over, but I never saw them again. I was too afraid to ask him for them. Mom never had any idea about our finances or taxes, or if we even paid taxes. I didn't bother trying to ask her for help.

I recalled in Dad's memoir, that he wrote of the importance of education, and how proud he was of the one he got in prison. But now he was unwilling to help me pursue mine. The weeks and months ticked by, and I missed the application deadlines. Classmates all spoke with excitement about what they were doing the following year. I just remained silent on the subject.

. . .

All three of my brothers joined the school wrestling team. Jeff became friendly with another kid on the wrestling team, Dannie. He was a shy, skinny kid, his knees the widest part of his legs. Dannie Boy, as Dad called him, became a frequent fixture at our house. It was obvious that Dannie Boy looked up to Dad and Dad soaked up the adoration.

At the wrestling matches, Dad cheered loudest for his boys. And they often won. But he cheered for all the boys, including Dannie, while he flirted with Dannie's foster mom. Whether Dad gravitated to the bleachers near the moms or they gravitated to where Dad sat, I never figured out, but he was always surrounded by women.

By now, I knew better than to invite girlfriends over to my house. I arranged to meet them outside, on the street. Laura was my friend from our new church, Burton Assembly of God. We met on Saturdays to hang out, and one Saturday I was running late. Unfortunately, she was running early. She got to my house and waited outside for a while, but it was hot, so she knocked on the door, hoping to wait inside. I was upstairs getting ready, applying makeup in such a way that Dad wouldn't object to it. I had become an expert in subtle use of cosmetics products, but it was a process that was harder to rush. I didn't hear Laura knock on the door. Dad did, and I'm sure he liked what he saw. Laura was pretty, with long brown hair. When I opened my bedroom door to head downstairs, I heard Dad's voice talking with someone. With a sick feeling, I came downstairs and there were Dad and Laura sitting in the living room. Dad was chatting in his most charming way; I felt hopeful that he had been on his best behavior, which was rare but acceptable when it kicked in. When Laura saw me, she popped up out of the chair and we left the house.

She didn't seem rattled as we walked down the driveway, so I thought things were okay. But the next minute Laura looked at me and said, "Wow, April. I'm never coming to your house again." I didn't ask her for specifics. I didn't know what Dad had said to her and I didn't want to. I just hung my head in shame. He hadn't changed at all.

. . .

During the years Dad was in prison, his sons grew bigger and stronger. I had grown, too. I was now technically an adult and built like a woman. Dad was interested to see how the power dynamic between his children had changed and what a fight would look like now that we were nearly grown. We hadn't had a formal fistfight since before he'd been arrested four years earlier. My brothers and I had no interest in pounding each other to oblivion, but my father wanted to see it again.

Generally I was moody and miserable that year. I would yell at my brothers to get out of my room. I'd even yell at my sister to leave me alone, and she and I shared a room, she on the top bunk and me on the bottom. I hung a sheet, creating a cave for myself in the bottom bunk, where I could read in peace and pretend no one else in my family existed.

But despite our occasional squabbles, my brothers and I had actually grown closer while Dad was in prison. Dad couldn't stand that. He tried to put wedges between us. He began setting us up to argue. He set traps for us. Telling us that one of us said something bad about the other or lied about another, trying to instigate a fight.

I was becoming increasingly icy toward Dad. When he yelled at me, he would get right up into my face, trying to get a rise. His spittle would splatter my cheeks. He made me look into his eyes. I know he could see what I was thinking. I would say to myself as I met his stare, "I hate you I hate you I hate you." I think he really wanted to see my brothers finally pummel me. He wanted them to do to me what he wanted to do but could not.

Sometimes John would push against my door, and I'd push from the other side to keep him from coming in. We'd end up in a shouting match. During one of these through-the-door arguments, Dad intervened. He told us we had to fight.

"I don't want to fight," I said. I thought it was barbaric. It felt creepy.

But Dad called me and David and John into the living room. He pitted me against John. "Work it out," he said, standing in front of us, his hands on his hips. He meant "fight it out," and we knew he'd beat us if we didn't beat each other.

I held back as John pulled my hair, literally coming away with fistfuls. My heart was not in it, and this infuriated Dad. The fight wasn't real. He wanted to see a real fight. He demanded that I fight with all my strength. I glared at him with venom, and something snapped inside me. I attacked John. I fought with a vengeance. I wasn't angry with my brother. It was Dad's face I saw when I punched him again and again. Dad let the fight go on and on. He wanted to prove that I couldn't take it. That I'd break it off first, like a coward. He wanted to see how far I would go. He got his answer, surprising us all, most of all myself. When I fully unleashed my fury, I fought like a crazy person. I scared myself. I scared my brother, and I was scared for him. For the first and only time, Dad stopped the fight. My brothers never forgot this fight, and they held my savagery against me. So in the end Dad won. He'd divided us. Divided, we could never unite against him.

Dad was a different parent to Jeannine and Jeff. He was hardest on his three oldest children. We were his minions. We had always been made to do the hardest labor, we were the ones he had forced to fight, we were the ones who got punished the hardest. It was as if the last two children were precious in some way that his first three were not. Jeff, who was still the favorite, could tease Dad, and even talk rudely, but in a jokey way. Jeff could defuse and deflect arguments with sarcasm or humor. "Old man, be quiet," he might say, and Dad might at first look like he wanted to smack him, but instead he'd just say, "Man, oh man," and shake his head and start laughing. I would have been too scared to talk to Dad that way. If I had, he might have thrown me across the room.

To get out of the house, I rode my bike past the cemetery to a park along the river. I brought a book, and just for an hour or so, I would feel far away. Then I got an after-school job at Lambert Chevrolet, a car dealership in downtown Burton, which was a few blocks from school. Dad would pick me up on his way home from his construction jobs and he charged me for gas. We were far beyond the days when we were a team, when he would burst with pride as he collected the bets on the campground races I won. We were no longer partners. It felt like centuries since the days of snuggles and naps on his chest. Now we were less than strangers. We were enemies.

The room I shared with Jeannine was a typical messy teenager's room when I was in a rush. The house was always messy and disorganized in general, but Dad wanted us to keep our rooms neat. Every now and then, I'd go through a purge and clean it. But it was messy on the day Dad made my brothers pick up all my stuff on my floor and throw it on the burn pile in our backyard. Not Jeannine's stuff or the stuff on my brothers' floor, just my stuff.

That day, when I got home from work, Dad wasn't there. I went up to my room as I always did when I got home to change my clothes. I saw that my side of the room was almost bare. Where there had been clothes on the floor, there was nothing. At first I thought, *Did someone put away my clothes?* But then I saw David and John hovering in the doorway to see my reaction.

"Where's my stuff?" I asked. I tried to act like it was no big deal.

"Look out back," John said, barely containing a nervous laugh.

I went out behind the house, which was where the burn pile was. The fire wasn't lit yet, but my clothes were tossed on top of the heap and coated in the ash from previous fires that had become slick like mud in a recent rain. My beautiful doll with black hair was there, too, her hair clotted with ash. The little treasure chest was on the heap. It was broken and the happy grams were scattered and wet. I knew the doll and the chest had not been on the floor. They lived on the windowsill, like they had in every room I'd slept in. This meant that my brothers, or maybe Dad himself, had taken not only the clothing pile on my floor but the most precious relics of my childhood and thrown them on the pile to burn. I felt a tight band around my chest and I started to breathe too fast. There was nowhere I was safe here at home. None of what I cherished was safe. Everything and anything or anyone I cared about was vulnerable to Dad's cruelty. And it was all to hurt me. He took pleasure in inventing ways to hurt me, to punish me for seeing him for who he was—a pouting, dangerous child.

This was when I understood that I was more mature than my father. He was stunted. I had surpassed him as the adult. I looked at my discarded childhood treasures and turned away. I could say goodbye to my childhood now. My father was almost worthy of my pity. But not quite.

That year in Burton, I would hear Dad talking to Jeff or Jeannine about me. He would recount nasty things that I'd said about them that I had never said. I sat on the stairwell listening to him, wondering if he was poisoning my relationships with my siblings forever. By this time, I realized that Dad was recording our phone calls. While I still wasn't allowed to call boys or girl-friends, they were allowed to call me. I began to suspect this when he'd blurt out information that I'd only spoken about while on the phone, such as who was dating whom or what grade I'd gotten on a paper.

But I never let him know I was on to him. Phone conversations were just another layer of perceived privacy that had been an illusion. In my father's house, there was no such thing as privacy. There was no such thing as my own life.

As graduation day approached, I was offered a full-time job at the car dealership. Dad said I had to start paying rent. But I had been saving my money for college, and with no college on the horizon for me, this was my ticket out of the house.

No one in my family said anything as I packed my meager belongings. Just my clothes and toiletries, a scrapbook that had somehow missed being thrown on the burn pile, my clarinet, and a camera I'd bought with my own money. I looked back at this room I shared with my little sister. I'd worry about her, but I wouldn't miss this room, or this house, or living with Dad. This had never been my "home." I wondered if I'd ever had one.

I rented a room in an apartment above the pizza parlor down the street from the car lot. My roommate was the manager at the pizza place. The apart-ment smelled like pizza, but I found the yeasty smell of the pillowy dough comforting. I loved my small bedroom and lying on my new twin bed listen-ing to the radio without worry that Dad would come barging in. I didn't have to fear the crunch of tires outside. I felt safe.

The eat-in kitchen was freshly painted a cheerful yellow. It was small but recently renovated, with new appliances. It was the cleanest kitchen I'd ever cooked in. I made my first meal—lasagna—in my own place, careful not to burn my fingers as I pulled hot noodles from the pot. I'd perfected the dish while Dad was in prison. My roommate and I sat down at the little round oak table, and I savored the aroma of the hot, bubbly dish that I'd labored over with pleasure. I ate with deep satisfaction and helped myself to seconds that I couldn't finish, which was perfectly okay. That might have been the best part.

Monday through Friday I worked at the dealership, sometimes until 9 p.m. I worked at the pizza parlor Friday and Saturday nights and Sunday afternoons. I went to church Sunday mornings. I was busy and making money, but I knew I needed full independence, so I took drivers ed. At the end of the course, I borrowed a car from a coworker and got my driver's license.

I put my college savings toward a 1984 blue Renault Alliance. I had a place to live, two jobs, and a car. At last, I never had to see Dad again.

PART THREE

Author's note: The events in the following chapters are told chronologically, even though some of the source materials—including police files, recordings, and articles—were made known to me only years later and over the course of time.

PART THREE

28

Checklist

My first morning in my new apartment felt luxurious. I got ready for work with no interruptions, wore what I pleased, and applied my makeup as I saw fit. I made my lunch, grabbed a granola bar and my purse, and was about to head out when I heard a knock at the door. I peeked through the peephole and stepped back when I saw Dad, his face looming large in the distorted lens.

Now what? I yanked the door open and Dad greeted me with a big grin and a bag of groceries.

I was too stunned to speak.

"Thanks," I finally said, taking the bag from him. He took a seat at my table and eyed the kitchen.

As I put away jars of peanut butter, a box of cereal, a loaf of bread, and boxes of spaghetti, I braced myself for him to ask me to cook him something. Or some other diversion that would make me late for work.

But Dad stood and said, "The place is nice."

"Thank you," I said, this time with more actual appreciation in my voice. "I have to leave for work in five minutes," I added. I was seized by the irrational worry that he was going to say he was moving in.

"Okay, sure, honey," he said. "Just wanted to see your new place."

And with that, he left. I didn't trust him further than I could throw him, but I did appreciate the gesture even as I feared an ulterior motive. He didn't stop by again.

I felt pretty good about having an independent life. I saw Mom and Jeannine at church every week, so I still kept tabs on them. David had joined the military when he graduated. John was talking about going to college. I asked

Mom how John was going to afford college. She said that Dad was helping him get loans and scholarships. I was speechless. Dad wouldn't lift a finger to help me when I had wanted to go. He'd withheld his help as a way to punish me for being fed up with him. Well, I didn't need him or his help now.

I had a boyfriend named Ronnie, who I liked a lot and maybe even loved. But he had no interest in attending church with me. I had a mental checklist for any guy to be considered marriage material. First on the list was that the man would have to be a Christian. Ronnie was not, and this was an absolute deal-breaker. It didn't matter that he met all my other criteria. My future husband also had to be a hard worker and he couldn't have a criminal record. He would have to be good with children, because I wanted children, but there was no way I was going to have five children like Mom did. I was not going to have more children than I could properly care for and more than adequately feed, clothe, and house. In every way, I wanted my life to be different from Mom's.

By then I had moved on from Lambert Chevrolet for a job as the office manager at another car dealership. I made good money. I paid my taxes and paid my bills on time. I felt like I was doing okay. But the car dealership turned out to be running a scam: when customers bought the extended warranties, they kept the money. Soon I discovered that a bank owned all the cars, but when the dealership sold a car, they didn't tell the bank. The bank had become suspicious. When I caught on to this, I grabbed my purse and walked out of the office. I had found myself with rent to pay and no income for the first time on my own.

Each morning I combed the newspaper classified ads. One day I saw that a family was hiring a live-in nanny in another town. The next week I got the nanny job after a single interview and moved in with the family—a single father, Bob, and his adorable, well-behaved three-year-old son, Bobby, and four-year-old daughter, Michelle. I moved into the basement apartment in their little ranch house in the town of Conneaut on Lake Erie.

On my first Sunday, I attended the Conneaut First Assembly of God. Sitting in the pews during the service, I noticed a young man walking into the sanctuary with a young-looking woman who I assumed was his wife. After the service, the pastor introduced me to other congregants as they filed out into the sunlight. Up walked this young man, and I was introduced to Michael Balascio and learned that the woman was not his wife, but his mother.

I really wasn't interested in meeting my spouse that day, but Michael was. He asked me out after the next week's service. Our first date was to a mom-and-pop hunting supply store that had an archery range in the back. Michael was an avid hunter and fisherman, and he knew the folks who owned the place. They looked me over when they saw me. I wondered if he'd ever brought any other woman here on a date and if it was an initiation of sorts. If so, would I pass? Did I want to?

He had brought his hunting bow, and I watched closely as he demonstrated how it worked. The target seemed far away as Michael positioned the bow in my hands and told me how to stand. "Turn your body perpendicular to the target," he said. "Now look at the target." I did as he said, held up the bow in my left hand, pulled back the arrow with my right, and let it fly. I missed the target entirely, but I was more focused on the burning of my inner forearm where the arrow had raked it. Michael took a look at the blue and red mark rising and went into the gun shop. He returned with a can of Coke for me to hold against my arm.

Another date was rifle shooting practice in Michael's parents' backyard. I didn't like guns, personally, or how careless people could be with them. But I knew some people took guns and gun safety seriously and that hunting was more than a sport. It put meat on the table. I admired responsible hunters, in theory. In practice, I didn't see the appeal of killing an animal with a gun or a bow. But Michael was eager to show me his own prowess with a rifle, and I watched as he took his stance and hit the target.

On another date, Michael took me fishing. He had his car packed with rods and waders. When we got to the river, Michael parked and began to unpack the gear. He handed me a pair of waders and I put them on. They were too big, and I felt like a clown at the circus lifting my legs high with each step so I didn't trip over the felt-bottomed boots and baggy rubber legs. At the river's edge, I watched what Michael did and imitated him, walking into the stream with my fishing rod held forth. I tripped on the rocky bottom, fell to my knees, and the waders filled with water. I spent the rest of the day trying to warm up in the shafts of weak sunlight on the bank, watching Michael fish.

Even if I didn't share his passion for hunting and fishing, I considered Michael a good catch. As for being a Christian, he hit the ball out of the park. When he first laid eyes on me, he heard the voice of God saying, "You're going to marry that woman." As for the second item on the list, Michael had a strong work ethic. He *expected* to work hard, never looking for the next person he could scam. And as for making a good father, Michael was already volunteering as a Ranger leader in the church, and the boys loved him. And Michael was, in fact—not fiction—a law-abiding man. Whereas Dad was a charlatan pretending to have been "metamorphosed" into an upstanding citizen. Check. Check. Check. Check.

I placed my checklist above all other considerations. My job started early in the morning when the kids woke up. Michael worked the second shift and got off at midnight. He would come over after work for a few hours. I was always exhausted by the time he arrived. Once, he showed up as I was washing off my makeup.

He said, "Do you have to do that?"

"Do what?" I asked.

He said, "Do you have to take your makeup off? I like you better with it on."

I felt a stab of alarm, but I refused to linger on the memories of Dad's belittling attempts to get Mom to wear makeup. I told myself that Michael thought I was attractive. He frequently complimented me when he liked what I was wearing. But tonight wasn't about clothes that a person could put on or take off. This was about my face. He was a far cry from my tenth-grade boyfriend. Unlike Mark, Michael didn't think I looked "pretty" without makeup. My list of husband-qualifications obviously didn't include "loves me just the way I am."

I didn't bring Michael to meet my family until the day he asked Dad for my hand in marriage. Before they met, I told Michael, "I have to warn you. My dad's a piece of work. Don't believe anything he says." I had told him *some* stories of Dad's temper, like the times he overturned the dinner table, but I didn't admit the worst of it. I left out the times Mom had gone to the hospital because of him, or the times I couldn't go to school because I couldn't sit down. I didn't mention he had been on the FBI's most wanted list. Or that he was a convicted arsonist. Or his memoir.

"Oh, don't worry about me," Michael said. "I can handle him."

We were married nine months after our first date. I was twenty-one. Michael was twenty, not old enough to legally drink at his own wedding. We had a daytime wedding at the church. Michael had just been laid off and I was only making a hundred dollars a week, so we kept things simple. My old friend Jennifer had been married the year before, and I borrowed her decorations. I had no bridesmaids. Just one maid of honor, the wife of Michael's best man, who loaned me her long off-white satin dress with puffy sleeves and a V neckline that she'd worn for her wedding the year before. My family was all there—David on leave from the air force base and John on break from college. Nellie and Don came, and Nellie made the wedding cake. Jennifer and her husband came, as well as a few friends from church. It was a small country church, and my circle of friends was even smaller. Little Bobby was ecstatic that he was given the honor of being the ring bearer and his sister, Michelle, was my enthusiastic flower girl.

Dad walked me down the aisle, and as we passed the pews, I heard soft chuckles. I didn't know why until I reached the altar and turned to watch him walk back down the aisle. His polka dot boxer shorts showed clearly through the white tux pants he wore.

After the brief ceremony, the church served a brunch with eggs, pancakes, and sausage. We couldn't afford a honeymoon, but I knew Michael would get a new job soon. He was the hardest worker I had ever met, which proved I had not married someone like Dad. No, sir. I was definitely doing things differently than my mother had—from top to bottom. My mother had her first child in her first year of marriage. I wasn't going to do that.

And then I did.

I got pregnant within months of my wedding night. I suffered with morning sickness twenty-four hours a day. I could not abide the smell of most food, but worst of all was chicken. I was too focused on feeling physically ill to realize how devastated I was that I had gotten pregnant so quickly. I had expected it would take a while. I told myself I would space the next one out.

Michael and I lived an hour from my parents in a rented single-wide mobile home in the country. From time to time I felt the need to see Mom and Jeff and Jeannine, and I was always curious about what Dad was up to, though I dreaded the thought of seeing him.

I was a few months into my pregnancy when I decided to visit my parents. I arrived before Mom got home from her job at Value King, a grocery store. Jeannine and Jeff were still at school. As soon as I entered the house, the stench of oily fried chicken hit me, and I retched and ran to the bathroom. I came out a little unsteadily and lay down on the couch, feeling dizzy. I pulled a trash can close by just in case. The house smelled like Dad had been cooking chicken all day.

"Hey," Dad called out from his bedroom. He emerged wearing only a baggy white T-shirt. He greeted me by handing me a pair of his boxers.

"My back is killing me, April," he said. "Help me put these on."

I refused to get up from the couch. "No, Dad, I'm not putting your underwear on for you." Instead, I grabbed the trash can, trying not to vomit. He stood in front of me, his genitals dangling, groaning and moaning with pain while he struggled to pull on his boxers.

He called me selfish. He said I was an ungrateful, faithless daughter. *Faithless?* Ha! That was rich coming from a man who only ever stepped into a church to con its members. If anything, I was *too* faithful a daughter. I trusted him too much. I kept coming around, unable to break the cord that bound us. I closed my eyes and threw up.

Just a couple of weeks before my due date, Michael and I hosted Thanksgiving dinner at our home. Mom, Dad, Jeannine, Jeff, John, David, and David's wife, Erin—also pregnant—arrived in two cars. Michael made a huge turkey dinner, rivaling the best of Dad's Christmas feasts of my childhood. I baked two pies. It was the first time Michael and I had my entire family over.

During dinner, Michael and my brothers kept up a rapid stream of funny stories and made each other laugh. It seemed like Dad couldn't get a word in edgewise. After dinner, we settled into the living room for a rousing game of Spades, while Dad stayed at the kitchen table, sulking that he wasn't the center of attention. Dad didn't like that he wasn't the host of the party. This wasn't one of his shindigs. It was mine and Michael's. The card game was boisterous with laughter and more loud stories, and now and then Dad would try to interrupt and divert the conversation to one of his own stories, but no one paid attention to him.

At one point, I looked up and Dad was gone. Mom said he'd gone to the bathroom down the hall. He was gone for so long that I went to check on him. I saw the bathroom door was open, but he wasn't there. I went to the back door, which opened to a patio, expecting to see him outside smoking. Michael and I didn't allow smoking in the house, a rule that annoyed Dad. But he wasn't out on the patio smoking. I took a walk around the house and saw that his car was gone. Dad had driven off, leaving six adult-sized people, one of them in late pregnancy, with just one small car to drive the hour home.

I came back into the house and announced, "Dad's left."

That pretty much brought the evening to a close. It was late and I was wiped out anyway. David, Erin, John, Jeff, Jeannine, and Mom squeezed into David's car and drove back to Mom and Dad's house. While they were on their way, the phone rang. Michael answered it.

"It's your dad," he said.

I waved him off. My legs were aching and my feet were swollen and I just wanted to go to bed.

"April!" Michael hissed at me. "Your dad says he has a gun." Michael's eyes were wide. He whispered to me, "He's threatening to shoot himself."

Into the receiver, Michael said in a soothing voice, "Okay, hold on now, Wayne," but he was pacing the room. "Let's just take a deep breath and think about what you're doing. Kay and the kids are on their way home . . ."

I rolled my eyes. Here we go again. I'd been down this road before. My dad was definitely not going to shoot himself. It was all theatrics.

Then Michael covered the receiver with his hand and said to me, "Your dad just shot himself." It took a while to sink in. "In the arm."

Michael actually smirked and shook his head in disbelief and relief. As an avid hunter, he knew by the sound of the shot that Dad had used a small caliber like a .22, not the gun of choice or the part of the body for a person serious about suicide. Had Dad been serious, he would have gotten the job done, but this was purely staged, a blatant bid for attention. While Michael was on the phone with Dad, the rest of the family returned home. They walked in to find blood splattered everywhere.

Dad was taken to the ER in an ambulance, but after he was admitted he escaped, despite being on a suicide watch. The hospital staff must have called his house alerting the family of the escapee, because Jeff got in the car and drove around till he found Dad walking home.

Three weeks later, my first child, Brody, was born.

The next few years were a whirlwind of diapers and bottles and strollers. After Brody, in quick succession came two more, first a daughter Brynn, and then a second son, Bryce. I had three children in three years. Just like Mom.

29

Marriage, Motherhood, and Murder

1991–1996

While I was busy having babies, my siblings were all moving on. David was doing well in the air force. John had graduated from college and become a teacher. Jeff and Jeannine had each joined the army after graduating high school. Without any kids to boss around, Dad took in a sort of foster son, Dannie Boy, Jeff's friend from back in middle school.

When Dannie finished high school at twenty-one, he moved in with a guy named Ralph. Dannie and Ralph had a falling-out, and that's when Dad and Mom took Dannie in.

I thought it was kind of strange when I heard that Dannie Boy had moved in, but it made sense when I considered that with all my siblings gone, Dad had no one to shout at to fetch his cigarettes or a cup of coffee, or fix the clogged sink, or mow the lawn, while he sat back in his recliner, feet up, watching TV or chatting endlessly on the phone. I figured, too, that Dad was charging Dannie rent. Dannie was too old to be legally adopted by my parents, but he legally changed his name from Dannie Law Gloeckner to Dannie Boy Edwards. In the petition to change his name, Dannie wrote: "I have been living with Mr. and Mrs. Edwards for over a year and have been supported by them. I call them Mom and Dad. I feel they are Mom and Dad. They treat me like a son." Therefore, he wrote, he wanted to change his last name to theirs.

Dad encouraged Dannie Boy to join the army, too. He coached and tutored him so he could pass the entrance exam.

Dad also put Dannie into a rigorous training program so he would pass the physical exam. He even duct-taped soup cans to the bottoms of Dannie Boy's feet so they wouldn't be as flat. Dannie passed both tests. Dad helped him fill out the enlistment forms, including signing up for the maximum military life insurance policy—$200,000. Dannie Boy listed my father as the beneficiary. Dannie took out another policy for $50,000, also with Dad as the beneficiary.

Dannie Boy had just started basic training when I visited Mom and Dad with my three small kids. I walked in the door carrying six-month-old Bryce in one arm, holding my almost two-year-old daughter, Brynn, by the hand with the other, while Brody stuck close to me.

My parents' small living room was cramped with a couch and two recliners. Now Mom had her own recliner. And for better or worse, she had Dad to herself now. I can't imagine it was for the better. Who was fetching Dad's coffee and cigarettes? I guess she was. Dad had acquired a large, overweight Rottweiler named Misha, who sat by his feet. The house reeked of dog. I sat on the couch, which was covered in dog hair, holding my children close to me. After a bit of idle chitchat, I was about to stand when Dad barked an order, "Misha! Get 'er!"

Misha lunged at the couch, baring her teeth, growling and drooling. Bryce cried and Brynn and Brody crawled on top of me in fright. I pulled my feet up.

"Dad, knock it off!" I glared at him.

He gave Misha a command and she sat quietly, vigilant, watching us. But when I lowered my feet to the floor, he gave the attack command again. She lunged at me, snarling, and the kids screamed and I shrunk back on the couch.

This went on and on, back and forth. Every time we tried to get up, Misha would be told to "get 'er." Finally, Mom intervened.

"Come on, Wayne. That's enough. You're scaring the kids," she said. She said this in a tone that made it seem like a suggestion. Like perhaps he shouldn't talk with his mouth full. As if this were a matter of manners and nothing more.

Dad laughed, but he called Misha to him.

I stared at Mom in disbelief. *This* was her response to his sadistic act of terrorizing his young grandchildren? In her life, she had sat back and watched him do much worse, of course. I had taken her beating for the nail clippers, hadn't I? And there had been so many beatings she did nothing about. I don't know why I was surprised now, but I was shaking with rage at my father and my mother.

I left the house sobbing, holding Bryce and Brynn, who clung to my neck. Brody held on tight to my leg. My kids were trembling. And I was almost choking on my fury. Dad was still laughing when I shut the door behind me. We had provided him with his entertainment for the day. I sat in the car with my head on the steering wheel and wept. I didn't want to be so angry. At least not at Mom. Shouldn't I take pity on her? I could walk out of that house, but Mom could not. I vowed never ever to visit my father's house again.

But I did. About a year later. Michael and I and the kids were invited to dinner. Brody, our oldest, wasn't yet four. My parents still had Misha, but I knew that Dad wouldn't pull any stunts with Michael around.

We walked in and were greeted by the aroma of fried chicken. Not being pregnant, I wasn't bothered this time. This smelled like KFC, a good thing in our book, and sure enough, as we came in through the kitchen we saw, in the trash can, containers from KFC. Well, I thought, with some relief, at least my kids would happily eat what was put in front of them, which would avoid conflict with Dad. In my own house, no one was forced to finish anything on their plates. But here, I had been bracing myself for a fight. The fight came. It just wasn't the one I expected.

We sat down to dinner and the table was laden with platters of chicken, biscuits, and a bowl of creamy mashed potatoes.

Michael said, "Great, we love KFC."

Dad said, "What KFC? I made this chicken myself."

Oh, boy, I thought. Here we go. I kicked Michael under the table, hoping he'd get the hint to leave it at that. I never called my father out on lies, but Michael wouldn't let it drop. "This sure is great KFC, isn't it, kids?" He looked at them and winked. "Finger lickin' good!"

The tension at the table grew unbearable as Dad stared daggers at Michael.

"*I . . . made . . . this . . . chicken . . .*" Dad snarled, as if daring Michael to call him a liar directly.

Michael was undaunted. "What was in the containers in the trash, then?"

Dad said they were left over from last night's dinner. Still, Michael would not let it go. "So, what is that secret recipe, Wayne? You must have gotten it from Colonel Sanders himself."

I kept kicking Michael under the table, trying to keep us from wearing the food, trying to keep my kids from getting traumatized by a table being flipped in front of them. Bryce was still in a highchair. Was it possible I had married a man even more stubborn than my father? Michael seemed to relish the absurdity of the argument. Or maybe he just couldn't stand that my father got away with shameless lies. If my father was like a dog with a bone, holding on to his lie, Michael was like Scottie locked in on a chipmunk.

Finally Dad stood up. I expected the table to go flying, but he just walked out into the living room and flipped on the TV and called Misha to his side.

That was the last time I went to that house.

But it wasn't long after that KFC dinner that Dad called me with the news about Dannie Boy. He had injured his ankle in basic training and would have received a medical discharge, but he had run off two days before his discharge. It made no sense. Why would Dannie have gone AWOL? What could have made him choose such a reckless act.

Dad said that Dannie called Dad after running away from the military base to let him know he was okay, but he refused to reveal his location. Dad taped the call, like he taped so many. The conversation went like this:

Dannie tells Dad a strange story about getting a threatening letter from Ralph, his former housemate, because he owed him money. He admits to breaking into Mom and Dad's house through an unlocked window and stealing Jeff's money that was kept in a big glass jar.

"Jeff won't appreciate that. There was about 260 bucks in that," Dad says.

Then Dad asks Dannie a series of questions that begin, "So let me ask you something . . ." Their voices are conversational. Dad asks: "Did you take any of Jeff's clothes?" Yes, Dannie says, he did. "You know they weren't yours to take, son." Dannie says he took Jeff's credit cards and checkbook, too. Dad says, "Uh-huh," as if checking off an inventory list.

"Let me ask you something else," Dad asks. "Misha give you any trouble?"

Dannie answers with unnatural calm, like he's answering a prompt. He says he found a bag of dog treats, and that helped.

The call sounds like an oddly unemotional exchange between a rational youth who has just gone irrationally AWOL two days before being released from the military, and his equally calm and kindly mentor. Several times during the call, Dad says, "Turn yourself in, son."

Then Dad says, as if enumerating Dannie's offenses, "I don't want to tell the police that you broke in. I don't want to tell the police that you stole Jeff's money or you stole his credit cards or his clothes . . ." (He will do exactly this by turning over the tape to the police.)

Dad asks Dannie again about Ralph, confirming that Dannie was worried about him. Dad ends the call, "I want you to stay safe," and "Call us," and, finally, "We love you."

That was the last anyone ever heard from Dannie Boy.

After Dannie went missing, Dad called me. It was a baffling call. It was the middle of the day. I was in the living room, lying on the floor. My youngest, Bryce, was just a year and a half. All three of my children had gone down for naps and I had been looking forward to one myself.

Dad told me that someone had just left a duffel bag on his porch. He said it contained toiletries and clothes, a photo of Dannie Boy, and, most disturbing of all, teeth.

We hadn't spoken in a while, and I was surprised he was calling me at all. Was I supposed to think someone was harassing Dad? Were those Dannie's teeth? That was a horrible thought. Was he trying to tell me that Dannie had been killed and the killer was taunting him? Why would he be calling me about this and not the police? Why would he have pawed through the bag, getting his fingerprints all over everything? Most confusing to me was that I recognized something in Dad's voice. It was his lying voice. I felt my old sense of unease returning. Why was Dad telling me this? What was he up to?

Dad said he was so worried about Dannie, that he had called the Army base and spoken to Dannie's friends searching for clues about what happened to him. Specifically, he asked if Dannie ever got harassing letters from Ralph. He recorded these calls, too.

When my three kids were all toddlers, they kept me too busy to think about anything but getting through the day. I didn't have the perspective to see that I'd done exactly what my own mother had done. In my days of early mother-hood, memories of my childhood began to surface even as I tried to shove them away. I had to somehow stop the memories from overwhelming me. I kept insulating myself from my pain, self-medicating with food. I began to eat compulsively, choosing foods that were most fattening. Periods of binging alternated with periods of dieting that made me irritable and only caused me to eat more. Objectively, I didn't like what was happening to my body, but that didn't stop me from using food to comfort myself. Any action to stop myself felt too punishing, and life was exhausting and difficult enough.

The one person from my childhood who I wanted to see was Aunt Lucille. She was such an important figure to me growing up, that I wanted my young children to meet her. Uncle Al had passed away and she lived alone. I thought she could use the company, so Michael and I took the trip to Cuyahoga Falls with the kids. She greeted us at her side door.

There she was, a sight for my sore eyes, standing before us in her dark poly-ester pants and short-sleeved white blouse, wearing her red lipstick and the hair-net she had always worn indoors. She was eighty-four and her eyes looked tired and her cheeks sagged. But I couldn't have been happier to see her. I hugged her gently, as if she were fragile. I felt safe and like I belonged. In some way, I did belong to Aunt Lucille. I realized then, standing before her slightly stooped body, that she had been an anchor for me all my life. As a child, I knew she would come visit with Uncle Al at some point in the year and we'd be as close to normal as we could be when she was there, and this was a kind of insurance for me. At least when she was there, nothing bad would happen to us.

Stepping into her house I was overwhelmed by the scent of Murphy Oil Soap. I loved that smell. The house was just as orderly as I remembered it was from my childhood. Lace curtains hung in the windows. There was no clutter of papers and bills on the dining room table. No overflowing waste baskets with candy wrappers tumbling out. No overstuffed ashtrays.

She took a seat in a living room chair, and I sat at her feet, with my kids playing with the toys we'd brought with us. Michael took a seat on the couch and said little, just watching, listening, and taking it all in.

Lucille pulled out a stack of photo albums and set them on the coffee table. I picked up one of them and opened it gingerly and flipped through the pages of the album. There were a few photos of our young family on Avon Street and Doylestown, from the time I was born to the time Jeannine was born. In one photo I'm riding a large Great Dane dog as if it were a pony.

Aunt Lucille pointed to the photo. "That dog once busted through the picture window to protect you from the mailman who was coming onto the porch," she said.

I didn't remember this dog. "I still miss Happy," I said. "She was the best."

"She was a saint, that dog," Aunt Lucille said. "A gift from God." She shook her head as if to say, *Lord knows you needed one.*

I opened another photo album, and this one was filled with pictures of Dad as a child. I stared at his impish, adorable grin at seven. Before he was sent off to the orphanage.

"Boy, he was cute, wasn't he?" I said.

"He sure was," she said wistfully. "But that child was a handful."

She sighed. "Me and Al had the opportunity to adopt your dad when he was a boy. We were so young ourselves, and newly married, and Wayne was just too much for your grandmother. But he was too much for us, too. I felt terrible, but I said we couldn't take him, and he went off to the reformatory." She took out a tissue from her sleeve and dabbed her eyes. "And, well, I guess I always felt pretty bad about that."

"Oh," I interrupted her, "you were always good to Dad. You made every Christmas special! You were always good to all of us." I couldn't bear for her to feel bad. She had done so much!

"Oh honey, I'm glad you remember it that way." I didn't like the regretful tone in her voice. I wanted our visit to bring her joy, not sadness.

I pulled the photo album onto my lap. Michael leaned over my shoulder to get a better look at young me.

I pointed to a photo of our Christmas in Colorado. "Remember when I ruined Christmas by exposing who Santa really was?" I said.

"Oh yes!" she laughed. "I thought Wayne was going to blow a gasket!"

"He didn't because you were there!" I said. "I loved when you visited for Christmas," I told her. "Those were always the best times."

She took my hand in hers and spoke to me in a low voice so the kids wouldn't overhear. Her hands felt soft and cool.

"You know your father has done some bad things," she said.

"I know," I assured her. "I read his book."

"No, I don't mean only back then," she said. She needed to tell me something, and I was sure I didn't want to hear it.

Michael did, though, and he leaned in closer.

"There's one time," she said, "that I don't like to think about, when we visited over the summer."

"When was that?" I asked.

"When you all lived in Wisconsin," she said. "Your dad did something . . . I don't know what, but I have a bad feeling about it."

I sat frozen in fear. Wisconsin. I knew we hadn't lived there very long. I had almost no memory of going to school there. I didn't remember her and Uncle Al being there.

Then she said, "One night he came home covered in mud, and his face was bloody. I wondered what he did to get dirty like that so late at night."

Oh God, I did not want to think about this. *No no no no*, my brain said, and shoved my memories down. *Don't go there*, I told myself. *Don't go there.*

I changed the subject and asked Aunt Lucille about church. She said, "April, when the Lord comes for me, I'll be ready to go."

When she died of a bleeding ulcer within the year, I realized that she had known she was ill during our visit but kept it to herself. She hadn't wanted us to make a fuss over her, I guess.

I learned that she had passed away when a lawyer called to tell me that I was one of her beneficiaries. In her will, Aunt Lucille had not left her estate to Dad. She left one sixth to him and a sixth to each of his children. Dad was outraged that he hadn't inherited it all.

This woman who had helped us out so much by funding Christmases and birthday presents throughout my childhood, who had lived a modest life otherwise, had saved over half a million dollars. It broke my heart. As a kid, the Christmas gifts and holiday cheer seemed like miracles set against the day-to-day poverty of our lives. Now, even after death, she was offering us miracles. The inheritance helped me and Michael renovate our home, a fixer-upper not unlike some of the homes I'd grown up in.

When I heard that she'd died, I felt ashamed that I hadn't kept in better touch with her in the decade since I'd left home. She had stopped coming to Christmases after Dad was arrested in Atlanta. I called Mom to express my guilt about the inheritance and say how grateful I was for Aunt Lucille's final gift.

"I'm heartbroken to think that she's no longer in the world," I said, "but I'm glad she's not suffering."

Dad recorded the call, characteristically. He had recorded plenty of conversations with Aunt Lucille herself over the years. But these tapes often had a motive beyond recording for posterity. Dad liked to edit his tapes to benefit whatever scheme he had in mind.

He edited the recording of my expression of sorrow and gratitude to Aunt Lucille, so that it sounds as if I said I was glad Aunt Lucille had died. Then he mailed a cassette with the edited recording to each of my siblings. He sent a copy to me as well. He wanted me to know what he had done, to hurt me. We may not have lived with him anymore, but he was still trying to get us back in the arena to fight. He was pitting us against each other so we wouldn't trust each other. He wanted us close to him, but not close to each other. Maybe he was afraid of what might happen if we ever bonded together and turned against him.

Trying to control his kids was something Dad felt he was an expert at. But he was also trying to control outcomes, like the recorded call that he had with Dannie Boy, which he gave to police as evidence to help them solve the mystery of what happened to that poor young man.

Dannie Boy had disappeared in May 1996. Nearly a year later, in April 1997, his decaying body was found in a shallow grave in a cemetery near my parents' house—the same graveyard I rode my bike past during my senior year in high school to get away from our crowded house.

Dannie Boy had been shot in the head, from behind, twice. He was twenty-five years old. The death was declared a homicide, and Dad, as well as everyone else in Dannie's life, was questioned by police. Dad conducted his own investigation that paralleled law enforcement's. He told police that he thought Dannie's former housemate, Ralph, was responsible. In the recorded call with Dannie Boy, hadn't he mentioned being worried about Ralph? No arrests were made.

Dad was asked to come in for a polygraph test, but upon entering the police building, he was struck with chest pains and couldn't take the test. Instead he wrote a seventy-two-page summary of everything he knew about Dannie and sent that to detectives.

A funeral was held. Dad bought a sheet cake that said, "We love you, Dannie," to the gathering after the burial ceremony. He even taped the phone call to Dannie's foster mother where he tells her all about the cake in great detail, down to the color of the frosting.

Mom and Dad moved to Arizona shortly after the funeral, and Dad bought property outside of Tucson. After the move, Jeannine called my parents, and of course the call was recorded by Dad. In the call, she asks him a question all his kids had uncomfortably on our minds.

"Did you get that insurance money from Dannie?" she asks casually.

"From who?" Dad asks.

"Dannie"

"No," Dad says.

"No?" she says.

"No, as far as we know . . . see what happened there . . ." He hems and haws and rambles, then says, "No, nobody got anything there. Nope. And besides, he was AWOL." Then his voice lifts, and he brags, "No, most of my money comes from investments!"

But none of us believed him.

30

Deal with It

1997–2009

Each year, at Christmas, my siblings and I took turns hosting a gathering. By now, we all had kids of our own and we lived in five different states. We felt it was important that we gather at least annually and get the cousins together. Years after Dannie Boy's death, Mom and Dad had left Tucson and moved to Kentucky. They weren't celebrating Christmas with us. We had gathered at Jeff's house, and Dannie Boy's relationship with Dad became the topic of conversation. After our kids were excused from the table and ran off to play together, we spoke in hushed tones as we pondered a monstrous question—did Dad kill Dannie Boy for the money? Was he capable of doing such a thing? We knew he had committed arson, committed violence, and we admitted that we fully believed he was capable of murder. I thought about what Aunt Lucille had said to me. That she had suspected him of something in Wisconsin when we lived there. I didn't tell my brothers and sisters about Aunt Lucille's suspicions. I wasn't ready to believe Dad was heartless enough to kill the young man who he had mentored. A stranger, maybe, but not a boy who called him Dad.

After that Christmas gathering at Jeff's, I couldn't get this question out of my mind. It began to grow its own kind of weight and validity. Could Dad have killed Dannie Boy? The question began to seem less absurd the more I asked it. Once I acknowledged to myself that I *might be* willing to believe that my father killed Dannie Boy, the boy he gave refuge to and took in as if he were one of his own, then I had to believe my father could have killed other people. And because we lived in so many places, he could have left a trail of victims. But I wasn't ready to do anything with these terrible thoughts. I kept denying my own memories, pushed them deep down, I protected myself by putting a buffer around my past. I focused on the present, my children, my church activities, and the community. I continued to put on weight, as if to bury memories inside myself. I had gained nearly two hundred pounds.

On many days, I struggled with a sense of panic and chronic gastric distress—I'd had stomach troubles for as long as I could remember—and no matter what I tried, I was unable to get rid of the weight that I'd gained. I saw a surgeon to discuss having gastric bypass surgery. He was a small, middle-aged Indian man with kind eyes. At the end of our consultation, he closed my file, crossed his legs, and folded his hands on his lap.

He peered at me over his glasses and said, "Mrs. Balascio, it's been my experience that people with your symptoms often have had a traumatic childhood." Then he asked me in a gentle voice, "Did you have a traumatic childhood?"

I blinked and stared back at him with a straight face, and said, "No more than the average dysfunctional family."

I watched him look down at his hands, disappointed. I knew I had missed my opportunity to unburden myself. But I couldn't allow myself to do it. There was just too much bottled up inside. I was like that party toy that my kids loved, the can that had a coiled fabric snake you had to stuff inside with great effort. And when you took the lid off the snake shot out of the can, out of control, surprising everyone around. That's what would happen to me, I thought. I'd be out of the can, out of control, surprising everyone. But I also knew I was only barely in control. Held in place by the thinnest of lids.

I homeschooled all three of my children for elementary school. They were on sports teams and in musicals through the church-affiliated homeschool groups, so I never felt they were missing anything by not attending the local public school. They played the piano and the boys were Rangers and Brynn was a Missionette. Our school day was spent at our dining room table. As a child I remember Mom helping my brother David with homework. I was both homework helper and homeroom teacher to my children. I learned more teaching them than I had when I was a student in school. They were so close in age, they were often learning the same things. Academics came easily for them. Brody was reading by the time he was four. Brynn, a year younger, kept in step with her big brother. She was reading by the time she was three. I was proud of them.

But when I was angry with them, I used a paddle that Michael and I had for the purpose of punishing our kids. When I was really angry, I feared that I'd spin out of control. The memory of getting thrown across the room by my father as a young child would burst forth in my mind like the first bubble on the surface of a pot of water coming to boil. I became afraid of my own temper.

One early morning, when the kids were asleep and Michael was packing to go hunting, I confessed my fear that I had the capacity to hurt my own children. But Michael didn't want to hear about my worries.

"Deal with it," he said, and then he walked out the door.

Hearing him say that was devastating. I had no one else to turn to for help. I felt utterly alone.

We had recently moved to a new town and didn't have close neighbors. We had one car that Michael used for work and to go fishing and hunting. I was as isolated as my mother had been. I didn't know anyone in the new church we had just joined well enough to confide in them. And I knew Michael believed that family problems should stay in the family, so it wasn't like he would have approved if I sought church counseling. We couldn't afford private counseling. To cope, I put enormous pressure on myself to be the perfect mom, to make sure my children were dressed impeccably, and behaved impeccably as well. They had to be perfect in every aspect of their lives.

When they entered the local middle school, they excelled in academics, in athletics, in whatever extra activities they participated in. They liked to win. Just like I did. Just like my dad. How else was I just like Dad? I was afraid to know.

When my children became independent teenagers, I panicked every time they left the house that they would never come back. I knew that bad men lurked in the shadows, waiting to do them harm. In fact, one of these bad men might be their grandfather. Weren't there hundreds of other men like him out there? All those *True Detective* magazines I read as a child had taught me that.

Sixteen years after the Thanksgiving dinner when my father left my house and shot himself in the arm just a few weeks before my first child was born, I decided it was time to make a change. My youngest, Bryce, had turned thirteen. I had no more little kids. They were growing up. And now it was my turn.

I had gastric bypass surgery. I began working out twice a day, some might say obsessively, and with the pounds that began to shed, memories came flooding back. In my dreams I saw Scottie and Happy. My father's contorted face as he grabbed me and threw me to the ground, my mother's hand in bandages, a barn in flames, screams in the night. A dog hanging. Terrible memories I had managed to suppress all these years.

The words of Aunt Lucille a decade earlier began to echo in my head. She had confided her fears about Dad. But back then I wasn't ready to do anything about that. The discussions with my siblings had also been swirling around in my head for years, but I had not been willing to fully embrace their suspicions. Now I was.

I began to search the internet at night when Michael was at work. I searched for cold case websites looking for any murders that might align with the town names that would pop into my head in the middle of the night. I knew what states we lived in, but I couldn't remember all the little towns.

It was 2009 during a sleepless night, that the name Watertown suddenly came to me and I stumbled out of bed and got on my laptop. Michael wasn't home; he was working that night. I typed "cold case 1980 Watertown Wisconsin" into my search bar. And the August 1980 "Sweetheart Murders" in Concord, Wisconsin, popped up. The unsolved double murder case had just been reopened because police had DNA evidence on file for this crime. I read every article I could find about the murders online.

On August 9, 1980, at the Concord House, just outside Watertown, Wisconsin, nineteen-year-olds Kelly Drew and Timothy Hack attended a wedding reception. They had agreed to meet friends later at a carnival, but they didn't turn up. They were last seen leaving the reception somewhere between 11:00 and 11:30 p.m. Tim's car was still in the parking lot, his full wallet inside. It was two months before their bodies were found. Two months of their families wondering what had happened to them, who was responsible, were they still alive?

Now I stared at the photos on my screen of two apple-cheeked nineteen-year-olds who looked like the picture of health, the American ideal: a young couple barely older than my own kids about to embark on the rest of their lives together. They were last seen leaving a wedding at the Concord House. I remembered the Concord House!

We had lived just a few miles away from the Concord House that summer, but by the time Kelly and Tim's bodies were found by squirrel hunters in the woods by the edge of a field, my family and I had already moved to Pittsburgh.

Memories started sparking, sending shocks through my brain. I remembered the Simons and the Uttechs and the house with the stained glass window. I began to recall things my father said. "I bet they find them in a field," and his obsession with this missing young man and woman. I remembered his busted nose. The image of his triple E wide muddy boots popped into my head. Hadn't Aunt Lucille said something about Wisconsin and muddy clothes? I began hyperventilating. Now I was faced with a decision that no child should ever face. Should I call the Cold Case Hotline to tip them off? I had no solid proof that my father had killed Timothy Hack and Kelly Drew or any proof that he was a murderer. I only had my suspicions.

I paced my bedroom, even jumping on the bed in my frenzy. I saw my reflection in the mirror. I looked like a mad woman. My hair was a mess, my red-rimmed eyes looked wild. Maybe the police would think I was insane.

I looked at my phone. My shaking fingers hovered over the dial pad.

I called Jeannine instead. My relationship with my brothers was strained. I was the bossy older sister who they never quite forgave for enforcing Dad's rules while we were growing up. But I had always felt close to Jeannine. I wanted her blessing to finally make our father accountable for crimes he committed. *If* he was innocent, there would be nothing to fear. If he was guilty, then our world would blow up, but he would be convicted like any other killer would be. He should not get away with murder. No one should. *Didn't she agree?*

She did not.

Jeannine said, "He's our dad."

"I know," I said.

"Think of Mom. What will this do to her?" she said.

It would destroy her, I thought. But maybe it would liberate her. If I was right, that is. If I was wrong, then my family would hate me for my suspicions. But they might hate me either way. What would it do to us for the world to know, if it was true, that our father was a murderer?

"Think about what this would do to our kids," Jeannine said in reaction to my silence. "This is their grandfather we're talking about."

I knew she was thinking of their emotional response, but also their reputations, their futures. I knew she was right. It would be terrible for all of us. There was nothing for us to gain from this. Only everything to lose. What I was thinking of was traitorous. The ultimate betrayal.

"But what if it was our kids?" I insisted. "Wouldn't we want justice for them?"

Jeannine was a devout Christian too.

"Is it really up to us to withhold suspicions about Dad if he did wicked things?" I pushed. We weren't talking about domestic abuse, which he was guilty of. Or theft or arson, which he was also guilty of. "We are talking about murder," I said.

Finally, Jeannine said, "Just think about it, April. Don't do anything rash."

I hung up after talking with Jeannine, unsure of myself. My kids were asleep, safe in their beds, dreaming their teenage dreams. I looked at the faces on the computer screen again. There was the scrubbed face of a red-haired farm boy and the bright-eyed smile of a beautiful girl ready to launch into womanhood. And they never had the chance. They died a violent death the night they disappeared.

I paced the room again and silently screamed into the night. I knew what

I had to do. I called the hotline number and waited nervously, hoping it would ring and ring and no one would pick up.

But a woman answered and I was put straight through to Detective Chad Garcia, who was working late. I was stunned. I didn't expect to actually speak to a detective. I wanted to hang up. But when he answered the phone, I had to speak. I said, "You might think I'm crazy or I might be leading you on a wild goose chase, but I think I have some information for you."

"Okay," he said, measured.

"My family lived in Watertown, Wisconsin, the summer of 1980. My dad came home with muddy clothes and a broken nose one night in August." I rambled on and on. I told him first we had lived in the campground next to the Concord House and Dad had worked there. I explained that we moved to a house in Watertown and even described the house's two spiral staircases. And I told him that my dad had been in prison before and mentioned his book, *Metamorphosis of a Criminal.*

Detective Garcia just listened. I didn't know how to read the silence on his end. I kept talking. Garcia asked if he could call me if he had questions, and I said yes, that I would provide whatever information I could.

But three weeks went by without hearing a word from Garcia. I guessed I had sent this guy off on a wild goose chase after all. I felt both relief and guilt. What a terrible person I must be to have suspected my father of such evil, but what a relief to know that I was wrong. Because if I had been right and I had not said anything until now, when my suspicions of my father had been festering like a wound in my mind for years, how many people died because I had stayed silent. With every day that went by without hearing from Chad Garcia, I felt that burden of guilt lift a little tiny bit. And then he called seemingly out of the blue and the dominos began to fall.

31

Kelly and Tim

2009

Weeks after our initial conversation, Garcia called to ask if I would be willing to meet in person. What I didn't realize then was that he had been busy since our first conversation. He'd ordered and read Dad's book and he'd found in the police records that Dad had been on the list of Concord House employees interviewed more than once after the couple disappeared. The Concord House and the location of the bodies and the place where we had lived were all within an eight-mile area.

Garcia and I set a date and time to meet in my home in Jefferson, Ohio. He would be coming from Wisconsin with another detective. As we were about to hang up, he asked if they could get a sample of my DNA while they were there. I said, "Of course."

On the day of the meeting, I paced my living room waiting for their arrival. My house looked like I was expecting company. It always looked that way. I kept it spotless, like Aunt Lucille's. Growing up in filthy homes had given me an intense aversion to dirt and clutter. From my very first apartment, my homes were always immaculate. This one had an off-white living room carpet that was always vacuumed and the shelves always dusted. The green gingham dining room tablecloth matched the curtains. The kitchen wallpaper had a print of climbing ivy, complementing the dining room colors. Michael and I had renovated this house with care. We chose warm oak cabinets and white tile for the countertops and floor. Having a clean, well-decorated home made me feel in control. I was desperately in need of feeling in control now that I had opened the floodgates of chaos. I waited impatiently for Garcia to show up.

The knock on the door startled me even though I'd been expecting it.

"Good morning, ma'am," the man with a military bearing and buzz cut introduced himself as Detective Chad Garcia and he introduced another detective by his side.

They stood there in their suits and ties, looking formal and uncomfortable. I invited them in and led them to my kitchen table. Michael was leaning on the counter, and he greeted them and offered them coffee, which they accepted.

The detectives were polite, sat stiffly, and once the obligatory talk of weather and traffic was over, Garcia placed a tape recorder and notepads on the table. Michael took a seat to listen to whatever came next.

"Do you have news?" I asked.

"Not yet," Garcia said. I didn't know if that meant he had none or just couldn't share it yet. I realized they were not here to share information with me. They were here to get it from me.

Garcia asked if he could record our conversation. I nodded and the session began. He spoke my name, the date and time, the purpose of the visit, and by the time I started talking I had forgotten the tape recorder was rolling.

"Have you remembered anything else that could help us," he said.

I had printed a timeline of all the places I had lived with my family. I started with the first town, Akron, and began to tell my life story.

"When my father was in prison in Pennsylvania for setting fire to the house in Portersville," I told them, "my mom told me that Dad's arson was usually for insurance fraud. But the Portersville fire may have been to cover the fact that he'd sold all the homeowner's furniture."

I shared with the detectives what I'd learned—that Dad had burned the barn on Taylor Road because he claimed that he'd had lumber stored in the barn, but he'd actually moved the lumber to the construction site on Kevin Drive before he started the fire. He burned the farmhouse down after he insured the contents (most of which he didn't own). And he burned the house down, not once, but twice. The first time the volunteer firefighters must have done too good a job putting the fire out. Investigators had suspicions of arson.

But Dad knew how to get rid of the evidence. He'd returned to finish the job he started, going back to the house, shoving rags into the electrical box, and setting them on fire. He figured people would think only vandals would burn a house down twice. The finger of blame was never officially pointed at him.

I was on a roll. "He got twenty thousand dollars in insurance money from that fire. Like with so many of his crimes," I told the detectives, "he was questioned by authorities and then walked away. This happened again and again." It had happened in Wisconsin, too.

Garcia listened without expression, taking notes.

"I think there's more than Wisconsin," I said.

"What do you mean?" Garcia asked.

"I think there might be more victims," I said.

Garcia looked up at me. "Go on," he said.

"When we lived in Doylestown, on Kevin Drive, I remember hearing about two kids that had gone missing," I told him. "Just like in Wisconsin." I remembered and described in detail the time Dad took us on an uncomfortable outing through tall weeds at a nearby park.

"There were other 'missing' kids, too," I said.

I relayed my concerns for the boys in Florida, Curtis and Chris, who disappeared, and the boy who bullied Jeff in Pittsburgh, whom we heard had been killed.

"What else do you remember about Wisconsin?" Garcia asked, bringing me back to that summer when I was eleven. I was able to give more details about the Concord House next to the campground, and described the rented farmhouse we lived in. I shared my memory of seeing the blood and bruises on my dad's nose that he told me he'd hurt while hunting. They listened, without interrupting, until I'd talked myself out.

I handed them my list of the places we lived.

"Who knows how many more there are," I said, "in each of these places." I was fully ready to believe my father had murdered people in every town we lived in. Might that be why we fled every one of them? I hoped that this list would help other cold cases be reopened.

Garcia said nothing in response to my theories. I was certain he thought I was crazy. Or at least overzealous. But he took the list and said, "Are you ready to give a DNA sample?"

"Definitely," I said.

Garcia pulled out a DNA sample kit. He explained the test was so sensitive that he had to ask Michael to step back. He turned his own head away when he swabbed my mouth and slipped the Q-tip into a cylinder quickly and sealed it in a plastic bag. And then they stood and thanked me for everything. Garcia gave me his cell phone number and told me not to hesitate to call him if I had any questions or thought of something else that seemed important. We said our goodbyes, shook hands, and the detectives walked out the door.

Again, weeks went by with no word from Garcia, and again I was left doubting myself, wondering about the DNA results. I questioned my own memories. I was worried I'd wasted the detectives' time. Maybe I had been crazy after all.

But while I was stewing in self-doubt, Garcia was growing more certain. He was in possession of both state and county police reports and was able to cross-reference them, something that detectives at the time had been unable to do. State police reports indicated that Dad was one of the many people interviewed immediately following the disappearance of Tim and Kelly. His busted nose was noted as well. His name also appeared in the county's file, because John Simon, the farmer we'd rented the house from, had gone to the sheriff after my family split town, to express his suspicion that my father was responsible for the murders. He said that my family left one night, without warning, not long after Kelly and Tim went missing. He said Dad kept a handgun under the seat of his van. He recounted a story about Dad chasing off teenagers who were making out on the bridge at the back of our property. He'd held a handgun to the guy's head and bragged about it. Apparently, this statement went no further. By the time John was giving his statement, my family was hundreds of miles away.

Garcia was gathering evidence in favor of Dad as a suspect. He had my suspicions, and something better: my DNA.

When Detective Garcia paid a visit to Dad in Louisville with a Wisconsin state agent, I had no idea it was happening. But long after the fact, I had the opportunity to listen to the tape of this visit. I have listened to it at least a dozen times and can picture it exactly.

The recording begins with Dad, having just returned home from a mundane trip to the grocery store with Mom, being greeted by a group of police officers at his front door. For most people, this would have been alarming to say the least. Two of the men had driven 435 miles down from Wisconsin to Louisville, Kentucky. But Dad took it in stride, like this was something that happened every day.

I should add that Dad, at the age of seventy-six, was in poor health. He was morbidly obese, had diabetes, and was confined to a wheelchair on oxygen. But in the recording you can't hear any infirmity in his voice. He sounds strong as he greets the officers without a trace of surprise or concern, as if they were passing by asking for directions. Or stopping to borrow a cup of sugar. He welcomes them into his living room and invites them to sit down. I can envision the mess on the coffee table and how the officers must have had to clear off the couch to sit down.

First, they chat idly about the humidity. Then one of the agents says, "We're with the Wisconsin Department of Justice."

"Wisconsin," Dad says, as if confirming he'd heard correctly. I imagine he was thinking, *Uh-oh.*

The Wisconsin agent continues. "The reason we're here is we're working on some cold cases, and your name came up in a case file from 1980."

Dad chuckles at this, as if he's thinking, *Oh, what antics I got up to when I was a younger man.* I can imagine his face here perfectly. His coy smirk, the slight tilt to his head.

"We're following up on . . . ," the agent says, "two teenagers—a guy and a girl—that disappeared from the Concord House."

"The Concord House . . . ," Dad repeats, drawing out the words.

Then Mom's voice pipes up for the first time on the tape. "Don't look at me," she says. "I don't even know what the Concord House is." I picture her sitting on the couch here, a pile of knitting on her lap, which is the same image I have of her throughout much of my childhood.

"That's what I'm saying," Dad says. "What is the Concord House?" Then he says, in full con man mode, "Tell me something. I'm curious. Ah . . . how in the world did you end up . . . you guys coming here, or whatever?" Listening to this tape, I thought, *Ah, here's the lying voice.* I'd been waiting for it.

Garcia fields this question. He says something vague, like they're interviewing all the people who worked at the Concord House at the time. And Dad admits that he now remembers working there, as if his memories have just been sparked. Listening to the recording, knowing the outcome of this visit, hearing Dad put on the act of the doddering old man with the faltering memory made me feel ill. If there's one thing everyone in my family knew, it was that Dad had an incredible memory. I wanted to reach through time and space and scream, *You are not fooling anyone! You think you're so smart! The jig is up!*

Then Garcia asks Dad if he remembers that two teenagers, a nineteen-year-old boy and girl, came up missing. "I don't know. I gotta think about that," Dad says. You can hear him stalling for time, calculating how much to reveal. He sounds cagey, weighing every word. When I was growing up, Dad would always comment while we were watching crime shows that if a person was guilty of a crime, it was best never to admit it, and that the best strategy was to keep the story as close to the truth as possible. Listening to this tape, I can hear Dad doing that.

Garcia tells him that his name appears on a list of people interviewed in August 1980 following the disappearance of the two individuals. "Wait a minute," Dad says, and then admits that he recalls being interviewed, pretending that it's all coming back to him.

Most people in Dad's shoes would be a nervous wreck or sweating by now if they were guilty. But Dad remains cool and friendly to the strangers who showed up unannounced at his door, asking questions about a thirty-year-old murder case. Garcia later told me that Dad's mild manner was not how an innocent person usually responds to a surprise visit by the cops.

But then they throw him a curveball. Garcia explains that because they have DNA evidence on file, they're asking for biological samples to rule people out. The Louisville detective who has come along asks if they can get a DNA sample from Dad.

"Oh, I don't know if I can go for that," Dad says. You can hear him thinking, *Oh, crap!* He didn't see that coming.

Then—here's the shocker—Mom speaks up and says, "If you don't have anything to hide, you shouldn't worry about it . . ." When I heard that for the first time, I nearly fell off my chair. I didn't recall her ever challenging my father before. Was she emboldened by the crowd of law enforcement officers in her living room?

But Dad says he's seen TV shows where people are falsely accused after giving DNA. He's flustered for the first time during the visit. He says to let him think about it, and they can come back another time.

Garcia and the Louisville detective are ready for this. They have brought a warrant, which legally compels Dad to give the sample. Having run out of options, Dad submits. The analyst, who has been waiting outside, comes in to swab his cheek.

In the recording, you can hear the detectives bring the visit to a close. As they are walking out the door, Garcia adds a parting question, Columbo style. He says, "Do the names Kelly Drew and Tim Hack mean anything to you?" Dad says, "No, the names don't ring a bell." And then in a surreal super-friendly voice, as if guests were leaving after a chicken dinner, Dad says, "Thank you now! You have a safe trip back!"

Five weeks after Garcia's visit to my parents' living room in Louisville, I received an angry email from my brother Jeff. "Are you happy now?" he wrote. I had no idea what he was talking about.

Jeff had received a phone call from Mom that Dad had been arrested. Garcia and another Wisconsin agent, returned to Kentucky on July 30, 2009. This time they brought a crew of *seven* people to read Miranda rights to an old man in a wheelchair and take him away. In a search of his home, they found fake social security cards, forged birth certificates, and phony ID cards claiming he was a private investigator and a professional security guard. Disabled, maybe, but Dad was still in the scam game.

As soon as Jeff told me that Dad had been arrested, I knew I needed to be with Mom as soon as possible. She was ill-equipped to be on her own. Mom had never lived alone in her life. I knew Dad paid all the bills, still drove them everywhere despite being in a wheelchair. Dad controlled their money. She had always turned everything she earned over to him. She would have no idea how much they had in the bank. I doubted she made a single household decision for herself. I couldn't imagine how she was coping now that she was suddenly alone, with her husband held in jail under suspicion of murder.

I jumped in the car with Brynn, now sixteen, to offer my mom support in whatever way we could. Brynn and I were close. Normally, we would have loved a road trip together, but I was too distracted for our usual comfortable conversation. It was a seven-hour drive from Jefferson, Ohio, to Louisville, and I had too much time to think.

I called Garcia's cell number as I drove. "Are you sure?" I asked him. "Was his DNA a match?" He told me yes, they were 99.9 percent sure it was. I ended the call and began to shake. All the guessing, all the suspicions, could not have prepared me for the confirmation that my father was a killer. I had always hoped I was wrong. Because if I wasn't wrong about this murder, that meant that my other suspicions might be right too. How many lives had he taken?

I abruptly took the next exit ramp. I pulled into a gas station. I stood by the back of the car, my body turned to hide my wracking sobs from my daughter. There was no mistake. My father was everything I feared he was, and worse.

When Brynn and I pulled into the small parking space in front of my parents' worn-down trailer, I noticed that it had a new front porch. We walked up the wheelchair ramp to the front door. The heavy smell of dog urine permeated the air. We knocked on the door. My heart pounded. Now that I was here, I was afraid Mom wouldn't want me there. But she answered the door with a smile.

"How was your drive?" she asked cheerfully.

We set our suitcases inside the living room. A little dog yapped his greeting, too. Mom had dinner waiting for us in the kitchen; it was meatloaf and mashed potatoes. None of us mentioned Dad. Mom just asked how everything was at home. We tried to keep the conversation light and talked about her dog, church goings-on, and recipes. We enjoyed Mom's meatloaf with ketchup and floated our corn kernels in gravy in the pools of mashed potatoes. I told her how delicious everything was. She seemed pleased.

Later that night, after Brynn had gone off to bed, Mom and I sat on the couch and finally talked about Dad.

She told me that Jeff had gone to see him in the Louisville jail right after he had been arrested and told him, "If you can look me in the eye and tell me you didn't do it, I'll post bail." Dad couldn't do it.

Then Mom said something astonishing. Something I had waited my whole life to hear. She said that the day before the police came to arrest Dad, she'd cried out to God, "I can't take it anymore!" God had answered her prayer. Finally.

Mom told me this without emotion, but I wept for her liberation, and for the awfulness of her life with him. My mother never hugged me, and now I forced myself to reach over and hug her. It was awkward, and she soon pulled away. I was so stunned by her confession that I didn't press her for more.

I wanted her to keep talking, to finally open the vault of her stories that she'd kept secret for the forty years she'd been married to him. But she told me only that she'd come to the end of her tether and begged God for help. And she told me one more thing. She'd been pregnant with me when she and Dad married. I'd always assumed she'd gotten pregnant on her honeymoon. Now I saw that she had been trapped. I wanted to ask her if she felt regret back then. Did she already know what Dad was? But I didn't want to put her in a position of telling me she wished I'd never been born. I didn't know how to encourage her to open up. I realized I hardly knew my mother at all. We sat quietly for a while and then she went off to bed and I lay on the couch, exhausted, drained, and sad.

Brynn and I spent a few days with Mom after doing some cooking, cleaning, and shopping. While cleaning the house, I found much that the police missed. There were boxes of photos and tapes and newspaper clippings that my father had saved. And I found gallon-sized ziplock bags of prescription drugs. These were controlled substances. *Was Dad dealing?* Mom was clueless, or pretended to be. The "business" end of her life was Dad's turf.

Jeannine was on her way. When Brynn and I pulled out of the driveway, Mom stood waving goodbye, her little dog by her side.

After Dad's arrest, he was taken to the Louisville Metro PD, where an excruciating eight-hour interrogation began. I was able to watch the video years later, seeing Dad toy with detectives, dodging questions, and infuriating Garcia. He was also interrogated by a team from Louisville, seasoned detectives with their own true crime show. But Dad was more than they could handle. He had been playing with cops for fifty years. In the video recording of the interrogation, you can see and hear them become enraged. They hated that they couldn't get him to confess.

Finally, when asked to explain how his DNA matched the semen found on nineteen-year-old Kelly's clothes, he said that he'd had consensual sex with Kelly that night. He even claims they'd been "seeing each other." Listening to this, I thought two things: First, of course he wasn't going to admit to rape or anything else. Never admitting to a crime was a guiding principle for him. And we all knew he was a pathological liar. But, on the other hand, back in 1980, he cut a charismatic figure and had many affairs throughout his marriages, including his marriage to Mom, with women of all ages. And according to Dad, Kelly was one of them. But he denied killing her or Tim. He said, "I've never killed anyone in my life."

After eight hours, as infirm as he was, he outlasted the professionals—they still hadn't gotten him to confess. He concluded with this story: While he and Kelly were having sex in the parking lot that night, Tim Hack and two other guys came out of the dance hall and caught them in the act. He said those other guys beat Tim to death, and Kelly too, because she was screaming. (The injuries evident on Tim and Kelly's corpses tell a different story.)

When asked why he didn't tell the police at the time, if he had witnessed the murders, he answered, "I'm no snitch."

When I heard that line on the video—"I'm no snitch"—I nearly burst out laughing. Wasn't that exactly what he was?

I had been avoiding the news, but now I had to see how the local news outlets were talking about Dad's arrest. A Kentucky TV news station's website posted an article: LOUISVILLE MAN ARRESTED IN WISCONSIN COLD CASE DOUBLE MURDER. Neighbors were interviewed, and one is quoted as saying he was shocked. "He didn't fit that attitude at all. He was a real soft, pleasant guy. You would almost want to go over and visit him every single day. He was just that nice." Another neighbor said, "He seemed neighborly. . . . He seemed like a Boy Scout."

Reading the neighbors' responses to his arrest, I was struck by how familiar it all sounded. Dad could be charming and convincing. On a sort of masochistic impulse, I found online the 1972 episode of *To Tell the Truth* that Dad was on. Watching it brought me back to that living room on Avon Street, nestled on the sofa between my parents during what now seems, in retrospect, to be a time of innocence. Mom's attention was on the screen as the host introduced the three contestants.

When it was time for the four celebrities on the panel to make their choices, they each drew out the decision-making process as they tried to outsmart the show's producers and figure out who the real ex-felon-turned-writer was. Alan Alda and Kitty Carlyle chose one of the imposters. Gene Rayburn, correctly chose Dad, referring to him as a "young all-American-looking boy." He said Dad was the most unlikely-looking of the three to have a prison record, so that's why he voted for him. The last panelist, Peggy Cass, also picked Dad because he looked like someone "you'd trust with your life." The grin on Dad's face when she said this goes ear to ear. He seemed genuinely pleased as punch. And I'm sure he was. When the host, Garry Moore, asked, "Will the real Ed Edwards please stand up?" Dad stands, looking bashful and sweet. This moment was proof that he fully embodied the man he pretended and wanted to be: reformed, trustworthy, honest, and earnest.

When I think about how many people believed in his metamorphosis back in 1972, and how many people, even thirty-seven years later, believed him to be a kind and harmless man, it helps me understand how a naive twenty-one-year-old Kay Hedderly fell for it too. By the time we watched the show as a young family snuggled on our couch, she knew better, but she still didn't—couldn't—know it all.

32

Billy and Judith

From the outside, my life looked pretty good. My work with the church was fulfilling—my days were full of helping other people, running children's activities and parties, collecting for the community Christmas fund, restoring furniture in my workshop, and raising fine young teenagers who excelled in school, took early college courses, and had bright futures. I told no one in church about my father. They hadn't known him, and I never talked about him.

When his arrest in Louisville, Kentucky, for the Wisconsin murders hit the news, my world began to come apart. Friends called me and told me how shocked and sorry they were.

During the period after my father's arrest, other events in my life converged, creating a storm of emotional upheaval. My daughter's behavior abruptly changed. She and I had loved cooking together, doing crafts together, going to church activities together, but now she wanted nothing to do with me. I barely recognized her. She wrecked the car and lied about it. She lied about where she was going when she went out. She kept threatening to run away. Michael took the door off her room so we could keep a closer eye on her.

Michael worked so much and was hardly home at all, and I was on my own to deal with managing three teenage kids, and now one of them seemed to be heading for serious trouble. I blamed myself. I was failing as my daughter's mother.

One afternoon, when Brynn was out at a friend's house, I walked into her bedroom and sat on her bed, smoothing her white ruffled comforter with a trembling hand. I needed to do something, to take action, because I was afraid we were losing her.

I looked up at the bookshelves filled with some of my own favorite series. The Babysitters Club, Little House on the Prairie, American Girl Doll novels. Beneath her bed, I knew were bins of once well-loved Barbies—real ones—and every accessory a Barbie could need. I understood that there were no substitutes for the high-fashion strappy outfits that Mattel made. And I had happily supplied my little girl with authentic Barbie paraphernalia for each birthday and Christmas. My daughter would never experience the humiliation I did as a child, when the mother of my friend came to retrieve the suitcases of her daughter's Barbie gear, not trusting it in my care. But now Brynn was too old for Barbies, and I didn't know how to protect her.

She had told me she was spending the night at a friend's, but I had learned from another parent that she had stayed somewhere else so she could go to a party. The idea that I didn't know where she had been filled me with terror. Anything could have happened to her at the party and I would never even have known where she was. I feared for her safety. Even for her life.

When she walked in the next day, I told her she was grounded and couldn't leave the house other than to go to school for the next month. She screamed at me in protest and stomped into her doorless room.

In a split second, I made a desperate decision that I will always regret. The old paddle we had used when the kids were young had been gathering dust in the utility closet. When I say "we used" I mean "I used" because, while Michael believed punishment should be spankings with a paddle, he wanted no part of being the disciplinarian. It had been years since that paddle had been used, but I grabbed it now.

I walked into her room and said, "Bend over!" and I hit her with the paddle, on the rear, the way my father had beaten me. After everything I had been through as a child, I resorted to my father's method of discipline. After all this time, I fell back on his example.

With each strike of the paddle I became more overwhelmed by nervous anxiety and I began to shake and a strangled sound came out of me, like an ugly high cackle, drowning out my daughter's cries. Horrified, I couldn't stop myself. I was tipping toward hysteria. When I finally put the paddle down,

Brynn looked at me with confusion and pain, "Why are you smiling!?" she screamed at me. I realized my face had contorted into a crazed grimace. We were both shocked by what I'd done, and I was overcome with shame. Later that night, I apologized to her profusely. She was so hurt and angry that she couldn't hear my apology. And how could my apology ease the emotional and physical agony that I knew so well.

Like John, after the final fight forced upon us by my father, Brynn did not forgive me.

Another schism in all our lives occurred at the same time. Just as I had done in high school, as an adult I gravitated toward people who seemed to be outsiders and I wanted to help them feel included. I had noticed that the thirty-six-year-old son of one of our church leaders was awkward and often stood apart at church activities. I'll call him Cal. I made him my personal project, encouraging him, going out of my way to be friendly, and I pushed him to become a coach for our church youth soccer teams. And for the next several years it seemed like he was thriving with his new responsibilities.

Until the day I discovered that he had been, for years, grooming and preying upon an underage girl within our church community. His coaching position had given him access to this girl—and potentially others—and because I had urged him to become the coach, I believed myself to be responsible. I thought it was my duty to confront him. When I did, he insisted that he was in a long-term consensual relationship with the girl, despite being more than twenty years older than she. What was wrong with me, that I'd been so absorbed in my quest to save this man that I'd been gullible enough to endanger the girls within the church community by inviting a pedophile into their midst? I exposed Cal. The girl's family prosecuted, and he was convicted and received the maximum sentence.

Half the church congregation took Cal's side, blaming me for his downfall, and half the congregation defended my decision to expose him. My family was asked to leave the church. These were the people we socialized with, vacationed with. Now we were pariahs. We felt like our church community was our family and they had cast us out. The rupture was excruciating. Michael blamed me and the church equally and he began pulling away. I was losing everything I held most dear.

In the midst of my family crises, I received another email from Jeff that knocked me off my feet. This new email asked me a strange question: Had I been molested during my childhood? He was asking because Dad had written to him from prison and told him that I had been. And Dad had also told Jeff that he had killed a man because of it. I was stunned.

My answer to Jeff was one word. *Yes.*

I knew that I had been molested in Doylestown at the age of seven or eight, I wasn't sure exactly how old I was. I had tried to forget the details. I hadn't told anyone and certainly would never have told Dad about it. But Dad must have known. How else could he have told Jeff? And he killed the man? I felt sick to my stomach.

Thanks to Jeff's email, I was not surprised when I got a call from another detective, John Canterbury of the Norton, Ohio, police department. He asked if he could come to my house to ask me a few questions about a new case involving my father. I told him to come, but I dreaded the visit. Ever since turning my dad in, I had begun to have migraines. I cried all the time. I had trouble eating. Memories came to me that I didn't want to have, and they physically wrecked me.

Detective John Canterbury showed up at my door with another detective, Amanda Burnette, who smiled kindly and said little. John was a burly man with a warm smile. He was unlike the stiff and square-shouldered Chad Garcia. I brought them into my kitchen and we took seats around my table.

John Canterbury asked if I was in touch with my dad. I wasn't. I hadn't been in touch with Dad for a while even before I turned him in. Dad wrote letters to my brothers from prison, asking them for money for the commissary, but he was furious at me, so it didn't surprise me that Dad hadn't written. In one letter Dad wrote Jeff, he railed against me. *Jeff, I am sorry but I will never talk, see, or write to April. I wish you could see all the lies she has told this Det.*

When I read that line, I just shook my head. All the lies *I* had told? The irony was painful. I wished that Jeff could see all the lies my father told.

Dad had written to the Norton Police Department, however, and that's why Detective Canterbury was in my kitchen.

Canterbury asked me questions about our life in Doylestown. Did I remember anything about a young couple who had been murdered in our area? I told him I did remember that two "kids" had gone missing and were found dead. And that my brothers and I were scared for a while when we played in a field next door. We thought that we could get kidnapped because we assumed that the "kids" were our age.

Canterbury told me that they hadn't really been kids but young adults, and they were killed in August 1977 near us, in Silver Creek Metro Park. And I *did* remember that park. I also remembered with perfect clarity the strange trip to the park that Dad had brought us all on, to walk through weeds while he muttered and that we'd had no fun at all. I told Canterbury about that day.

He said, "Your father has just confessed to killing that couple in that park."

I had the urge to run to the sink and vomit. I just clutched my stomach and stared at him. My temples began to throb. He looked at me almost apologetically through his glasses before he went on.

"Does the name William Lavaco sound familiar?" he asked me.

"No," I said, because it did not.

"This is someone you might have known," he said.

He told me that Dad claimed to have killed him because Lavaco had molested me as a child. I flicked a glance at Detective Burnette. She gave me a reassuring nod. I took a deep breath as a face came into focus. It was Billy's. That was his name. Billy Lavaco. He had stopped coming around. Now I understood why.

"Yes," I said. "I knew him."

After the detectives left, I ran to the bathroom, doubled over, and vomited. William Lavaco was Billy. My mind began to play a reel of unwanted memories. Of sitting on Billy's lap at parties until my dad told me to get up. Of

Dad calling me downstairs after Billy had given me a piggyback ride and . . . I shuddered, remembering now, after all these years, that he had reached into the wide legs of my skort. If someone had done that to my daughter when she was eight years old, I would have wanted to kill him, too.

I went to my bedroom, closed my door, and opened my laptop. I began to search for what happened on the night of August 6, 1977.

According to the archived Akron *Daily Record* news articles, that Friday night, William Lavaco (21) and Judith Straub (18) drove to Silver Creek Metropolitan Park in Norton, Ohio, on the border of Wayne and Summit counties, just a few miles from Doylestown, where we lived on Kevin Drive. I learned that Billy, as he was known in our family, worked on the B&O Railroad. The articles didn't mention that on the side he was helping Dad finish up the construction on our house. Judith had just graduated from vocational high school and already had a job as a dental assistant.

According to the articles, late that night, they sat in Billy's 1975 Monte Carlo, in an area in the park where young couples went to be alone. They might have been fighting. People were quoted as saying he was jealous of the other guys she was seeing. Or maybe they were making up. Whatever they had been doing, the *Daily Record* reported that police found an empty car in Silver Creek on Sunday. Inside the car were Judith's shoes and her purse with over four hundred dollars in it. Just like the full wallet found in Tim Hack's car. When the Monte Carlo was still abandoned by 9 p.m. Sunday night, police ran the plates and found it belonged to William Lavaco. A call to his mother and his roommate revealed that he had not been seen since Friday night. Judith Straub's mother hadn't seen her daughter since then either. It was after dark when the search for bodies in the park began. The area was dense with weeds and difficult to examine at night. Visibility wasn't much better in daylight. But from a helicopter, two bodies were spotted in an overgrown area about three hundred feet from the abandoned Monte Carlo. A young man and woman had been shot point-blank in the neck with a 20-gauge shotgun. No gun was found in the woods. Scuba divers searched the nearby pond and came up empty-handed.

I turned away from the screen. Killed by a shotgun. I remembered with a violent shudder the shotgun Dad showed up with one day on Kevin Drive, the one he told me to shoot at the barrel in the front yard without actually telling me how. Had I held a murder weapon in my own hands as a little girl?

I wanted to stop reading and just crawl under my covers and never come out. But I read on. The Norton police chief was quoted as saying, "We are working on the assumption that it was a double homicide." They had no suspects. Billy was described by a friend as "a nice guy and even-tempered. He didn't seem like a person who'd have enemies." Judith was said to be a wonderful person, kind and generous. The consensus about both Billy and Judith by everyone who knew them was that no one could have had reason to dislike them, let alone kill them. The money in the car ruled out robbery as a motive. I put my face in my hands. Another young couple dead at my father's hands. Two more grieving families.

I thought back to when we had left Kevin Drive. It wasn't right after these August 1977 murders. In Wisconsin, he'd fled before the bodies were discovered. Here in Doylestown, Dad hid in plain sight for nine months until we sold the house, bought the van and the Winnebago, and drove south the summer of 1978.

Back in August 1977, police interviewed everyone connected to the young couple but had no leads. Dad was never even questioned about these murders. A friend of Billy's was arrested two years later, but a grand jury found no evidence and dismissed the case. Like so many others, the case grew cold.

I soon learned that when Canterbury had come to see me, he had already met with my father. He had received a crazy letter from a Wisconsin prisoner named Edward Wayne Edwards and wasn't sure if it was a hoax or for real. The letter claimed to have information about a 1977 double murder near Doylestown, Ohio. John Canterbury knew exactly which murders were being referred to. It was Norton's only unsolved murder case. In the letter, Dad concluded by saying that when they were done talking to him, they would be "wanting to put the needle in my arm."

Dad hadn't even confessed to the Wisconsin "Sweetheart Murders" of Tim and Kelly, and police wondered why he now wanted to confess to a double murder in Ohio instead. For someone who didn't know my dad, this might have made no sense. But it made perfect sense to me.

Now, as a sick old man aging fast behind bars, he was looking at the only possible escape route: death. And he was going to play games with detectives until he got what he wanted—the escape and notoriety of the death penalty.

Dad was making demands, even from his seemingly helpless position in prison awaiting trial in a Wisconsin jail, where, if found guilty, he'd be facing two life sentences there. He would die behind bars like a caged animal. Wisconsin had no death penalty. But Ohio did.

Dad knew Garcia and the prosecutors wanted him to plead guilty to the Sweetheart Murders. They wanted to wrap the case up. Why drag the Hack and Drew families through a long, painful trial? But Dad, always looking for the advantage, teased the promise of a confession if two conditions were met. One, he wanted a guarantee that he would be extradited to Ohio. The second demand was the promise that if he pleaded guilty to killing Billy Lavaco and Judith Straub, he would be guaranteed the "needle," as he put it. Canterbury agreed to bring Dad back to Ohio.

In the video recording of Dad's confession in April 2010 to the murders of Billy and Judith, Dad looked like he had lost over a hundred pounds in the nine months he'd been in prison in Wisconsin. But more shocking was the flat tone in which he delivered his confession.

"Billy was a nice kid," he told Canterbury. "I liked him, I really did, but he had a *problem*. At the time, my daughter April was *quite* young. He liked to *handle* her."

He claimed to have warned Billy to cut it out, but Billy kept paying me an unnatural amount of attention, and once, Dad said he saw Billy coming out of my bedroom during a party on Taylor Road. Billy said he was looking for the bathroom, which was next to my bedroom. But Dad said he was suspicious. He waited and observed until he was sure.

Watching the story unfold as Dad told it, I wondered if the last straw was what he heard or witnessed in the house on Kevin Drive, when he called me from downstairs and asked me directly, had Billy touched me where he shouldn't?

The detective asked Dad why he didn't go to the police with suspicions of child molestation. And Dad said, "My mind functions a little different than most people . . . You don't mess with one of my children." He was going to take matters into his own hands. In the confession, Dad recounted that with the intention of murder, he rode his bike late one night to an area in Silver Creek Metro Park where he knew that Billy and Judith would be parked at a spot popular with lovers.

He said he watched the parked car, and when Billy got out to relieve himself, Dad meant to shoot him. But Billy heard him and quickly returned to the car, and then Dad had to confront Billy in his car. At gunpoint, he told Billy to get out, and he told Judith to stay where she was. But she followed. In his confession, he actually blamed Billy for Judith's murder. Not that Billy pulled the trigger—Billy was killed first. It was dark and Dad claimed that Judith didn't recognize him. But Billy called him by name, saying, "Wayne, there's five hundred dollars in the car. Take the money." Judith, he told Canterbury, was collateral damage. "In the wrong place at the wrong time." Now that Judith knew his name, he had to kill her. After he shot Billy in the neck, Judith began to run, and my father described, with cold detachment, how he had to reload the shotgun while he talked to Judith, telling her to come back, telling her that he wouldn't kill her. She stopped. And then he killed her.

"I shot her and made my exit," he said without emotion in the video.

You might think that would be the end of it. But what Dad didn't know was that in 1977, Ohio had temporarily suspended the death penalty. Dad wasn't going to get the needle for killing Billy and Judith. He had confessed for nothing.

The man who delivered this bad news in person was not John Canterbury, but one of Dad's old police pals from Burton, Ohio, Brian Johnston. Back when we lived in Burton, Dad had befriended Brian, and they would meet for coffee at a little gas station/convenience store near our house. Dad would tip Brian off to any criminal activity he had gotten wind of.

Now Brian got to pay his old friend a visit in prison, and he had his own motives.

Brian said to Dad in their recorded session, "There is no death penalty for the crime you committed in Norton . . . *However*, there is the death penalty for capital murder from '81 on. So"—he takes a big sigh—"that's the skinny of it." Then he said, "Whether or not they told you that, shame on them." The "they" means John Canterbury here. In this recorded conversation, I can almost hear Dad wanting to whip out his belt and beat someone. He was furious. "I don't like what I'm hearing," Dad said. "I wouldn't have done any of this . . . I wouldn't have even talked to Norton!"

Dad wrote furious letters at this time to Canterbury, to Brian, and to anyone else who would listen.

In one letter to Canterbury, he wrote: "Did you know about that when you were here? Would you please give me an answer? . . . What makes you think WI will turn me over to you? I'm just an old man wondering where my life is going! I would really like to know . . . because there is another state that would love to have me & they did, & still do have the death penalty in 1977."

The first thing about this letter that amazes me is the line: "I'm just an old man wondering where my life is going!" *Where is your life going?* I want to say to the ghost of my father. *Nowhere! You're in prison!* He seems not to grasp that he is in the custody of the judicial system, no longer able to call the shots. And yet he's still trying to do just that.

The even more astonishing thing to me is that *no one* appears to have followed up on the last sentence of his letter, which is a direct admission that he committed murder in another state in 1977. One that had the death penalty then and still does. Which state fits that description? In which state could he have easily committed murder at lunch and been home by dinner? Pennsylvania, where my father had history. In 1977, we lived in Doylestown, which was just over an hour from the Pennsylvania–Ohio border. In my online search for unsolved murders in Western Pennsylvania, there were so many in 1977 that one newspaper article describes the phenomenon, listing the cases, many involving couples, young people, women raped and strangled. How many of those were at my father's hand?

Dad continued to write to my brothers, especially Jeff, often asking them for money, but also to vent his frustration about how Norton had lied to him, and about me—the traitorous daughter who turned him in. He complained about Chad Garcia, too. Never did he seem to consider that it was he himself who was responsible for landing where he had never wanted to be again: in jail.

The only letter I received from him was a torn scrap of paper that said, "Hold on to this. It will be worth something someday." And in the envelope was another small piece of paper with his signature on it. I ripped it up and threw it away.

33

Dannie Boy

2010

Now, with Dad fuming at Canterbury, Brian pulled out the card he'd been holding. He told Dad on the tape that, to get what he wanted, Dad needed to admit to a more recent murder. One that would qualify for the death penalty. Brian had one picked out for him—a 1996 murder that he suspected my father had committed but had never had proof. Now's the time to admit it, Brian told him. And so began a series of meetings and phone calls with Brian that became more and more absurd and grotesque as time went on.

The murder Brian wanted my father to confess to was one that Dad didn't want to admit to because even for him, it was too terrible. He would be confessing to the murder of a young man who he'd taken under his wing and given his last name: Dannie Boy Edwards.

There were other unsolved murders in the Akron area, but Dannie Boy's murder had been bothering Brian Johnston since 1996. Brian had been to Dannie's funeral and watched my father's behavior. He thought he'd acted like a showman. And he observed that Dannie's foster family kept their distance. He also noted that Dad had a tape recorder at the funeral and was interviewing attendees, doing his own investigation. It seemed like a stunt to Brian.

Fourteen years later, Brian saw his chance to get Dad to admit to it once and for all. In one recorded meeting Brian said, "If you are bound and determined, Wayne, to get executed, you need to tell me the truth. And I know what the truth is and so do you. We will charge you with capital crime on Dannie's death and you can go to death row in [an Ohio prison]. And I promise you, you'll get the f#@%ing death penalty."

"You get me back there . . . and then I'll work with you," Dad said. He was still trying to get away with not admitting to killing Dannie. Brian told him he was putting the cart before the horse. He tried to flatter and appeal to Dad's humanity.

"I'm going to be straight up. I think for the most part over the years you were a decent human being. I think you raised a great family. You have kids who are successful. April's a good person. Your wife's a nice lady. But along the way, I think you had periods . . . I'm just talking man-to-man . . . I think you had periods when your brain was broken. It didn't function right. You did some crazy sh-t. You did some crazy sh-t in Doylestown. You did some crazy sh-t up here in Wisconsin. Bottom line is, some families need some closure. Your good family needs some closure. It's better they know you did something than always f#@%ing wondering if you're responsible."

Of course we would never stop wondering what *else* he'd done. Jeff wrote to Dad asking him directly, *Did you kill Dannie Boy?* Jeannine wrote, too, asking Dad, exhorting him to confess to everything, to ask forgiveness, and to think about his salvation. Their letters did not move Dad to confess, and neither did Brian's argument.

All summer this conversation continued, with Brian telling him he couldn't get him back to Ohio until he plead guilty in Wisconsin and confessed to Dannie Boy's murder. But still Dad didn't want to do either. Dad was afraid that if he confessed before he got to Ohio, he'd be betrayed and would end up dying in a Wisconsin jail cell, unable to control his own fate.

Yet Dad was confident enough to tell Brian that when he finally got to Ohio and gave his full confession, he wanted to be served a dinner of Maine lobster and a loaded baked potato. He also had a request for the ride to Ohio.

In their taped conversation, he said, "Give me a bucket of Colonel Sanders chicken and I'll sit there in the back seat of the car and I'll just eat my bucket of chicken."

Brian asked, "Regular or Extra?"

Dad said, "Regular."

As chummy as they sound on the tapes, I can tell that neither trusts the other. Brian wanted Dad to provide some proof that he wasn't lying. Because he needed to know for sure that Dad pulled the trigger and killed Dannie that night in the cemetery. You can't execute a man without evidence, just because he says he committed the crime. What could Dad tell him, he asked, that no one but the murderer would know? Here's where the conversations got even stranger, worthy of one of Dad's favorite horror movies.

"Where's his head?" Dad asked in one of the calls, which remained light-hearted despite the gruesome details, as if they're having a minor dispute over Park Place in a game of Monopoly.

"We have his head," Brian said, bluffing. "We have pieces of it, what's left."

"You have pieces of his head?" Dad asked, skeptical.

"Uh-huh," Brian said.

"No you don't either," Dad said.

"Okay," Brian said.

"Where'd you get it from? Not from the gravesite."

This was true. Parts of the skull and jawbone had never been recovered. Brian needed more. Dad didn't want to give it to him and kept teasing him.

"I know where his head's at," Dad said. "So that's reason right there to get me back there so I can tell you. So, when are you going to get me back there, tomorrow?"

On another call that sounded like a script from an Abbott and Costello skit. Brian asked where "the head" was.

"I put the head in a feed bag," Dad said.

"Where'd you put the feed bag?" Brian asked.

"It's with the head," Dad said.

Both men chuckled—they are playing a sick game. But it's not moving things forward fast enough for Dad.

"You just don't under- *f#@%ing*-stand . . . You wouldn't even know about the God damn head if I hadn't mentioned it to you . . . You guys want to know where the head is? You get me back there. ["There" is Akron, his hub, of course.] That's my ace in the hole . . . I ain't going to tell you guys sh-t . . . 'til you get me back there."

Then Dad announced that he's tired of being toyed with and he's going to confess to an AP reporter. He wanted it to be known to the press, not just the cops, because he wanted to be sure that public outrage would carry him to the gallows in Ohio.

Dad went through with his threat. In the June 17, 2010, AP video, he gave a full concession. He said, "I'm responsible for it, and I'm wanting the death penalty." He told the AP reporter that he'd told the police this, but they hadn't followed up. In his public confession, he said that Dannie Boy was stealing from his children—a lie that Brian eventually would get Dad to retract—and he told Dannie to meet him at the cemetery and, once there, shot him (this part is true). He said he pulled a sawed-off shotgun out of his jacket and shot Dannie as he knelt in front of him looking for cigarettes in the duffel bag. He reloaded and shot him again. "He fell over," my father said in the video. "He didn't know it was coming. I felt bad," he said. "But apparently not bad enough to keep from doing it."

"I'm not new to crime," he went on. "I've been in crime my whole life. I made up my mind a long time ago that I wasn't going to go back in the penitentiary for just, you know, anything . . . I don't feel good about it . . . You got to remember something else, too. I'm thinking also of my family . . . I have put my family through God knows what. They don't deserve . . . They're good people. They've been kept in the dark, for example, my wife . . . I want to provide closure for my family. I've done it and I deserve the death penalty. As a matter of fact, uh, I have a daughter—" and then the video jumped, cutting out whatever he said about his daughter. I presume that I was the daughter he talked about, but what had he said to the AP reporter who chose to edit it out of the taped confession before it aired?

Dad was so furious at me that I don't believe he included me in his notion of "family" in that interview. In one of his angry letters to Brian he wrote, "Please don't call or tell or ask April anything about me or my case . . . she is not a part of me and I want no part of her. If you do, you're going to find me very hard to get along with."

But even the video confession didn't get him to Ohio. It got the case enormous notoriety, though.

Brian returned for an in-person talk with Dad for the last time and said, ". . . this stuff is all over the newspaper right now. There's a stigma about the missing head, and it portrays you as being somewhat of a monster besides being a killer, and I am just appealing to you as a father . . ."

Dad threw Brian a new tidbit. "Hey, here. You want something else? I did it for the insurance money. Now there. Now you got something."

Dad finally got to Ohio in August 2010 and confessed to everything. I don't know if he got KFC on the ride there, but he did get his lobster dinner. He admitted to Brian that he had played the long game with Dannie. This wasn't an impulsive scam. He'd coached and tutored him and got him into the military and made sure Dannie's life was insured for the maximum amount possible. He'd planned to murder Dannie when he was home on break after basic training. But the injured ankle and the medical release would have meant that Dannie was soon no longer going to be in the military, and the life insurance policy would no longer be in place. He had to move fast and improvise. He told Dannie to go AWOL with just two days to spare before he was released. He coached Dannie for their performance on that taped phone call. Dannie was using a pay phone close by. Dannie's admission on the phone call of breaking into the house, taking Jeff's stuff, and his fear of his former housemate, Ralph, was all a carefully rehearsed script, written by Dad.

It breaks my heart to imagine what Dannie was expecting the night he met Dad in the cemetery. Probably shelter and guidance from his father figure. But we do know that this happened: Dad asked Dannie to get his cigarettes from a duffel bag he'd brought, and when Dannie bent down, Dad pulled a shotgun from his jacket and shot his "son" in the back of the head. Twice. Then he buried the body in a shallow grave.

But the body would have to be found within a year of his disappearance or there would be no payout to the beneficiary of the policy. In the recorded confession to Brian, over lobster, Dad admits that he returned to the grave twice to disturb and scatter the bones, hoping to make them more visible. He took parts of Dannie's skull, intending to plant them in a stream by Ralph's house to frame him.

With only a month to spare, a hunter spotted a human leg bone with a shoe attached, sticking up from the ground.

"Ah," Brian said after the full confession. "It all comes together now."

And Dad finally confessed to the Wisconsin murders, retracting his earlier story. In the recorded video confession, Dad never admitted to raping Kelly, still insisting that she had gone out to the parking lot with him willingly to "have their fun." He said that he later came upon Tim and Kelly fighting, and when he approached, Tim attacked him. Dad said he struck Tim in the neck, possibly killing him. Kelly, horrified, turned on him now and he had to subdue her, too. He strangled her. Then he took their bodies and dumped them at the edge of a field.

I knew he was still lying. Dad's confession didn't match the evidence of stabbing on Tim's body or explain the ligature marks on Kelly's wrists and ankles that showed she was bound by rope. It didn't explain why she was nude or why strips of her clothes were scattered along the roadside, like intentional clues. He didn't admit this, but I believe in this case, too, Dad had picked out someone to frame. The road he'd scattered Kelly's clothing along led toward the house of a man who lived in the area and was somewhat of an outsider.

A June 21, 2010, AP article about the twenty-minute sentencing in Wisconsin after his confessions described Dad as "impassive, with head down." The courtroom was packed with family members of Kelly Drew and Tim Hack. Kelly's mother was quoted as saying to my father, "You are a lying, evil murderer and God is saving a special place in hell for you."

> "Tim's brother, Patrick Hack, who was 16 at the time of the murders, wiped away tears as he spoke about his brother's slaying. 'I've been waiting 30 years to face the bastard who killed Tim and Kelly and now I just want to leave my anger and frustration right here today and never waste another second thinking about you,' he said. 'May God show no mercy on your soul and may you rot in hell.'"

• • •

On March 8, 2011, Dad was granted his wish and sentenced to the death penalty in Ohio for the premeditated murder of Dannie Boy Edwards. His execution date was set for August 31. I was dreading the upcoming execution. But on April 7, Dad died of natural causes. His own body betrayed him, robbing him of his final performance. It was a small blessing that we—his children, grandchildren, and his wife—were spared the circus.

He died alone in his jail cell.

PART FOUR

34

Mythology of a Criminal

2010–2016

I had become estranged from my own family, but I knew that turning my father in for the Sweetheart Murders had given the Hacks, Drews, Lavacos, Straubs, and Dannie's foster family, if not closure, then at least answers. How many other families might find some degree of comfort knowing who did— and sometimes, more importantly—who did not take their child's life. Using Dad's memoir to map out his wandering course through the US, I continued to look up cold cases at each town where I knew he'd lived. I wasn't the only one doing this. Someone was as obsessed with my father as I was.

Seven months before Dad passed away, I got a call from a man named John Cameron, a retired detective working for the Montana parole board.

Cameron explained that when he had read about my father's confessions to Billy and Judith's murders in Ohio, he had immediately thought of the legendary 1956 double murders in Great Falls, which were still unsolved after more than fifty years. Having once been a detective on the Great Falls force, he was familiar with this famous case and was struck with the similarities. In both cases, the couples had been shot in lover's lane. Full wallets were found in the cars. Robbery wasn't a motive. Then while reading my father's book, he realized that my father actually had been in Great Falls at the time of the murders.

Cameron felt certain he was on the trail of solving the Great Falls cold case—*and* many others. There was also the 1960 Portland, Oregon, double murder of Larry Peyton and Beverly Allen. Like the young woman in Great Falls, Beverly's body had not been found near her boyfriend's. Like Kelly

Drew, Beverly had been bound and strangled. There were just too many similarities to ignore.

The police didn't seem to be making any progress with the timeline I had provided, but, I thought, maybe John Cameron was actually connecting some dots. I said, yes, I'd meet him. We made a date for him to come to my house in Jefferson, Ohio.

Michael and I had been coexisting in an uneasy truce. We didn't have a lot of overlapping interests these days and maybe we never had, but he was all in when it came to believing that my father had committed other violent crimes. He was more than ready to hear what Cameron had to say.

Cameron arrived a few days later having driven twenty-two hours straight from Great Falls. When I opened the door, I saw a clean-cut man—unrumpled despite his long drive. He was younger than I had expected, since he had already retired from being a detective. I guessed he was just a little older than myself.

Michael and Cameron shook hands. We all sat down at my kitchen table. I had my archives with me—which consisted of the timeline I'd made as well as clippings and photos. Cameron had his files with him as well and he already had most of what I collected, and much more.

Cameron began to share his theories. In addition to the Great Falls and Portland murders, he suspected my father of the January 1946 murder and dismemberment of a six-year-old girl.

Michael and I exchanged glances.

"But my dad was twelve years old then," I said.

Without any evidence, other than his own assertion that my father "loved to kill kids," he claimed Dad was also responsible for the May 5, 1993, killing of three eight-year-old boys in West Memphis, Arkansas. He said he thought Dad committed some of the most famous murders of the century—the murders of JonBenet Ramsey, the Black Dahlia, Sam Sheppard's wife, Laci Peterson, and finally, he said he thought my dad was the Zodiac Killer.

I thought he was out of his mind.

He pulled out his copy of *Metamorphosis of a Criminal*. The margins were filled with notes, sentences were underlined and words circled, as if Cameron were finding clues, deciphering a puzzle. He had already made up his mind that Dad was the world's most prolific serial killer. He had combed the memoir for anything—*anything*—that he could twist to confirm his suspicions.

Cameron was convinced that my father had killed many times on "EE Day" (Ed Edward's Day), May 5 (5/5), E being the fifth letter of the alphabet, representing the number five.

"What?!" I said, "The only EE Day in Dad's mind would have been his birthday, June 14, which he loved like a little kid. His favorite thing on 'EE Day' was a big party in the backyard and a cake that said '*We Love You, Dad*'." I couldn't believe I was now in the position to defend my father.

"And the two double murders he confessed to were committed in August," I added.

I tried to directly counter at least some of Cameron's claims, explaining that Dad couldn't have committed the West Memphis murders in 1993 because I knew for sure that at that time he was in Ohio, waiting for my daughter to be born any day.

"And I can prove Dad couldn't have killed JonBenet Ramsey in California, on Christmas of 1996," I said, "because I have a photo taken that Christmas in Burton and there he is, playing with my kids with the ball pit he gave them for Christmas."

But Cameron was undeterred. There was no reasoning with him.

When I waved goodbye to him that day, I expected I would never hear from him again. I was disappointed not to have found an ally interested in solving my father's crimes. I was definitely not interested in trying to force mismatched puzzle pieces to fit. I was interested in real answers.

After Cameron's visit, I realized that I didn't even know, exactly, what a person had to do to be called a serial killer. I needed to do some research. That night, alone in my bedroom when Michael was at work, I got on my laptop and found a report on the FBI's website from a multidisciplinary symposium on serial killers. I wondered how much of my father I would recognize. Was John Cameron onto something? How many of his theories were absurd?

According to the report, the common traits among serial killers were listed as: sensation seeking, a lack of remorse or guilt, impulsivity, a need for control, and predatory behavior. *Oh my God*, I thought as I read the list. *Dad was all of the above.*

The article also listed the traits consistent with psychopaths, or people with psychopathic personality disorder. Not all psychopaths are serial killers, and not all serial killers are psychopaths.

I felt a chill when I read that psychopaths "use a mixture of charm, manipulation, intimidation, and occasionally violence to control others in order to satisfy their own selfish needs." That description could have been custom-made to fit my father. Growing up, I thought this was just ordinary behavior. Now I read that it was in fact a sign of pathology.

I picked up my copy of Dad's memoir and flipped through to early psychiatric reports that he included in the back. I had skipped over these when I read the book as a child, but as an adult, I found them fascinating and terrifying. One Szondi test result from when my father was examined by psychologists at sixteen years old reads: *Our subject is socially maladjusted. He has a strong need for passive affection and attention. There is sexual conflict suggestive of sado-masochistic nature. Emotional outbursts can be expected, and Wayne is likely to show such reactions to outside experiences. Negativism and impulsive behavior are evident. It can be antisocial and of a criminal nature.*

Another assessment has this to say: *The personality picture is one of a highly disturbed individual who needs psychiatric help. This will probably be impossible since it would take a very long-term treatment to make any change. It is a case of a boy who has multiple difficulties most of which it is too late to correct. A positive directional program, such as the services, may offer much for him, but we cannot hope for too much. Wayne is neurotic and possibly psychotic.* His behavior was definitely psychopathic even as a teenager, and he had gone out of his way to include these reports in his book. Why? Did it make him feel special? Was he proud to be a psychopath?

I got up, paced my room, went to the bathroom, got a drink of water. I wanted to move on, do something else, pick up a book, turn on the TV, but I was drawn back to the FBI website by a compulsion. I found a list called the "Psychopathy Checklist." I decided to see if the father I knew checked all the boxes.

The checklist is divided into four categories.

The first is the "interpersonal category," which includes the traits of superficial charm, grandiose sense of self-worth, pathological lying, and manipulation of others. *Okay. Dad easily qualifies within that category*, I thought.

The second category is "affective" traits, which include lack of remorse or guilt, lack of empathy, and failure to accept responsibility. In his taped confessions for the murder of Billy and Dannie, he showed little remorse. And as for taking responsibility, I remembered my father crawling into my bunk after he beat me so badly that I could not even lie down on my back. He didn't say he was sorry. He said, "I hate that you made me have to punish you." He wanted me to tell him it was okay, that I deserved it, and that I loved him anyway. But he didn't feel guilty. I decided he qualified for the "affective" traits category too.

The third category is "lifestyle," and Dad qualified without a doubt. Traits include stimulation-seeking behavior, impulsivity, irresponsibility, and the lack of realistic goals. I recalled how he would spend roll after roll of quarters playing Pac-Man while his children didn't have enough to eat.

The fourth is the "antisocial" category, which includes poor behavior controls, early childhood behavior problems, juvenile delinquency, and socially deviant lifestyles. That one was a no-brainer.

A calm settled over me. Everything I had read confirmed that I was not wrong about him. I learned that, without question, my father qualified in every category as a psychopath. And even though that didn't guarantee he'd become a killer, he did. But was he a *serial killer*?

Serial killers, the FBI symposium report goes on to say, have common aspects in the murders they commit. They usually don't know their victims. They might be motivated by anger, status, power, excitement, and sex. They pick vulnerable victims whom they desire and can control.

As I read this, I tried to compare his known murders with the common aspects of serial killers. As for not knowing his victims? Well, he claimed to have known Tim and Kelly, and we know he knew Billy, Judith, and Dannie Boy. He was definitely motivated by anger and a desire to protect his child when he killed Billy. But the murder of Dannie Boy was in cold blood—for money. That killing was a deadly scam two years in the making. And we will never really know why my father killed Tim Hack and Kelly Drew. Maybe it was sex and power.

A person isn't called a serial killer unless they've killed at least five victims over a period of time, not at once. My father confessed to five killings over three murderous episodes. I closed my laptop. I still believed there were more than five victims, but I didn't believe John Cameron's fairy tales.

I didn't think too much about what Cameron was up to. I had my own troubles. My marriage was disintegrating, and I began having bleeding ulcers. Just like Aunt Lucille, I ignored the symptoms. It wasn't until I passed out in the bathroom and Brynn got me to the emergency room that I realized how serious it was. I was taken right into surgery, and I was in the ICU for about a week.

Meanwhile, John Cameron went public with a 2014 book called *IT'S ME: Edward Wayne Edwards, the Serial Killer You Never Heard Of.* Then in 2018 he released a six-part documentary called *It Was Him: The Many Murders of Ed Edwards.* He went on late-night talk radio, on websites—claiming his own wishful thinking as fact without any supporting evidence. And people were eating it up. He even appeared on the *Today* show with Megyn Kelly and declared that my father had killed hundreds of people. With every new documentary or national news article, my phone would start ringing off the hook. People I hadn't heard from in decades reached out to me on social media. *We had no idea that your dad was the Zodiac Killer!*

I was not receptive to the many salivating reporters and journalists who called me, but one was less pushy than the others. Josh Dean seemed nice, but when he asked me if I would work with him on an investigative journey into my father's yet unsolved crimes, I turned him down like I had all the others.

I was trying to put my life back together after my kids moved out. I joined a church of a different denomination. I had hoped and expected Michael would join with me, but he had sworn it off. I dove into life in my new church community, I worked as a house cleaner and decorator for small businesses and a few of my friends. I restored furniture in my barn. I continued to lose weight and kept it off with obsessive gym workouts, sometimes three a day. The rapid weight loss had resulted in skin that had nowhere to go. Michael encouraged me to have skin removal surgery. I was reluctant because cosmetic surgery like this wasn't covered by insurance. I was afraid Michael would use the expense as a source of resentment for the rest of my life, even though it had been his idea. Despite the cost, I had the surgery and Michael was pleased with the result. And I was too. We both felt optimistic enough about the future that we decided to buy a new house nestled in the woods on a beautiful piece of property in the nearby town of Kingsville, Ohio. The house had a huge master bedroom suite with a sitting room and a four-car garage and outbuildings for all of Michael's toys—his four-wheeler, his boats, his snowmobiles—and all my woodworking tools. I loved our new home.

My father had been dead five years and, still, the media frenzy churned in the background. I frequently received calls wanting me to appear on this show or that documentary, reporters wanting to interview me. I was determined to do none of it.

But then I got a call from Scott Peterson's lawyer, asking me if I had any information that could free his client, that could verify Cameron's assertion that my father had killed Laci Peterson. He had to pursue the chance that his client was innocent of killing his wife and their unborn son.

That was the last straw. I was tired of getting phone calls about crimes that my father didn't commit, yet no one was looking into the crimes I thought he had committed. I had turned all my information over to the authorities and expected them to do the investigating. Cameron had embarked on his own journey and was leading the public astray, while it seemed to me that the most likely connections were going uninvestigated by police. There weren't funds for legitimate investigations, but the thirst for sensational content provided plenty of funds for conspiracies.

Now Edward Wayne Edwards was a tabloid headline. It was time to set the record straight. Originally, I had no intention of going public, but if conspiracy theories could free murderers like Scott Peterson, I decided I needed to somehow push back against Cameron's narrative. If the police departments didn't have the resources to follow up on my suspicions, then I'd have to do it myself. But the task was so overwhelming, and I didn't know where to begin.

The journalist Josh Dean happened to message me again, right before I heard from Scott Peterson's lawyer. In an impulsive move, I messaged Josh back: "I'm ready to talk." I didn't know if I could trust him, but I was desperate to find the truth and I decided to take a chance.

I sensed that Josh would be respectful and dig into my father's story doggedly and in good faith. I believed he would go the distance with me. I was relieved that I finally had a partner, and that I was not alone in the attempt to make sense of my father's life and his crimes.

35

The Clearing

Our collaboration took the form of a podcast called *The Clearing*.

Josh showed up to our first official podcast meeting, at my house, in what I would come to think of as his uniform—a plaid button-down shirt. His producer, Jonathan Menjivar, followed, with his giant mic and recorder slung over his shoulder.

I ushered them into my home and into the kitchen, where I'd set out trays of veggies and dip, and cheeses. I offered coffee, thinking we'd sit down to get to know each other, but I realized that Jonathan already had the microphone on. We had begun.

They asked what materials I had to share, and I took them up to my bedroom and dug out two suitcases full of photos, documents, and cassette tapes I had found in my parents' trailer after my father was arrested. We sat in the seating area in my room, and I put the suitcases on the floor and ran downstairs, returning with the snacks while they began to explore the mountain of material that I had not had the energy or the will to dig through myself.

The biggest questions I had, I told Josh and Jonathan, were split into two time periods—before and after I was born. Dad's book might help with the early period, and my own memories might help with the later period.

By now, Josh had read Dad's memoir, so he knew all about Verna, Dad's pregnant girlfriend who Dad claims he left in Denver when he took off with Jeanette. I told Josh that in the 1990s, my brother Jeff was stationed out West in the army. Dad had asked Jeff to help him find Jeanette's son—his son. But he never asked Jeff to help him find the child he conceived with Verna. Why would he try to find one child and not the other?

Did he already know that Verna's child couldn't be found? I desperately wanted to know the answer.

Also, what about the 1956 Great Falls murders and the 1960 Portland murders? Cameron was sure my father was responsible, but he—and the police—had no proof.

As for the period after Dad published his book and declared himself a re-formed family man, what might he have done in each of the places we'd lived? I was entrusting these two young men with what felt like my life.

At each of our sessions, Josh would share what he'd learned or found, or play a snippet of tape, or present me with a list of questions. Looking into the artifacts of my past was like ripping off a scab covering a stab wound to my heart. Sometimes I would feel a migraine coming on and had to go lie down in a dark room.

In one box of cassette tapes, Josh found something he wanted to play for me. When he hit play, I was flooded with a sweet sense of nostalgia. I had heard this tape before, but it still hit me hard when I heard the voice of Aunt Lucille. The call had been recorded back when I was a baby. It was after Dad learned that he'd been adopted and he had actually found and called up the woman who turned his birth mother in for stealing a hundred dollars when Dad was a baby. On the recording, he's telling Aunt Lucille about the call to the woman who ruined his mother's life. Aunt Lucille sounds worried. She thinks he should leave the past alone. He tells her he thinks it's important, and someday his children should know his whole story. "You want to tell April *everything* about your past?" she says.

"Yes," he says, "I do."

"Well," Lucille says in a scandalized tone. "Well, I don't think that's *normal* in a person."

I had to laugh at that through my tears. I could perfectly picture her say-ing this. Dad was hardly a *normal* person. But I knew what she meant. She didn't think it was normal for a person who had been a convicted criminal to share his past life experiences with anyone, let alone his children. But he'd shared it with the entire world in his book.

One day, in a box of papers, I found a brochure for one of my father's church retreat speaking engagements, where he lectured to Christian youth about staying out of trouble.

I held it up and showed it to Josh and Jonathan. "Look," I said with disbelief. "The retreat was just eight days before he killed Billy and Judith."

I felt freshly humiliated with each revelation. How much of my childhood had been a farce? Each day I learned something new that turned my stomach. My ulcers were getting worse.

BURTON, OHIO

We made an itinerary of all the places we would need to go to interview people involved in my father's cases and in my past. We tackled Ohio first, where Dad had always felt most at home. Our first visit was to meet with Brian Johnston in a conference room in Burton. There, Josh asked Brian when he began to suspect my father of killing Dannie Boy and Brian shared his recollection of the case, going over the crime in detail all over again. I listened with dread, knowing each detail already—I had watched Dad's confession; I knew what he had done. I sat wishing I didn't have the gruesome images branded in my mind.

And then the four of us visited Dannie's gravesite. He was buried in the same little cemetery that I used to ride my bike past as a senior in high school. Dannie's gravesite is so close to the spot where he was killed that I thought, *How could he find any peace after death here?* It seemed such a cruel irony. A flat stone marker with "Dannie Boy Edwards" engraved on it lay across his grave. We all stood solemnly, saying nothing.

I fought back tears, the terrible weight of what my father had done, pressing down on my chest like a fist. What he had done to that poor young man. I couldn't get the picture out of my head, the promise to help, the gun, Dannie's head. A plan two years in the making. Cameron was right. My father really was a monster. Maybe not Cameron's monster. But one nonetheless.

DOYLESTOWN, OHIO

Our next trip was to Doylestown, where I had lived from the ages of five to eight, kindergarten through third grade. Some of my most indelible memories are rooted here, in this little rural part of the world. Josh and Jonathan met me at my house in Kingsville and we drove the two hours together. We went in their rental car. My head was hurting too much to drive. We had to stop at a gas station for Tylenol. My head felt like it was going to pop off. Lately my headaches had been keeping me up at night. I was so exhausted I fell asleep on the way. They let me sleep. They knew the toll this was taking on me. On every outing we took, I fell asleep in a car, and they did not disturb me.

On this trip, I wanted to test my recollections. For example, had I really remembered the trip to the park where Billy and Judith had been murdered? Could it really be true that Dad had taken his wife and children to the place he'd just killed two people? My memories of that day were clear and sharp. If they weren't accurate, what else was suspect? Norton's Silver Creek Metro Park was just a few miles from where I'd lived on Kevin Drive. The park was our first stop.

When we arrived at the entrance, I worried that I'd made a mistake. I recalled a parking lot, a pond, and weeds. There was a parking lot and there were weeds, lots and lots of tall grass, but I didn't see a pond. I strode through the weeds, Josh and Jonathan in tow. The scale was all wrong. I had to remind myself that I had been eight years old at the time, so I squatted down to look at the world from four feet high. The grass and weeds were nearly at eye level now, as I remembered. I relived the memory of stumbling after my father as he took long strides. I walked away from Josh and Jonathan and stopped where I expected the pond to be. I didn't see it. I was starting to doubt everything. Then I turned around and looked behind me and saw a berm. I walked to the top. And there before me was a familiar scene. There was the pond with lily pads and cattails. And beyond the pond was a row of trees. The trees were much bigger now—thirty years bigger—since I had last seen them. The pond was more a muddy water hole than I remembered it to be, but still it was the pond. I had been right. I felt enormous relief. This was validation. I could trust my memories of places, and, as importantly, so could Josh and Jonathan.

This pond, these weeds, this park was the last place Billy and Judith had been alive. This was the place my father shot them. Such a violent death. They must have been so frightened. In my father's confession, he mentions that he and they had been to the same bar that night in August 1977. Billy and Judith had come to this parking spot from the bar, probably glad to get some time alone. In the evenings, Dad had often played pool, yakking with other patrons, hanging out just to eavesdrop. He had known where to find Billy and Judith that night. He had known Judith would be there. And that didn't stop him. He had never valued her life. She was expendable to him.

Our next destination was the farm on Taylor Road. It was just a few miles away, but Taylor Road is long, and as we pulled onto it, I told Josh that I wanted to find it without GPS. As we drove, nothing looked familiar. We went through an intersection and at once I knew where we were. I said, "Keep going. It's going to be on the right side; we'll go down a dip, across a bridge over a stream." And finally, "Stop!" There it was. Not the house—that had not been rebuilt. But I recognized the big tree in a field, and cherry trees—now much bigger—still lined what had once been the driveway. But even the driveway had become overgrown with grass. Time had covered up traces of our lives there, but I still remembered it as a magical place. I still thought of Cindy as forever grazing in those fields. We can't ever go back, really, but it was reassuring to see the trees in my memory still standing.

The house on Kevin Drive was less than a mile away from the Taylor Road farm, which surprised me. An easy walk from one to the other, if Dad had not been so lazy. I recognized this house right away, even though it now had blue siding with white trim. There was a new deck and sliding glass doors off the kitchen. Someone had done a nice job with landscaping and maintaining the big, beautiful lawn. The house looked neat and tidy, and smaller than I remembered. But the woods behind the house were familiar. I told Josh and Jonathan, "There's the tree that we built the treehouse in. The tree behind it, to the right, was the one with the tire swing. That's where the vines were, where we swung like monkeys. Here was where the woodpile was." Memories of living here in poverty bombarded me. Remembering sleeping in the bunk beds in the living room, lugging firewood into the house, just two logs at a time. It made me grateful for my house in Kingsville. Michael and I had both worked hard to have what we had. And we had so much. I thought of that little girl, swinging on the tire swing; she had no idea that the life she lived here would someday be just a memory, that things would someday be different. She had no idea what her father had done, what he would do, and that someday she would come back here long after he was gone.

On an ordinary day, when I wasn't walking—or stumbling—down memory lane with Josh and Jonathan, I would be either cleaning a house or wood-working. One day, a few weeks after our return from Doylestown, I was in my workshop, refinishing a bedroom set for a client, when I felt a sharp burning sensation in my abdomen. I went inside to make a work-related call and the pain became so severe I realized I needed to call 911 instead. I was rushed into surgery again. This time, it was much more serious. The ulcer had perforated. The surgery resulted in an incision from my breastbone to my navel. That expensive flat tummy was sliced open. The incision was glued shut, and after several days I was sent home. Michael had visited me once, for five minutes, after the surgery. The day I got home from the hospital, I vacuumed my living room. No matter how well or ill I felt, I was anxious to have the house perfect for Michael when he came home from work. Like Mom must have felt anxious that Dad would come home and find fault. I felt that way myself before my father came home. Michael was not my father, not by a long shot. But still, the instinct to anticipate his disapproval was there, even if it wasn't warranted.

Two weeks later Michael went with me to a follow-up appointment with the surgeon. I wish he hadn't. I was lying on the exam room table, the fresh scar red and angry. My stomach was swollen, puffy, ugly. It looked ghastly. Michael grimaced at it and said, "Well there goes twenty-one thousand dollars." Tears sprang to my eyes. I turned my head away from my husband. The surgeon patted my arm in sympathy.

My surgery and recovery put the travel for the podcast on pause, but as soon as I was well enough, we were back on the road. Our next destination was the Geauga County Sheriff's Office.

This was close enough to be another day trip for me. Josh and Jonathan flew in from New York and I met them at a hotel nearby. We had learned that sixty tapes pertinent to my father's case ended up at the Geauga County Sheriff's Office. Josh had run into trouble getting anyone in the office to help. But when I called the office, I identified myself to an incredibly helpful clerk named Sharon as the daughter of Edward Wayne Edwards, and she agreed to help us out. Josh sent her a box of blank tapes, and she copied all that she was legally able to copy onto them. Our mission on the day of our visit was to pick up the tapes and to look through the files that contained transcripts of meetings, police reports, and who knew what else.

When she handed over the box of tapes, Josh asked her if she'd listened to them. She said she had listened to just the first few minutes of them. "He sounded like a Creepy John Wayne," she said. Dad would have liked the John Wayne part of the comparison.

We made photocopies of everything Sharon was allowed to copy in the files. I saw copies of letters that Dad wrote from prison and those that he received. There were even some letters to and from my brother Jeff. Letters from Dad to Brian Johnston. Interview transcripts with other detectives' meetings with Dad.

We went back to my house and began listening to the tapes. That's when we realized that my father's taped, scripted phone conversation with Dannie Boy had been preserved, as well as the bizarre conversations between Brian and Dad, where Dad teased Brian with clues about "the head." Also among them were the tapes Chad Garcia had gathered from his investigation. Back in 2009, I, too, had turned over all the tapes I had found in Dad's trailer to the Geauga County Sheriff's Office. Now, almost a decade later, I had them back. There were prison interviews with police from several states, his confessions, the whole works. It was a treasure trove.

WISCONSIN

A few weeks later, we were in Wisconsin to interview Detective Chad Garcia at the Jefferson County Sheriff's Office. He was just the same as the day he sat at my kitchen table nine years earlier. Still sat ramrod straight with his military bearing. We all set out together to visit Tim Hack's father, Dave. Tim's mother had died twenty-two years after her son was killed. She did not live to see Tim's killer caught.

I had met Dave and his second wife, Judy, the year before. They had reached out to Chad Garcia nine years after my father was arrested for murdering Dave's son and Kelly Drew. They asked for my contact number, and I had given Garcia my permission to share it with them. When Dave and Judy called me to ask if they could visit, I was amazed at Dave's bravery in wanting to meet me—the daughter of the man who killed his son. I said, "Yes! Please come."

When they arrived, I was nervous. I wiped my palms on my pants to shake their hands, but Dave and Judy reached out to me with hugs and big smiles. They sat close together on my couch, and I sat on the floor at their feet, gazing up at them. They looked at me, radiating love and acceptance, as if I was their own child.

"We didn't tell our kids we were coming," Judy said. They weren't sure how their family would feel about it, so they'd kept their plans to themselves. They told me that between the two of them, they have over thirty grandchildren.

"*Thirty!*" I said. "That's a lot of cousins."

"None of them know their uncle Tim," Judy said. Or the woman who might have been their aunt Kelly. Dave recently sold his large dairy farm. Tim was the one who would have taken it over, and without him there was no need to hold on to it when it became too much for Dave. He and Judy still lived in the farmhouse. From the house, they could see the cemetery where Tim and Kelly were buried.

Then they asked me how I was coping. *Me?* I felt I almost had no right to answer them. "I'm fine," I said, my stock response, but they saw right through me.

"I am so sorry you had to go through the pain of turning your father in," Dave said, his eyes steady on mine. My own eyes welled with tears. I don't know why I expected them to be angry with me—to hold my father's actions against me. It was just the opposite, and I was filled with gratitude. And humbled at their grace.

Before they left, they invited me to visit them in Wisconsin, and they presented me with a gift, a wooden box that Dave had made, about the size of the treasure box that held my happy grams, the one that Dad had thrown on the burn pile.

Dave's wooden box was carefully crafted. The top was made of strips of oak and cherry, with a knob made of wooden beads. He'd made one for each of his children and grandchildren that year for Christmas. There was a note inside. It read:

> THANK YOU
> *We are grateful for your courage and your honesty.*
> *You are a wonderful person. We will not forget your kindness.*
> *Dave and Judy*

And now, a year later, I was taking Dave and Judy up on their offer to visit them in Wisconsin, but I was bringing along the podcast crew and Chad Garcia to hear and record Dave's story. We stopped on the way to buy sandwiches and cookies to have lunch with the Hacks.

We were warmly greeted and ushered to a large table in the kitchen where we had our lunch. Chad and the Hacks had been through a lot together. Their trust in him was reassuring. He had been the right person on the other end of the phone when I had called the hotline ten years earlier.

I admired the kitchen island's butcher block top and asked Dave about it. "Judy and I made that," he said. I smiled, and thought it was the most romantic thing I'd ever heard.

After we ate, we moved to the living room area and Dave talked about the morning of August 10, when Dave and his wife noticed Tim hadn't come home the night before. The Hacks called Kelly's parents, hoping they knew whose house they'd gone to, to crash after the carnival perhaps. But Kelly's parents were worried too. Kelly's bed had not been slept in.

Dave and his younger son, Patrick, went to the Concord House and found

Tim's car still in the parking lot. That was odd enough. But what really raised the alarm was that Tim's wallet and keys were still in the car. Dave knew this meant that Tim and Kelly hadn't just run off, but the sheriff said, *Oh, they'll be back soon.* I can only imagine the panic that Dave Hack had to overcome as he knew that something sinister had happened, even while investigators were trying to reassure him.

Missing persons reports were filed. The search was on. Attendees at the wedding and Concord House employees were questioned. Someone mentioned there was a van spotted leaving the parking lot. For over two months, the Hacks and Drews waited for the phone to ring with information on the couples' whereabouts. Misleading reports of sightings and rumors of elopement were only distractions. Dave practically set up an information center at police headquarters, becoming part of the investigating team. There had been two weddings at the Concord House that night. Dave kept an index card for each person who attended the weddings. With every bit of information gained, Dave felt he was accumulating data but getting nowhere.

Seventy agonizing days later, Kelly and Tim's bodies were finally found, discovered by chance by two Milwaukee squirrel hunters in the woods at the edge of a cornfield about eight miles from the Concord House. Tim, fully clothed, had been stabbed to death; and Kelly, naked, had been strangled and tied up and likely raped. No arrests were made. For thirty years, Dave Hack couldn't look at certain community members without wondering, *Was it you?* The not knowing took a terrible toll. Now he knew, finally, and that was a relief. But he never got the answer to the gnawing question of *why, why, why?*

When we were done recording, I asked Dave what his latest woodworking project was. He took me down to his basement workshop, where I looked around in amazement. Along the shelves were samples of his Christmas gifts past and present. Each one was a carefully crafted wooden treasure—a box, a figurine, a plaque. His latest Christmas gift lined the shelves—little reindeer ornaments, ready to adorn trees. He invited me to try my hand at making one. I was honored. He stood beside me as I moved the bandsaw along the marked block of wood, making the intricate cuts. Standing beside this gentle man, working with wood, was such a contrast to my life with my father—who taught me plenty about working with wood and tools—in his own brutal way.

It should have been Dave's son Tim who was learning from his father. Not his killer's daughter. I concentrated on making the next cut just right.

When we left the Hacks, Chad said he had something he wanted to give me. Back in the sheriff's headquarters, while Josh and Jonathan waited in the car, Chad greeted me differently. I saw compassion in his eyes as he handed me three CDs with the interrogation and interviews with my dad. And then he let me look through a box of photos and papers he had not turned over to the Geauga County Sheriff's Office back when he'd turned in everything else. In the box, I spotted one photo that called to me. I picked it up and held it close. It was a photo of Dad and Jeff. Jeff was just a little boy, his thumb in his mouth. He's sitting on Dad's lap, looking at the camera, and one hand is resting on Dad's stubbly cheek. A sob rose in my chest. I had to sit down. "I'll just take this one," I said.

That night, a huge snowstorm grounded planes. I spent the night in the airport, curled up sleepless in a plastic chair, trying to process everything I'd just seen and absorbed. I pulled out the photo of Dad and Jeff and gazed at the tender expressions on their faces. Such love between a father and son. So much sadness. It was just too much. I wept for Dave and for Tim and the future they never got to share. And I wept for my brother, too.

36

Great Falls, Montana

It was time to tackle our biggest questions about Dad's early life. We started with the one that had brought him to Cameron's attention to begin with. The big case we hoped to explore was the still unsolved double murders of Patricia Kalitzke and Lloyd "Duane" Bogle in 1956 in Great Falls, Montana.

Before we flew out to Great Falls, I had to refresh my memory of the case. I looked up anything I could find online about the Great Falls murders. An AP article published in a Montana paper read, "Indications at the scene were that [Patti], like her boyfriend . . . had been forced to kneel before the brutal killer, who then fired a bullet into the back of her head." She was "fully clad," and the preliminary investigation by the county coroner "failed to show any signs that she had been criminally molested, either before or after she was killed." Another account of the murder says her body did have injuries consistent with a struggle or even a sexual assault. In the autopsy, semen was found on a vaginal swab—a standard procedure for female autopsies at the time—and preserved.

I recalled that Dad had a clipping of these murders in one of the boxes of papers I had found at my parents' trailer. I knew he was familiar with the case. I reread the account in Dad's memoir of his time in Montana to see if he had said anything about it. In 1956 he was on a crime spree with his wife, Jeanette, under the alias of James Langley, robbing gas stations throughout the West. They stopped in Great Falls, where Jeanette's brother lived. Dad pulled an armed robbery there as well as in Billings, where he was caught and arrested in March of that year.

The fact that my father was arrested for armed robbery just two months after the shocking Great Falls murders, coupled with the fact that he was wanted in Akron for jailbreak and in Florida for fraud, means he was very likely questioned about the double murder when he was picked up by the Billings police. The murder would have been fresh on detectives' minds. Strangely, he didn't mention this murder in his book at all. He didn't shy away from mentioning the Portland murders. In fact, he goes out of his way to include them. Why would he not mention the Great Falls murders when it was nearly the same pattern: high-profile double murders, followed by his arrest soon afterward for another crime?

The story Dad tells in his book about being arrested in Montana for robberies was that when he confessed that his real name wasn't James Langley but Edward Edwards, the detective dashed out of the room. He said the man returned with a Wanted poster with a picture of Dad, saying, "This is you!" And he included, as he did throughout the memoir, what he considered to be flattering headlines. The one in the local newspaper read, EDWARD EDWARDS CAUGHT IN BILLINGS, MONTANA. HOTTEST CHARACTER TO HIT BILLINGS IN MANY YEARS. Dad also reveals that while in police custody he somehow slashed his wrists—not too deeply—wanting to be sent to the hospital instead of prison. He wrote that he figured it would be easier to escape from a hospital than a prison. It was a trick that didn't work in 1956 or in 1982, when he pulled his stunt with the pill-studded chewing gum in Pennsylvania before he was sent to prison for arson. But this was more evidence that he was a creature of habit.

On a crisp day in January 2019, Josh, Jonathan, and I found ourselves in front of the Great Falls, Montana, Cascade County Sheriff's Office. We had no appointment. They wanted to come in with me, with their mic and gear, but I knew if we went in with guns blazing we'd be turned away. As the killer's daughter, I could open doors with police and speak to people who had been involved with old cases. Whereas a true crime reporter would probably be turned away.

So I walked into the Sheriff's Office by myself and spoke to the receptionist, who raised her eyebrows when I explained why I was there, that I was a murderer's daughter, and I thought my father was a suspect in an old unsolved double murder. My mouth felt dry, like I'd eaten a stick of chalk. I felt pressure building in my head. The receptionist looked at me a moment too long, as if she could see the cymbals clashed behind my brow. Then she left to retrieve Sergeant Jon Kadner, who brought me back to his office. As I was telling my story I began to sob. The sergeant listened patiently and then went to speak to his captain, Undersheriff Scott Van Dyken. He returned to tell me Van Dyken was willing to sit down with me and my team.

I texted Josh and told them to come. And in they marched with the tools of their trade. Josh had a simple notebook and pen, and Jonathan had the big microphone and recorder strapped across his shoulder—he was a walking recording studio.

The Sheriff's Office was like the set of a TV western. Van Dyken wore a tall cowboy hat to greet us. Deer antlers were arrayed along the wall the way straw baskets adorned my kitchen. The lawmen were friendly yet reserved. They gestured for us to sit at a large conference table. They nodded as we told them what we were hoping to find—clues that my father may have been responsible for the murders of Patricia Kalitzke and Lloyd Bogle. All we knew was that Dad had definitely been in the right place at the right time. They didn't ask questions, just let us do the talking as if waiting for us to say something interesting that they didn't already know. I guess we didn't, because they didn't seem impressed. We left disappointed and deflated.

Next we were due to pay a visit to the man I had been avoiding. But he was too important to the Great Falls story to ignore.

When we walked into John Cameron's home, the first thing we saw was a big mirror with the words "It Was Him" written in red, as if in blood. *It Was Him: The Many Murders of Ed Edwards* was the title of his six-part documentary. *Oh, boy,* I thought. He had three little dachshunds, and that seemed to somehow offset the foreboding mirror.

Cameron brought us into his dining room, where he had piles of files and boxes and binders on the table. His binder on Dad's years between 1955 and 1960 was so thick I was intimidated. Before we delved into it, I had to ask about the mystery that was most urgent in my mind: What had happened to Verna?

I already knew that Cameron believed my father had killed Verna and her unborn baby. But had he found proof? He had done his homework here.

One of the most surprising things about Dad's memoir to all of us was that he used people's real names. And this allowed Cameron to do what detectives do: he found Jeanette and Theresa in the phone book. He called them, recording his calls. He played those tapes for me, Josh, and Jonathan as we sat around his dining room table.

In the memoir, Dad wrote of Jeanette's devotion to him. When she visited him in prison, she said, according to him, "I'll be waiting for you . . . I'll stick by you and I'll write every day. When you get out, we'll give up this life and live for our child. Believe me, I won't leave you under any conditions." He wrote, "That was what I longed to hear. I knew that if there was anything trustworthy in human nature, at all, I could trust Jeanette's love for me." Knowing how Dad treated the other women in his life, I think we can take his recollection of her words with a grain of salt, but it was hearing her speak for herself that brought us nearly to our knees.

In 2012, Jeanette was still alive and living in Idaho Falls, Idaho.

Here's the conversation, when John Cameron called her up fifty-seven years after she last saw her former husband.

JC: Are you the Jeanette . . . who was married to Ed Edwards?
Jeanette: I am . . . I've tried to put it behind me. [She sounds flustered.]
JC: Are you willing to speak to me? I've been . . . He was a horrible man.
Jeanette: Sure was.

She confirmed that they were married on October 20, 1955, after knowing him for just two months.

Jeanette: How I survived, I don't know . . . He was very domineering. I
learned in a hurry not to cross him.

She recalled that he let her talk to her mother only a few times. He would call her mother and talk to her first, without Jeanette being in the room. Then he would let Jeanette get on the phone. Her mom would always cry during these calls. Years after she left him, her mom told her that my father had said, "I'll let you talk to your daughter, but if you tell anyone where we're at, I'll kill her."

Josh sucked in a breath. Cameron stopped the tape. Jonathan said, "Whoa." I looked at their faces—they were truly horrified. We all sat in silence. Josh and Jonathan both shook their heads and then admitted they were stunned.

"Why are you shocked?" I almost yelled. Their reaction was as much a shock to me as my father's words were to them.

They were investigative reporters. They had listened to tapes of his awful confessions. They knew what he had done to Dannie Boy. How could anything my father have said or done shock them? And yet this had.

"Why are you shocked?" I said again. "Really, why?"

They both became thoughtful. Cameron said nothing, watching them struggle with this contradiction. Then Josh spoke and said that hearing my father's words repeated by Jeanette, he sounded like a monster. But listening to his playful voice on his home recordings made them think that while he was a bad man, a confused and twisted one, he wasn't evil. They'd heard him talking to Aunt Lucille on the phone, as he described trying to learn about his mother's life. They'd heard him practice his lectures on family values. They'd heard the tape he'd made while he was in the hospital waiting for me to be born, telling the tape recorder in an adorable way that it was keeping him company. They had found him difficult to despise. And after all they had learned, the strange warmth that my father seemed to inspire in people, like a rosy veil, still lingered. But Jeanette's words had cut through that cloak and shocked them.

Dad's charm was how he fooled neighbors. It's how he fooled law enforcement. It accounted for the almost affectionate portrayals of his prison escapes in the newspaper articles he was so proud of. And this, above all, was one of the most puzzling and enraging aspects of my father's legacy. People thought my father was a likable guy. And everyone thinks likable guys can't also commit heinous crimes. Who says these opposite personas can't be possessed by one person? What my father did to Dannie Boy is public knowledge. If that's not a monstrous crime, I don't know what is. How could anything he's done surprise anyone who's familiar with that case? But I hear this shock registered again and again. "Your dad was such a likable guy—the life of the party; could he really be *that* bad?" Yes, I always say. Yes, he really was *that* bad.

Cameron continued the tape. When he asked Jeanette directly about Verna, Jeanette had no memories of what became of her or anything that would help connect my father to the Great Fall double murders of Lloyd Bogle and Patricia Kalitzke. But she acknowledged that she herself was lucky to be alive.

After speaking to Jeanette, Cameron called Theresa, the potato farmer's daughter who, in the recording we listened to next, was clearly surprised to hear from anyone asking questions about a man who worked for her father in 1955. She was upset to learn that her name appeared in a "trashy book." But Theresa remembered my father well. He owed her money, in fact. "If you know that guy, or where he is," she told Cameron, "he still owes me sixty dollars." When she'd worked at the Dairy Queen, he'd "borrowed" her entire paycheck. I can imagine how he told her some sob story to make her feel sorry for him. It had been her school clothes money. She remembered his pregnant companion, Verna, too. And Theresa knew with certainty that Verna wasn't Dad's sister. Of course she remembered introducing Dad to her friend, Jeanette, and how hard Jeanette fell for the charming stranger. Theresa wasn't enamored, though. Even Theresa's mother had misgivings about him. When he worked at the farm, he spent more time in the house "getting a drink of water" than in the fields. Her mom said, "I don't trust that man." She thought he might be casing the house. Theresa remembers when Jeanette left with my father and Verna. But she didn't know what happened to Verna. Cameron had hit a dead end.

We had specifically come to ask Cameron about the Great Falls murders, but Cameron had gotten stonewalled there, too. He said he'd tried to get the Sheriff's Office to focus on my father, but they were fixated on another suspect. An airman named Blackwell.

It was getting late and it was time for us to go, and Cameron surprised us by saying he had decided he needed to put the story of Edward Wayne Edwards behind him. I looked at Cameron and choked up. The feelings of anger that I had toward him drained away. I felt only empathy. What had my father done to him? I looked at this man who had given up so much—his reputation, his job, his health insurance—to be the chosen one to pin all the unsolved murders out there on one man, and I thought, *Cameron is my father's last victim.*

After we left Cameron's house, we sat in the car. This is what we did when we left each place we visited. We would talk through the conversations, each sharing what we had learned. But this time, we just sat in silence. A melancholy had settled over us.

That night, Josh sent an email to Sergeant Jon Kadner asking about Blackwell. A last name was all we had. But this immediately got a response. Kadner asked us if we could come back to the Sheriff's Office as soon as possible.

The next day we returned to meet with Scott Van Dyken and Jon Kadner again. This time they had questions for us.

The first thing they made clear was that my father's DNA did not match the DNA on file. Neither did this person Blackwell's. Despite the fact that the DNA evidence didn't match either man, the detectives had not ruled out the possibility that one or both were somehow involved. Why? Because both men—both with criminal records—were in the same place at the same time for two almost identical double murders in 1956 in Great Falls and Portland in 1960.

"Do you know if they knew each other?" Kadner asked me.

I said I didn't know.

Arnold Blackwell was an airman. The Great Falls victim, Bogle, was an airman too. They asked me if my father was in the military, specifically an airman.

"Well," I said, "he often pretended he was." I was able to tell them about my father being dishonorably discharged, and that he often impersonated military personnel.

They asked me if my dad traveled with another man, or perhaps hung around with a group of men during the period of 1956 to 1960? I told them I thought it was possible. In his younger years, I said I thought he might have been learning how to be a killer from others. I told them, "I heard him say many times, 'If you're going to commit a crime, you do it alone so there's no witnesses and no one to rat you out.'" As an adult, I've often thought, *Why in the world would you tell a child this?* Was he speaking from experience? Maybe.

Nothing definitive had emerged during our meeting, but we—all five of us—were more convinced than ever that my father had something to do with the Great Falls and Portland murders, and that the missing link was the relationship between the two men: my father and Arnold Blackwell.

When we got back to the hotel, the woman at the front desk said a man had stopped by and left something for us. She handed us a big bag and a carry-on suitcase. Cameron had turned over the entirety of his research files regarding my father, with a note that he was passing the torch, hoping I would carry on his work.

I surprised myself by feeling unbearably sad. Here I had wanted Cameron to stop his crazy quest, and now that he had, I almost wanted to call him and say, *Wait! What was it all for? Don't give up!* But I didn't. Instead, exhausted, I went to my room and tried to sleep. Josh and Jonathan brought Cameron's files to their rooms and began to excavate.

In the morning, I somehow had to fly home with this extra burden of a full suitcase plus tote bag full of research. I removed all the papers from their binders and stuffed the pages into every nook and cranny of my check-in luggage, my carry-on bag, and my purse.

37

Finding Johnny

2019

When I got back home after our trip to Great Falls, one thing was clear to me. If I wanted to know if Dad had a connection to a man named Arnold Blackwell while he was in Portland, we were going to have to find the one person who might be able to help—the man Dad had called "Johnny" in his memoir—if he was still alive.

First, I needed to refresh my memory of the Portland double murders. There were plenty of news articles available online. The case was one of the most famous double murders in Portland. The crime was committed on Thanksgiving weekend in 1960, and Larry Peyton and Beverly Allan, nineteen-year-old sweethearts, were parked in a make-out spot. Larry Peyton was not shot, but he was stabbed twenty-three times. Peyton's mutilated body was found in his car with his skull caved in. One of the most puzzling aspects of the scene was a bullet hole in the windshield, as if someone had shot a gun from the back seat of the car. Beverly was missing. She was found over a month later, forty miles outside of town in a ravine, bound, strangled, and raped. Just like Kelly Drew. I shuddered. Like the Hack and Drew murders, the Peyton and Allan murders resulted in a massive manhunt. Over two thousand individuals were questioned over the course of the investigation. Hundreds of people were considered suspects. Detectives believed there had been more than one assailant.

Meanwhile, Josh had been reading about the Peyton–Allan murders, too, in a book written by a journalist, Phil Stanford, *The Peyton–Allan Files*. Stanford writes about one of the suspects, a twenty-eight-year-old "case-hardened ex-con" named Edward W. Edwards and his twenty-two-year-old buddy, "a chiropractic student named Wayne Berggren," who were "nosing around" the crime scene when it was all over the news. *Ah, well, now we knew who Johnny was.*

The crime scene was overrun with photographers, reporters and curious gawkers, and not very well secured. So it's not all that telling that Dad and "Johnny" were among the nosy public. But it didn't look good for Dad when he was arrested for the fire alarm stunt. In his book, Stanford writes that my father was a suspect who got away, and he describes the Larry Peyton and Beverly Allan killings as "virtual carbon copies" of the murders in Wisconsin of Tim Hack and Kelly Drew.

Josh noticed that there was no mention in Stanford's book about a man named Blackwell, and he contacted the author to ask him about it. Phil told him that it was in the second edition ebook. Josh read that, too, and shared with me that he'd learned this:

Two years after the killings of Larry Peyton and Beverly Allan, a woman named Barbara Blackwell turned her husband, Arnold Blackwell, in. She had been pulled over by police and used the opportunity to tell them she thought her husband was responsible for the Peyton–Allan murders. She said that he'd been discharged from the air force for psychiatric reasons. She also told them she thought he committed the 1956 Great Falls double murders as well. They were living not far from where the couple had been last seen. He'd been a taxi driver in Great Falls and always carried a revolver. Police had considered him a suspect for both crimes, but they had no evidence.

Then Barbara Blackwell recounted a story for the police that may be the only thread to link him to my father. She said that in Portland, Arnold brought another airman home and forced her to have sex with the man. Blackwell was convicted in 1962 of raping his wife and of forcing her at gunpoint to have sex with other men. He was never charged for either double murder.

What a creep, I thought. It wouldn't surprise me a bit if it turned out that Dad knew this guy.

The other penny dropped when Josh connected with Detective Jay Pentheny from the Multnomah County Sheriff's Office, in Portland, Oregon.

Police investigators from several states had visited Dad in jail, hoping to get him to confess to unsolved murders in their jurisdictions. One of those detectives was Pentheny. He met with Dad on March 9, 2011, the day after he had received the death sentence. Pentheny shared a recording of the meeting with Josh, who sent me a transcript.

He said he thought I should read it before I traveled to see "Johnny." Josh had found an address for Wayne Berggren in Idaho Falls, but no phone number, and I was determined that I needed to pay him a visit, even if it was an unexpected one. Maybe that was even better. Michael and I booked flights, and I sat down with the transcript to read.

Jay Pentheny begins the interview by saying, "I specifically flew out here to talk to you about your activities in Oregon during the 1950s and 1960s."

"All right," Dad says.

Pentheny says that reports show that Dad committed nine robberies in Oregon, California, and Montana before he was caught in Montana and sent to Deer Lodge.

"Uh-huh," Dad says, confirming. He then tells a story about buying a .32 automatic gun in a Las Vegas pawn shop and hitting up gas stations throughout the West.

When they get to the part of Dad's life in 1960 in Portland, he tells the most outrageous stories about how he convinced Marlene and her mother that he was with the CIA. He'd done such a good job of it that when the FBI came to her mother's door, she absolutely wouldn't believe that her son-in-law was not in the CIA. She told the FBI agents they had it all wrong.

I thought about Josh and Jonathan's reaction to my father. At every turn in my journey into the past, I was struck by how convincing my father had been all his life. Sometimes I didn't know whether to laugh or cry.

Dad tells Pentheny about working for the Kirby vacuum cleaner company. "I was a hell of a salesman, uh, one of the best that's ever went through there . . . they had contests and I'd win every [one]."

Visions of selling Girl Scout cookies came to me. My aching feet. Dad saying we couldn't stop until we had met our daily goal. He wanted me to be like him, "a hell of a salesman," the best there ever was.

I read on, wanting to hear about someone new. Pentheny did too. And Dad does mention someone else. He says "it was somebody that sold Kirbys, I can't remember any names . . ." Dad proceeds to tell a crazy story:

"There was one guy . . . he worked for me . . . his wife and me went to the dog races, to that track, I think it was outside of Portland . . . had a good time. We're on our way home, and, uh, uh, we're in his car and he says, Hey, do me a favor while we're driving, he says get my wife hot for me. I says, what? He says get my wife hot for me. So I'm in the back seat there with her and, uh, he's getting higher and higher and I'm having a hell of a good time and with his wife and, uh, so we get home to his place . . . and for some reason I want to say, there was somebody else, but we were all in bed together . . . while he's sleeping I'm over there banging his wife . . ."

Then Dad says that when he got up to go to the bathroom, he heard the guy and his wife arguing in hushed voices and he said, "Hey, it's late, I got to get home . . . to my wife and I was out of there."

I got up and paced the room at this point in my reading, my heart pounding. Dad had sex with another man's wife in their bed and then got up and went home to his wife, Marlene. I wondered if—or how many times—he had done that to Mom. I had to slow my breathing down consciously, close my eyes and tell myself to keep reading. *All this digging was for a good cause, right?*

In the interview, Jay Pentheny keeps asking Dad if there were any other people he hung out with. You can tell he's really hoping for a potential accomplice. Dad says he often had parties at his house, inviting people over, and when Pentheny asks their ages, Dad says, they're mostly younger. Marlene was just out of high school, and "Johnny" was still a student. He said he liked to have young people over for parties and be a big shot. He liked their admiration and was always trying to impress them.

I was struck at once that he had never outgrown the desire to surround himself with young people so he could be admired. Those young men, including Billy, whom he gathered around him when he was building the house on Kevin Drive, were the same age as the ones he hung out with as a twenty-eight-year-old con artist in Portland.

Pentheny kept fishing, but he never got a name. However, I had gotten something from reading that transcript, and I wanted to know if Josh got it too.

I called him. Sure enough, we had both noticed the parallels between the story Dad told about the night with his Kirby vacuum salesman friend and the story Barbara Blackwell told about her husband, Arnold. In her story, Arnold brought another airman home and forced her to have sex with them. It was easy to imagine Dad being that "airman." I was thinking, *This has to be the link*. Josh was thinking the same thing.

And then Michael and I flew out to meet "Johnny." I still thought of him as Johnny, even though I knew his real name. It was just too strange to call him Wayne, my father's name.

We drove from the Idaho Falls Regional Airport on a snowy February day. We were dubious when we arrived at a farm that this really was the right place, but the driveway was plowed and it appeared that someone was home. I walked up the steps of the farmhouse and knocked at the door. An older woman and a black lab greeted us. I asked if Wayne Berggren lived here, and the woman called to her husband.

An old but vigorous man strode into the room. He wore jeans and a big belt buckle. At eighty, "Johnny" had aged a lot better than Dad.

I explained that I was the daughter of Wayne Edwards, and asked if he remembered him.

"Well that's a name I never expected to hear again!" he said. "Oh, boy. That's a long time ago." Almost sixty years, in fact. He invited us in. His wife had been his girlfriend at the time Johnny had known my father. But she had lived on the East Coast, so she'd missed all the chaos Dad had stirred up. However, she did get a visit from the FBI after Dad pulled a runner.

Their living room was warm. Michael relaxed into a comfortable chair, just listening. He was there for the diversion, but also as a witness. I began to ask Johnny questions. He said he hadn't given my father much thought since he'd last seen him back in 1960. They hadn't kept in touch, and he didn't know anything about my father's life on the lam until the FBI came around asking questions.

I told him my father had been arrested for the 1980 Sweetheart Murders, and that he'd confessed to murdering five people before he died.

"I had no idea," Johnny said.

He hadn't known about Dad's criminal history when they'd been friends in Portland. Back then, he'd found him entertaining and couldn't quite figure him out. In the beginning, at least, he too believed Dad was with the CIA. I asked him if he'd read Dad's memoir, *Metamorphosis of a Criminal*. Johnny had never heard of it. He was surprised and not all that pleased to know he'd been immortalized in this way. Par for the loop-de-loop course of my father's story, Johnny grew up in the same town as Theresa and Jeanette. In 1959, Dad gave Johnny a ride back to his hometown from Portland for a visit, driving like a speed demon. Dad had been happy to drive eight hundred miles in a single day. They got there in an impossibly short time, Johnny recalled. I laughed. "Yeah, he never could drive anywhere slowly." But I wondered if Dad tried to find Jeanette at that time in '59. Or if he'd done anything else in Idaho Falls while he was there. I made a note to add it to my list of cold case cities to look up.

Johnny told me he and Dad were bowling buddies and he said my father was a phenomenal bowler. He said, "Wayne was good at everything he did." He called my dad a "thrill-seeker," and that explained, for him, why Dad loved pulling fire alarms and getting into all sorts of other trouble. But he never thought my father was a killer.

"One time," Johnny said, "Wayne pulled a knife on me, and I took it away from him." From then on, they were pretty good friends. Johnny looked up at me and said, "I been around the block myself a few times, too."

I asked him straight-out if he was the one who placed the call, pretending to be Dad's parole officer, the call that had allowed Dad to escape. He said, "You know, I've erased so much of that from my head . . . but it's possible. After he got out, I took them to the airport and then I took the car and parked it in a residential area in Northwest Portland and left it there."

My dad's claim in his memoir that Marlene's mother drove her daughter and my father to the Portland airport was false. Dad must have been protecting his friend. This is why he didn't use his real name. I wondered what else Dad had left out to protect someone else or himself.

Johnny admitted to something else Dad hadn't mentioned in his book—he had driven Dad around to cash checks. They even needed to wait a day to leave because it took a while to collect the funds.

"Boy, you're dragging out a lot of old memories," he said.

I remembered something that Dad had admitted to Pentheny in their meeting. After he got out of jail, thanks to Johnny pretending to be his parole officer, he swindled the bowling league's bank account. He was their treasurer! *Oh, the absurdity!* I didn't ask Johnny if he knew about this, though. I wasn't there to accuse him of anything.

Then I asked him what I'd really come to find out: Did he recall my father having a friend named Arnold Blackwell?

"That name doesn't do anything," Johnny said, shaking his head. "I don't think he had any friends," he added. "He was pretty much a loner."

Dad may have been a loner, but one who bowled in a league and had enough of a friendship with Johnny to care to protect him.

After we left Johnny's house, Michael and I mused on the visit. We weren't sure how much Johnny was omitting. But Johnny had been a student at the time, not a professional criminal like my father. If Dad had known and hung out with Blackwell, it's possible that Johnny and Blackwell would never have met. One was Dad's partner in fun. Was the other his partner in more serious pursuits? We know for certain that Dad left some pretty big events out of the memoir. Maybe Blackwell was one of his omissions. But we'll probably never know. It was time for me to let this mystery go. I was beginning to wonder if I would solve any at all.

VERNA

I was too late to speak to Jeanette. She had passed away. I had the name of one of her brothers who still lived in Idaho Falls, but no address or number. I grabbed an old phone book from the hotel reception area and saw there were three men with his name. Michael and I set out with the plan to show up at each address unannounced.

The first one on the list was a small ranch house out in the country. A man answered the door, and I introduced myself, saying, "I'm April Balascio. I'm sorry for the inconvenience—" He interrupted me and said, "Oh, I know who you are." He actually recognized me, from my appearance on Cameron's documentary. I had regretted appearing on that, but it came in handy now. Michael and I sat again in yet another living room, and I asked Jeanette's brother what he remembered about my father and if he remembered a woman named Verna.

He *did* remember Verna. He'd believed she was Dad's sister and didn't know anything about what had happened to her. What he really remembered was Dad's car, a snazzy convertible. Dad had swapped cars with him for a day. Immediately that raised a red flag for me. What had Dad done that day that he hadn't wanted to be seen driving his own car?

Next, I called Theresa, Jeanette's girlfriend, who also still lived in Idaho Falls. Cameron had given me her number. She didn't want to meet in person, and she was surprised to be contacted again about that strange time when her friend took off with a con man. I asked her specifically about Verna. What did she remember? Theresa told me that Verna confided in her. She had told Theresa that she was not Jim's sister and that she was pregnant with his baby. She also told Theresa that he'd punched her in the stomach to try to induce an abortion. But Theresa didn't know what had become of her.

I wished I had a last name for Verna, but all we had was her age and her first name and where Dad *said* he'd left her. Our next stop was to the Bonneville County Sheriff's Office in Idaho Falls. I asked the woman at the desk if they had any Jane Does still unidentified from the 1950s. I explained that I was the daughter of a murderer I believed may have taken the life of a young woman in Idaho Falls. I should have been used to saying it by now—"I am the daughter of a murderer"—but I wasn't. I still felt my words catch in my throat as I said them. I did not want that to be my mantra, but I seemed to be headed that way. Were the answers worth what they were costing me? My identity?

I was surprised at how often that introduction resulted in opening doors.

I was taken seriously. For some reason, I thought people would see me as a crackpot. The way I had seen Cameron. But in each sheriff's office I visited, I was treated with respect, and even if I didn't learn anything new, I was at least heard.

In Bonneville County, Michael and I were asked to empty our pockets before walking through a metal detector. We were greeted by Deputy Korey Payne and brought back to a small, windowless room with a metal table and three chairs. It was a typical interrogation room. But I wasn't intimidated. I was the one prepared to do the questioning. I explained that my father had lived in Idaho Falls briefly in 1955. He'd come here with a pregnant young woman and then ditched her. He'd written a memoir claiming that he'd taken her to Denver, where he left her, but I didn't believe him. I knew that he'd killed five people. I believed this young woman, whose first name I was fairly sure was Verna, could be a sixth.

"Do you have any Jane Does in her late teens/early twenties, possibly pregnant or had been pregnant?" I asked, trying to keep my disgust for my father out of my voice. In searching for a Jane Doe, what could I gain by knowing? Who could I comfort by knowing? The answer by this point was myself. I ached for Verna. I could almost feel her fear and vulnerability. I wanted to know what had happened to her.

There was a Jane Doe on file, Kayne said, but she had been murdered more recently. Finding a body more than six decades after a murder was unlikely. The detective said, "It would be easy to get rid of the body here and that body would never be found, especially back in the fifties. There's so many caverns and open spaces and animals to get rid of the evidence. It's easy to disappear in the wilderness, and there's a lot of it in Idaho."

In Dad's memoir, he claimed that he and Jeanette had driven to Denver with Verna and left her there. If that was true, the answer could be with the cold case homicide unit of the Denver Police Department. They were my next call. I spoke to Detective Sergeant Joseph Vasquez. He didn't have any cases that matched Verna's description either. He, too, thought the likelihood of ever solving my mystery was minuscule. The recordkeeping for law enforcement departments had not been accurate or detailed until the last fifteen years. He was kind, not at all dismissive, as I feared he might be. He encouraged me to contact sheriff departments in other cities in Colorado, but he agreed that the search was probably futile.

I've finally had to let Verna go. She was yet another of my father's victims—whether she was murdered or not. I prayed that if she survived that year, that she went on to have a better life than the one she would have had with him. I prayed that she found love, that she had the baby, and that the child—my half sister or brother—was alive and well somewhere in the world.

38

Ricky and Mary

It was time for me to shift my focus closer to home. In 2009, after I turned my father in, there was no shortage of online coverage of other cold cases.

An *Akron Beacon Journal* article from May 10, 2010, described the 1979 cold case of North Hill teens Mary Leonard, seventeen, and Ricky Beard, nineteen. They'd last been seen on August 24, and their remains weren't found for six years, about six miles from where the car was discovered at Northampton Road and Portage Trail. Leonard had been stabbed in the chest and shot, and Beard had been shot multiple times.

North Hill? That was the neighborhood we had lived in when we were on Avon Street in Akron. I did a quick count. If Mary was seventeen in 1979, she would have been twelve the last year we lived in that house. I tried to think, *Did I have a babysitter named Mary?* I couldn't remember.

I looked up archived articles from 1979 to learn more.

On a hot summer night, two teens—Mary Leonard and Ricky Beard—disappeared. Mary was about to start her senior year of high school. She and Ricky had gone to the local drive-in Friday night to see the movie *Amityville Horror* in Ricky's white Chevy Impala. Her curfew was midnight.

In the morning, both Ricky's and Mary's families realized they hadn't come home.

Police found Ricky's car on a farm road, not far from a make-out spot near a bar. Ricky's wallet was in the car. There was no sign of blood in the car.

Local county law enforcement thought perhaps that Mary and Ricky might have been abducted by a person who had driven the car there and left it. Nevertheless, police immediately released the car to the family without holding on to it as evidence. After the car had been released, a small bullet hole, possibly from a .22 caliber, was discovered in the passenger-side windshield. Police believed the gun might have been shot from the back seat. An eerie echo of the Portland murders.

Volunteers, bloodhounds, and helicopters searched the area. Nothing was found. Police settled on a theory that they had run away, not that they had been murdered. Two months later, police hired psychics. Three months later, the Leonard family hired a famous private investigator. No progress was made. Two young people had vanished with no leads or clues.

In May 1980, police claimed they got a tip that two bodies had been dumped near the woods, just a few miles from where Ricky's car had been found. One hundred and fifty people showed up and searched for eight hours and found nothing.

Then on May 29, 1985, a backhoe was digging trenches to lay cables, just a few hundred yards from where the search had been conducted in 1980, causing a skull to skitter across the ground. Forensic teams uncovered two sets of bones. They were the remains of Ricky Beard and Mary Leonard. According to the *Akron Beacon Journal*, "The most intensive missing person investigation in the city's history had ended—and a homicide investigation would now begin."

The coroner determined that the young couple had been killed by multiple gunshots, and Mary had also been stabbed. But her body was too decomposed for sexual assault to be determined.

The ditch where the bodies were found was on the property of a man who had a reputation of chasing teens off the land. The man, who was known to be mentally imbalanced due to a war injury, actually confessed to the murders, but the police didn't believe him.

According to the *Akron Beacon Journal* article of May 5, 2010, due to the similarities between this double murder and the ones my father had been arrested for, he had been considered as a suspect and dismissed because "Akron police said they cannot place Edwards in the area at that time."

When I read this I thought, *Are you sure he can't be placed in the area at that time?* I knew how far and wide we traveled, and I knew that Akron was the hub of Dad's wheel, where he returned again and again throughout his life. During the summer of 1979, we moved from Florida to Colorado. Was it possible that we made a visit to Akron before the start of the school year in Brighton? I thought of Johnny's story about Dad driving him to Idaho Falls from Portland in a day. A dash of twice that length—from Brighton to Akron—could easily be accomplished by driving all night, which was something Dad would have thought nothing of.

Maybe if we had all been in Akron in August 1979, it would explain a memory that I have trouble placing. I remember being in Akron, the Winnebago parked in a driveway—maybe Aunt Lucille's—and receiving a visit from Mom's parents, who I hadn't seen in a long time. Grandma, unlike Mom, was always dressed nicely. She had elegant blue eyeshadow, light pink lips, and always wore jewelry. Next to her, Mom looked so unadorned.

Grandma and Grandpa took me out to lunch all by myself. The restaurant was much fancier than any I'd eaten in, the kind of place where the waiter offered to grate cheese on my spaghetti and meatballs. Grandma spoke loudly so Grandpa could hear and she shared stories of my cousins, whom I rarely saw. After lunch, my grandparents took me to a shoe store and told me I could pick out a new pair of shoes. I was uncomfortable, even nervous. Everything I wore was either from discount stores or secondhand shops. I didn't want to be a burden to Grandpa and Grandma, so I picked out the cheapest pair in the store, beige sandals with straps and a low wedge heel.

Dad hadn't been at the Winnebago when they'd picked me up. He'd been off in the van. But he was there when they dropped me off—and he was angry.

He said to Grandma, "Why didn't you take the boys?" I had to look away. I thought he would have at least said thank you for buying me new shoes.

"April's ten years old. It's nice for a young lady to get some time away from her little brothers," Grandma said.

Dad went on accusing Grandma and Grandpa of treating me with favoritism. Why hadn't they bought presents for the other children? *Why this? Why that?* he berated them.

I don't remember Mom's reaction to Dad's outburst, or even how she behaved around her parents. Grandma and Grandpa left as soon as Dad's tirade was finished. Before they got in their car they didn't hug their daughter—they never hugged. They just said goodbye. I didn't want them to leave. And a part of me wanted to go with them. I wondered if Mom felt that way too. Even then, I didn't think Mom's parents worried about their daughter's safety as much as they should have. But on the other hand, did Mom worry about mine? I doubted it.

If I had those new beige sandals in fifth grade, and I think I did, it meant that we had stopped in Akron the summer of 1979. It is possible then that Dad was in the right place and the right time for the unsolved Akron double murder in August 1979. Aunt Lucille's house was just two miles from Northampton Road and Portage Trail, where Ricky and Mary's bodies were found.

These are the kinds of memories I wrestled with. Could a memory like this be a clue? *If* I was right, and Dad was again in the right place at the right time, and *if* Dad had killed two more young people parked in a car, then one thing Cameron had said rang true. This sounded like the MO of a serial killer. But *if* isn't *when*. And it isn't proof.

Back in 2010 Ricky's sister, Luanne Beard Eddy, had seen the news of my father's arrest for murders and she immediately went to the Akron police to ask if they considered my father as a suspect in the murder of her brother and Mary. They blew her off. They said Dad hadn't lived there in 1979, and that was that.

I visited Luanne in 2019 with Josh and Jonathan to interview her for the podcast. I hoped that together we might be able to connect more threads.

As Luanne brought us into her cozy living room, I gazed at the family pictures hanging on the walls. There were pictures of her children, and pictures with her parents and siblings as a child and as a young adult. I recognized Ricky from the newspaper articles.

Josh and Jonathan began to ask Luanne questions, while I quietly looked through a box of evidence her father had collected. Ricky's father, Bill, had gathered every piece of information that came his way concerning his son and Mary: tips from strangers, clippings, and police reports. I saw that the drive-in theater they'd been to the night they disappeared had been the Ascot. I had been there as a child. It was Dad's favorite. It was also just a few miles away from Aunt Lucille's house.

Bill had kept a journal, which had pages of notes per day. One day's note was short. It just said, "Today is Mary's eighteenth birthday." This struck me hard and I began to cry.

Luanne said that Ricky's disappearance destroyed his parents. They wondered where they'd gone wrong. Speculation in the community was rampant. No one wanted to believe they were dead. Was Mary pregnant, people wondered, and afraid to tell her Catholic family? Had they eloped? People called the families declaring that they'd spotted the couple. Luanne would get complete strangers approaching her saying things like, "I heard your brother was spotted in Mexico." But if they'd run away, why would Ricky have left his wallet behind? What about the bullet hole in the car window? It made no sense. Ricky's mother, Helen Beard, wrote to the FBI, pleading with them to get involved.

Bill Beard died two years after his son and Mary disappeared. He didn't live long enough to know they had been murdered. By the time the remains of Ricky and Mary were found six years later, Luanne's mother wasn't able to accept that the bones were her son's.

In Ricky's father's files, I found a note regarding a retired Ohio state patrolman who had worked with Northampton PD. The patrolman said he'd seen a car fitting the description of Ricky's Impala being followed by a van going west on Portage trail that night. They were going so slow, he passed them. This was the road on which Ricky's car had been found. And the "van" mentioned in the report? I read the note out loud.

"My dad had a green Econoline van," I said, looking up at Luanne.

Her eyes met mine. A hush came over the room. Was this a clue?

I couldn't get over the similarities. Ricky's body was shot, like Dannie Boy, like Billy Lavaco, like the young airman Lloyd Bogle in Great Falls. Bullet holes from shots made from within the car's back seat occurred in both

Ricky's car and Larry Peyton's car in Portland. The bodies of Ricky and Mary had been moved, like Tim Hack's and Kelly Drew's, like Beverly's, like Patricia's in Great Falls. The remains of Ricky and Mary were found on or near the property of an unreliable man. It would have been just like my father to place his victims near the home of the unstable man with a history of threatening teens. He tried to frame Dannie Boy's prior housemate, Ralph. And I believe he had scattered Kelly Drew's clothing on the roadside leading toward a man's house to point the finger at him. After Kelly and Tim went missing, a witness at the Concord House mentioned seeing a dark van leaving the parking lot. And hadn't we just read the report by the patrolman about a van being spotted following Ricky's car? Were we on to something?

Luanne told us that when the bodies were discovered, a young rookie detective, Bob Swain, was tasked with guarding the remains of the two young people. It must have been a solemn, spooky, and lonely assignment. He was deeply moved by the experience and kept in touch with the Beard and Leonard families. Whenever he got a tip, he'd pass it on to Luanne. It was clear he was frustrated with how sloppily the case had been handled by the Akron Police Department.

Years earlier, Luanne had turned over all her own research materials to the Akron Police Department, only to find out later that the files could not be located. Only Bob Swain seemed as committed to solving the case as the victims' families.

He even reached out to my father while he was in prison in Wisconsin. I found their letters in the files we got from Geauga County. In the letters, Dad toyed with Swain. He teased him with the promise to reveal information and asked him for money. Swain didn't fall for it. Dad didn't give him any information about the Akron murders.

In 2014, Bob Swain took his own life. He was sixty-four, leaving behind a wife and five children. Luanne lost her ally in the search for her brother's killer. I wanted to be her ally, but I didn't want to give false hope.

Before Josh, Jonathan, and I left, she told me something that I will never forget. In the thirty years since her brother vanished, the family mourned, and they still mourn. Ricky's siblings have children and there are many cousins. Ricky's children and grandchildren will never be among them. Ricky's children and grandchildren will never be among them. Luanne said one of the tragedies of his early death is that Ricky "didn't get to love all these other people."

Luanne is a grandmother now. She had three daughters—triplets. They and their children know all about Uncle Ricky. Though they never met him, they still think about him, include him on family trees, and still wonder what happened to him. Generational trauma has a long reach. My father caused this trauma to at least five families. "Yours too," Luanne told me. She said that I was in mourning, too. She lost a brother. Her family lost a whole branch of their tree. But, she said, "You lost a father"—or the notion of the father I'd had loved as a child. He was gone. We wept together for our losses, and for all the families whose loved ones didn't come home. She thanked me for trying to find answers. When we parted, we hugged and said we'd keep in touch.

I trudged back to the car with Jonathan and Josh, each of us wishing we'd learned something more definitive. The visit weighed heavily on us. Luanne's grief was still fresh after thirty years. Maybe this kind of grief always is. I wished I was able to help her. If only I could prove one way or another that my father had known Ricky or Mary or had at least some reason to encounter them like he had Tim and Kelly. Had Dad met them that night at the Ascot? Or had they known people in common?

I wanted to find that gray house that I lived in as a young child, the one I so helpfully climbed a ladder to paint when I was a toddler. The one where I burned my mouth biting into the electric cord. I didn't remember the exact address, so Josh and Jonathan indulged me as we drove around the North Hill neighborhood until we came to Avon Street. We drove up and down the block until I said, "There!" The house was now tan, but it still had white trim like I remember. I could still see myself walking down the sidewalk with the laundry basket bumping against my legs. In my mind, I could see my father's car, slowly rolling next to me, and I could hear his voice saying, "Where you going, April?" This had been the home where I had cuddled with Dad. Where I had run to him when he came home, with a candy in his pocket for me. How could that man be the same man who took the lives of at least five people? Five people who would never marry, never have children, never know their nieces and nephews, never grow old. Luanne was right. I was in mourning, too.

Ricky and Mary had also grown up in North Hill. I asked Josh to drive by their childhood homes. Each lived less than a mile from my house. Had Mary babysat for me, David, and John?

My mind began to race: Who could I ask? Who might know? But then what would it prove even if she had? I had to accept that there was much we would never know. I thought of the stories and the tears of the Hacks and Luanne. I wondered if *knowing* was really what this was all about. Maybe we wouldn't solve any mysteries. Maybe we were here to listen. I marveled at the warmth and compassion Dave, Judy, and Luanne had shown me. Maybe that was what I had been looking for all along.

39

Loose Ends, Loosely Tied, a Coda of Sorts

2019–2021

GREAT FALLS, A DNA MATCH

Two years after the podcast aired, the 1956 Great Falls case was finally solved, or at least considered solved. In June 2021, Detective Sergeant Jon Kadner of the Cascade County Sheriff's Office in Montana announced that the killer of the Great Falls couple had been found, thanks to DNA evidence on file, as well as the willingness of the suspect's children to give DNA samples themselves. The semen collected at the time of the murders from Patti's body turned out to be related to DNA found in a voluntary DNA database, like Ancestry.com or 23andMe. But the man himself, Kenneth Gould, a horse trainer who lived near the crime site, had died in 2007. Gould had no criminal history prior or after the murders. Whether he had an accomplice or accomplices, we'll never know.

PORTLAND, AND THE MYSTERY OF THE BULLET WOUND

One of the things that had been bothering me and the podcast team, like a stone in our shoe, had also puzzled Portland detectives since the 1960 double murders. It concerned the bullet hole through the windshield of Larry Peyton's car. Neither the gun nor the bullet was ever found. When my father was arrested in Portland, right after the murders, low and behold, he had a bullet hole in his upper arm. (Some accounts say it was his shoulder.) He makes no mention of this wound in his memoir—one of the glaring omissions, in my opinion—but he was questioned about it after his arrest in Portland. It was probably the real reason he panicked and fled the jail.

In his 2011 interview with the Portland detective Jay Pentheny, Dad was asked about it again. Because my father had told this story in different ways over time, I was eager to learn which version he'd told Pentheny.

Dad told Pentheny, very matter-of-factly, that he told Marlene to shoot him in the arm, and she did. "I lay in the bed, I showed her where to shoot me . . . to make sure it wasn't on the bone . . . and it went right through. I used Q-tips to go in one side and out the other to clean it out real good with peroxide and everything . . . Didn't hurt at all."

Pentheny said, "Your God's honest truth to me today is that your wife did that to you, based on you wanting notoriety."

"I did it for the recognition," Dad says.

Reading Dad's words, they sure sounded familiar. Then I remembered something the host of *To Tell the Truth*, Garry Moore, asked Dad. He wanted to know what the reaction in the neighborhood was when Dad was released from detention as a teen. Dad says, "They looked up to me . . . and this motivated me to go on to bigger things . . . I was out there committing crime for the recognition." I couldn't believe it. There was that word: *recognition*. My father had not changed since he was a teenager. All his life he had been seeking attention and recognition in the most destructive ways possible.

But that bullet wound story had a life of its own. At the time of his escape from the Portland jail, a newspaper ran an article and included the story that Dad told police when he was arrested, that his friend Johnny had shot him accidentally while they were shooting tin cans.

A neighbor read the article and called the police. She shared a different version of the story. She said her neighbor [my father] came to her saying that he had been shot and could she patch him up. He told her he'd been injured when he was accompanying a police officer friend on a burglary call. He didn't want to get his policeman friend in trouble, so he'd rather she not mention it to anyone else. The neighbor—a young woman—took Dad to Fred Meyer's to purchase first aid materials to disinfect and bandage the wound.

Regardless of how he got the wound, why couldn't Marlene have done the bandaging? The only explanation I could think of was that he wanted to have sex with the neighbor. He was once again pulling out the sob stories to get attention.

For years I've wondered how the bullet wound and the bullet hole in Larry Peyton's windshield had not been connected with Dad once and for all. And for years I had been missing a critical piece of information that would have answered my questions. In writing this book, I combed through police reports that I hadn't yet seen. Police files show that the Fred Meyer receipts for first aid purchases were dated two weeks before the murders. There was no way my father was shot the night the bullet blasted through the windshield of Larry Peyton's car, the night of his murder.

But that's all that means. These two facts of the bullet in the windshield and my father's self-inflicted wound are just two unrelated pieces of the same puzzle of my father. It isn't necessarily proof that he didn't commit the murders. It just adds nothing in the way of evidence that he was involved. This was how it often went for him: evidence that looked like it might mean something, really in the end did not prove anything. Was he a criminal mastermind or was he just lucky?

DOYLESTOWN

Lynn—our neighbor on Kevin Drive, and the mother of Diane, the babysitter who was there in the woods behind our house the day my father shot the gun above our heads—told two of the most bizarre stories I learned about my dad. He had knocked on her door asking if Lynn had a shotgun he could borrow. She told him she never loaned out her guns, so he asked her husband, who agreed to loan Dad his, one he'd had since he was a boy. I think Dad told a sob story about needing to hunt to feed his family. Lynn's husband never saw the shotgun again.

The second story is the oddest. Several weeks after we'd left Kevin Drive, Lynn received a strange visit from a man in a black sheriff's car. He was in uniform, wore a black hat and dark shades, and had a mustache. He had a sheriff's badge. He said he was looking for information on her former neighbor, Wayne Edwards. Did she know him? What could she tell him about Edwards?

She said she thought that his children and wife were nervous around him. His wife seemed especially detached. Lynn said she'd seen bruises on her and the kids, and she worried about them. She told him that Mr. Edwards had borrowed her husband's shotgun and never returned it. The uniformed man thanked her and left.

Only later did she realize that the sheriff who had come around fishing for details about her former neighbor was, in fact, Dad in disguise.

It was years before I could place my dad back in Doylestown after we'd left, when all I could remember was our life in Florida. But when Mom told me that Dad returned to Akron for Grandpa Fred's funeral in September 1978, the pieces fit. And that old police car sitting in the weeds back on Kevin Drive? That must have been stashed in a friend's yard when we left Doylestown, then called back into service for this occasion and who knows how many other times when he impersonated law enforcement.

AKRON

I reconnected with Mary Lou, who had been fourteen years old when she'd come to babysit me and David at the Avon Street house. She'd lived just down the block from us. Her son reached out to me after the podcast. Mary Lou wasn't sure she wanted to speak to me. She felt anxious whenever she thought of my father. And when she heard about the podcast, she had a panic attack. But in the end she invited me to her home. I asked her to tell me what she recalled about her experience with my family. She recounted a disturbing memory. She told me that one time she was babysitting, and when my parents got home, my father grabbed her and pulled her into a chair on his lap and asked her for a kiss. Mom had just laughed a nervous laugh and looked away. The next time she was asked to babysit, she refused and said she would never babysit again. But when I burned my mouth biting into the electric cord, Dad called her and begged her to come back to babysit for David. She did, but just that once.

I told her how sorry I was that my father had abused her, and I thanked her for sharing that painful memory with me. She told me later that our conversation was cathartic. She can now live with that memory without her heart racing wildly in her chest. It was as if she'd given the memory to me to hold for her. And I have, and I will.

PENNSYLVANIA

Among the documents and records I got from the wonderful clerk Sharon at the Geauga County Sheriff's Office, were copies of letters Dad wrote to Jeff from 2010, while he was still in prison in Wisconsin. The envelopes were addressed to Jeff Edwards. In one letter to Jeff, my father tells him that he must not open any letters addressed to *Mr.* Jeff Edwards until after his death.

Dad was playing games, even in the last days of his life. His letters to Jeff from prison ramble on and on for pages. Jeff wrote him long letters as well. In one of Jeff's letters dated May 10, 2010, while Dad was in prison in Wisconsin and before he had officially confessed to anything, he asked Dad directly a list of questions.

One was, "Did you kill Danny?"

Dad's answer: "No answer."

Another question was "When we lived in PA or Ohio, a black kid in my class ended up getting murdered that always picked on me did you have anything to do with that?"

Dad's answer: "The black boy that was killed in PA, who was in your class. A black man killed him and raped him. He is on death row at the prison I was at. I cannot remember his name. Jeff, I could never kill a child!!!"

And Jeff asks the big question that was on all of our minds: "How many people have you killed and what was the reasoning behind the killings?"

Dad's answer: "No answer. I cannot talk to you about alot of these questions in these letters because if I were to then you would by law have to talk to the police. So right now what you don't know won't hurt you. Plus you won't have to talk to anyone should they show up at your door."

I've never seen copies of the letters to *Mr.* Jeff Edwards. I believe these letters may have held clues, if not admissions, to his other murders. With all the cassette tapes, videotapes, letters, and clippings, Dad was documenting his life. He *wanted* his children to know all about him, like he'd told Aunt Lucille. For Dad to not tell his final story goes against everything I know about him.

The tidbit that my father dangled in his letter to the Norton Ohio Police Department—because they were too slow to have him extradited back to his hometown of Akron—was that there was another state with the death penalty that would want to hear what he had to say. To me, that was a confession of sorts that there were other murders.

I dove online to see what I could find. There are dozens of missing person's reports and unsolved murders in Pennsylvania and Ohio during the years we lived there, several involving young women and couples, but there are a few that keep me up at night.

One is the April 1978 Akron murder of a woman, a twenty-eight-year-old teacher named Leslie Barker. She had been found burned to death in her car after a night at Red's Bar. The news story made me think of Dad's account in his memoir of when he was thirteen, in love with the neighbor who had a boyfriend. He set fire to the boyfriend's truck in a twisted attempt to get rid of the competition.

We were living on Kevin Drive, in Doylestown, in April 1978. Dad was a regular at Red's Bar—it was also one of Aunt Lucille's favorites. Had Dad met Leslie at Red's? It is easy to imagine he did.

And then there's Michele Reidenbach, a sixteen-year-old high school senior, who disappeared on September 22, 1981. A newspaper article states, "The last confirmed sighting of Michele was at the Super Duper supermarket parking lot on South Main Street in Zelienople." The Super Duper was ten miles from the house in Portersville where we lived at that time.

Unsolved Pittsburgh area murders include: eighteen-year-old Debbie Capiola, who was raped and strangled on March 17, 1977; and several during the time Dad worked in the Pittsburgh area, including fifteen-year-old Christine Guenther who was last seen at a bus stop on October 26, 1981, and her body discovered five days later by a hunter.

I could go on and on. I could drive myself crazy. My own attempt to shed light on my father's crimes had become like the closet in the ghost stories I used to tell my brothers as a child, the blood spot kept growing bigger the more I peered in.

Again and again I was reminded of how hard it is to solve a long unsolved murder, and how easy it was to get away with one in the age before cell phones, social media, and advanced forensics techniques. Yet even now, new murders go unsolved and people go missing every day.

I still get calls from detectives, doggedly seeking answers for cold cases, even the ones no one is constantly pestering them about. In their heroic work, there are no happy homecomings, no bringing a child home to waiting parents' arms. Often the parents are long gone too. But the answers are no less important. Everyone deserves justice, even after generations have passed.

I hope that maybe, just maybe, some rusty wheel of justice that I've prodded to start turning again will come up with a new piece of evidence, and another family will have answers to the worst question of their lives.

Epilogue

One of the pilgrimages into my past that I needed to take alone was a trip back to New Castle.

Don Montgomery had passed away, but Nellie still lived in the cinder block house that my family had squeezed into back in 1985. When I called her to tell her I was coming to New Castle, she invited me to stay overnight with her. This time, I wouldn't be sleeping in the living room. "You can sleep in Jerry's old room," she said.

Walking into her home, I felt a comforting sense of the familiar. Her living room seemed smaller than I remembered. But it also seemed emptier. When I'd lived there, my family of seven had been camped out in it. It was when I went to use her bathroom and looked into the mirror that the waves of melancholy came crashing down on me. I stared into my reflection. It seemed like just yesterday I was getting ready for school in this bathroom. And it also seemed like a million years ago. Oh, how I had changed. And oh, how I was still the same. Still the same girl, holding my chin up so the world couldn't see that I was hurting.

I spent the next morning cooking in Nellie's kitchen, just as I had made meals there when I was an adolescent. I made a meat sauce—the same recipe I'd used when I made that first dinner in my first apartment on my own.

Nellie sat at the kitchen table, watching me work, chatting about the people I used to know from church and regaling me with funny stories about her grandkids. She was as warm and kind as always, just a little grayer than the last time I'd seen her.

I was at the stove, trying not to splash tomato sauce on my flowered silk pajama set and cream fuzzy slippers, when I heard the kitchen side door open.

I turned around to see my old boyfriend, Mark. I hadn't seen him in thirty-four years. He hadn't changed much. He'd gained a few pounds and lost some hair, but I would have recognized his smile and his bright blue eyes anywhere. I had not intended to be in my pajamas when I met up with him that day.

"Hey," he said when he found his voice.

"Hey," I said back. I couldn't stop smiling.

Mark and I had lost touch after high school, but he'd recently reached out to me on Facebook on my birthday and we began a correspondence. He told me he had married and had a family and then divorced. He was engaged to be married again. He had become a welder, like he'd trained to be in high school. This was a kid who'd had to work to give his parents grocery money. Now he had a well-paying career, and I was proud of him. I've often wondered what my life would have been like if we'd stayed in New Castle. I feel pretty sure I would have gone to college. My teacher and mentor Mrs. Houk wouldn't have had it any other way.

The week before coming to New Castle, I had asked Mark if he would accompany me on a driving tour of my childhood homes in Pennsylvania.

"Will you be my chauffeur?" I had asked. "It's hard to keep your eye on the road and on all the surrounding landmarks at the same time. I'll be rubbernecking every tree and road sign." Mark knew the area and I knew the landscape of my memories. Together we would make a good team.

"Sure! Happy to be of service, ma'am," he had said.

Now, here Mark was, blushing in Nellie's kitchen, still bashful and modest, even though I was the one caught in my pajamas. He was ready to indulge my trip down memory lane. I excused myself to get dressed. As I pulled on my sweater and jeans in Jerry's old bedroom. I thought of Jerry, who had lived here until his mid-twenties. What a good guy he was. There were good men out there like Jerry and Mark. I sometimes had to remind myself of that.

It was raining hard as Mark and I ran to his white Chevy Malibu. I looked over at him as he squinted past the swinging windshield wipers. He was a good sport, just like he had been when we were young.

First on my list was the house in Slippery Rock, the one in Portersville, PA. The house where my father brought the shivering horse into the dining room to warm him. The house where he stabbed my mother in the hand. The house he made my brothers help set fire to. That one.

I didn't have an address for the house, just the town name. But Mark was game. "If anyone can find it, April, it's you," he said.

I remembered that the Portersville Road intersected a highway. I knew the church we'd gone to had been on one side of the highway and our house was on the other side, down the road. I remembered the house sat on the top of a steep hill in a clearing surrounded by woods.

I peered out of the car window through the rain. But as we drove past a driveway I said, "This is it!" We stopped, backed up, and crept up the steep drive, which opened up to a field, as I remembered from all those days walking home from school. I could almost see that old horse cropping grass next to the house. But of course the horse was long gone, and even the house was gone. It had been replaced by a modern brick colonial. We rolled to a stop, and I opened the car door.

"What are you doing?" Mark said. He hadn't signed up for trespassing.

"I didn't come all this way to sit in a car!" I said, stepping out into the rain. I ran up the house steps and knocked on the solid door. No one was home. I got back into his car, soaking wet.

Mark was shaking his head and laughing, "You're just as crazy as ever," he said.

Next I wanted to go to see the uninhabitable house near McConnells Mill State Park. The one that we abandoned to sleep in the barn instead. I will never forget the makeshift loft bed I made for myself, and the musty smell that permeated the air, my clothes, and even my hair while we lived there. And the gnawing hunger. I can't forget that, either.

Mark patiently made every turn I shouted at him to make. *Turn left, Turn right!* I described the trees—I had remembered a border of evergreen hedges around the yard. I told him about the great big weeping willow. I described the small field and the chestnut trees.

"Make a U-turn," I said, feeling like we must be in the wrong place. But then I saw it.

"Stop!" I said. "That's the row of hedges; there's the chestnut trees; there is where the barn was! That's where the house used to be! That's where the spring was where we had to bathe! I used to play my clarinet in the big old echoey house." But it was now just a big empty lot.

We stopped at the ranger station in McConnell State Park to see if someone knew what had happened to the place. A ranger there confirmed, yes, there had been a house and big barn that had been torn down. The structures may have disappeared, but they still stood as indelibly in my memory as the image of Dad running at me with a plate of whipped cream, ready to pull one more "practical joke" on his daughter.

Mark and I stopped for lunch at a diner. I picked at my salad—I was always careful about what I ate, and I was saving room for tonight's lasagna. Mark ordered the same thing I did, though he wasn't staying for dinner at Nellie's. He had plans with his fiancée. He told me about his divorce, how his kids reacted, how crushed he felt. I was happy he had found someone new to share his life with. Michael and I were preparing to get divorced. Mark had been through all that and he'd come out okay on the other side. Maybe I would too.

That night back at Nellie's, I assembled my mushroom lasagna and popped it in the oven. Jerry and his wife, Michelle, joined us for dinner. Around the table, Jerry and I laughed, remembering that awkward prom. "I remember the dress I wore perfectly," I said.

"I remember how weird I felt walking back into that gym for prom after how many years?" he laughed.

"You were twenty-two!" I reminded him. "I was mortified!"

"Remember Jonathan?" Michelle asked. She had her own memories of my family. It had been her and her grandmother who had rescued that poor boy who rented out the chicken coop and nearly froze to death.

"Thank God you found him," I said, and shuddered.

Sitting in that familiar kitchen, I looked around. It felt good to feed these kind people who had taken care of me and my family in the best way they knew how. They'd given us a real roof over our heads. They had cared about us. They'd called the police when my brother ran away, worried for his safety. Nellie had given both my parents jobs, and my father had betrayed her trust.

Over dessert—Nellie was diabetic, so I made a sugar-free, almond milk cheesecake with strawberries—I asked her, "What in the world did you think of my father?"

"Oh, people making Goodwill donations would call to complain," she said. "They said some lazy man came in a truck to pick up their furniture and made his sons do all the work!"

"Yep." I nodded. "That was Dad. The Great Delegator."

Nellie said she had known he wasn't the most reliable person and that he wouldn't have won a Best Dad award. But she was absolutely floored by the revelations that he was a murderer. Imagine knowing you took a killer into your home. But on this night, none of us wanted to dwell on the dark—we were just happy to be together.

The next morning, I dropped off a gift for Mark. Tulips for his yard. I left a note that said, "Our friendship is like these tulips. It stays dormant for a time, but then blossoms in season." Every spring since, he has reminded me of this when they bloom.

Nellie and I hugged when I left. She said, "When you and your family moved out, we wondered what was going to happen to you kids."

What *had* happened to us? In those days we were a family—held together by the force field of my father. Now we were scattered. No longer affected by his gravitational pull. Unfortunately, in telling my story and the story of my father, I can't help but tell other people's stories too. Not everyone wants their stories told. Undoubtedly my siblings will remember things differently than I do. We each experience our childhoods through our own lens, and no child is parented in the same way. I know Dad treated his last two children with more kindness and less violence than he did his older children.

When I made the hotline call that night in 2009, I lifted the lid off Pandora's box, and for some of my siblings, it seemed that *I* was the one who had done something unforgivable. Not my father's crimes, but my revelation of them, was responsible for our fractured family. I do feel guilty for that. I also feel guilty I didn't come forward sooner. If I had put it all together sooner, would Dannie Boy still be alive? Might anyone else have been saved?

I woke up one morning from an unsettling dream about Happy. We had left her somewhere and couldn't remember where. She's often in my dreams, representing something vulnerable and unprotected. Maybe my children, maybe me, maybe my father's victims? My own three dogs snuggled into me, sensing my thumping heart as I awoke. They sleep in bed with me; their lives are so different from Happy's. I think of her under the trailer in Florida, covered in fleas, nursing those tiny kittens, and it makes me want to weep.

My love of animals was something I shared with my father, but he didn't know how to care for them. Even then I knew that dogs and horses should be tended and cared for beyond being given food and water. He didn't know how to care for children, either. But each of his five children figured out how to care for themselves. Each of us has led upstanding lives and given back to our communities. We've all had steady jobs and nice homes. I have those things, but they are not enough to make me stop digging into my father's past crimes—he will be a puzzle I'll always want to solve.

I may not know many more facts than I did when I started, but in shedding light on my father's life, I illuminated my own. I've learned so much from the generous people who have gone on this journey with me. I've learned the power of forgiveness, and that if you don't forgive the people in your life, it leads to bitterness and a hard heart. I forgive my parents.

I'm finding it more difficult to forgive myself. Do I want to be forgiven for betraying my father? Yes. But I think that's something only I can grant myself. I'm working on it. And I'm feeling like the future holds promise. I often think of the counselor, Wendy, who gave me guidance when I was sixteen years old. She told me never to forget what I had gone through, because someday God would use me to help others.

When I began this journey, diving deep into my memories, poring through police records and boxes of photocopies and letters and tapes, I didn't know what I was really seeking. I had to immerse myself in some foul waters of the past. And what I realized is that I wanted to not only bring answers to victims' families but to inspire others to find the courage to come forward and tell their own stories. What I hadn't expected was—after all the years of unanswered questions—how healing the revelations could be for families as well as for myself. And I received much more than I could have hoped . . . the blessing of friendship.

Acknowledgments

I can honestly say that writing this book was the hardest thing I have ever done in my life. I couldn't have done it alone. There were many people who made this journey possible. Thank you Lilly Golden, my collaborator, who helped me bring my vision to life. My agent, Jennifer Gates, for her unwavering support from the beginning. My editor, Hannah Braaten, for her excellent advice and guidance, and the whole Gallery team at Simon & Schuster. And Josh Dean, for being persistent and opening the door for me to tell my story.

And for my friends who were always there, I am withholding last names but these individuals will know who they are: Jennifer, Mark, and Paul. You guys didn't give up on me! Thank you for encouraging me from day one. Thank you to Detective John Canterbury, who was always willing to take my phone calls (no matter how late or early!). Thank you to Chad Garcia, and cold case detectives everywhere for their tireless search for answers.